best of GIFTS OF GOOD TASTE
CHRISTMAS

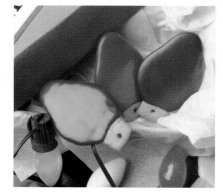

LEISURE ARTS, INC.
Little Rock, Arkansas

EDITORIAL STAFF
Managing Editor: Susan White Sullivan
Craft Publications Director: Deb Moore
Senior Prepress Director: Mark Hawkins
Art Publications Director: Rhonda Shelby
Special Projects Director:
 Susan Frantz Wiles
Special Projects Designer: Patti Uhiren
Foods Editor: Jane Kenner Prather
Contributing Foods Assistant:
 Rose Glass Klein
Art Category Manager: Lora Puls
Lead Graphic Artist: Dana Vaughn
Graphic Artists: Dayle Carozza, Angela
 Stark, Amy Temple, and Janie Wright
Editorial Writer: Susan McManus Johnson
Photography Manager: Katherine Atchison
Imaging Technicians: Brian Hall, Stephanie
 Johnson, and Mark R. Potter
Publishing Systems Administrator:
 Becky Riddle
Publishing Systems Assistants:
 Clint Hanson and John Rose

BUSINESS STAFF
Vice President and Chief Operations Officer:
 Tom Siebenmorgen
Corporate Planning and Development
 Director: Laticia Mull Dittrich
Vice President, Sales and Marketing:
 Pam Stebbins
National Accounts Director: Martha Adams
Sales and Services Director:
 Margaret Reinold
Information Technology Director:
 Hermine Linz
Controller: Laura Ogle
Vice President, Operations: Jim Dittrich
Comptroller, Operations: Rob Thieme
Retail Customer Service Manager:
 Stan Raynor
Print Production Manager: Fred F. Pruss

Library of Congress Catalog Number 2008924770

10 9 8 7 6 5 4 3 2 1

CANDIES
4-17

CAKES
& PIES
38-53

BREADS &
SPREADS
94-111

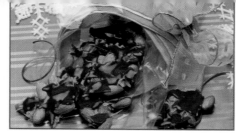

COOKIES & BARS
18-37

SNACKS & SIPS
54-71

SAUCES, SEASONINGS, & MIXES
72-93

CHRISTMAS CANDIES

Surely the most anticipated flavors of the season are the sweetest! And when those treats are simple to make, you can plan your entire gift list around boxes, bags, and cones of scrumptious candies. This collection of indulgent recipes and festive packages fits the Yuletide theme.

REFRESHING CHOCOLATE MINTS

Anyone with a sweet tooth will be thankful for your offering of Peppermint-Chocolate Creams! The luscious chocolate-covered mints provide a cool contrast to all the spicy foods of the holiday season. For a regal gift, package these refreshing candies in a pretty tin tied with Christmas ribbon and add a festive gift tag.

PEPPERMINT-CHOCOLATE CREAMS

    1 jar (7 ounces) marshmallow creme
  $^2/_3$ cup butter or margarine, softened
    1 teaspoon vanilla extract
  $^3/_4$ teaspoon peppermint extract
    6 cups sifted confectioners sugar
    8 ounces chocolate candy coating, chopped
    1 candy bar (7 ounces) dark sweet chocolate, chopped

In a large bowl, beat marshmallow creme, butter, and extracts until well blended. Gradually add confectioners sugar, stirring until mixture is well blended. Shape teaspoonfuls of candy into $^3/_4$-inch balls. Place on a baking sheet lined with waxed paper. Chill 1 hour or until firm.

In the top of a double boiler, melt candy coating and candy bar over hot, not simmering, water. Dip each candy into chocolate. Return to baking sheet lined with waxed paper. Chill until chocolate hardens. Store in an airtight container in a cool place.

Yield: about 9 dozen candies

HOLIDAY GIFT TAG

You will need red and green colored pencils, photocopy of tag design (page 114), red permanent fine-point marker, glue, and green paper.

1. Use pencils to color tag design. Use marker to write message on tag. Cut out tag.
2. Glue tag to green paper. Leaving a $^1/_8$" green border, cut out tag.

CHRISTMAS PRETZELS

A fun family gift, these easy-to-make Christmas Pretzels will bring holiday joy to young and old alike! The Bavarian-style treats are simply dipped in candy coating and sprinkled with colored decorating sugar for a sweet presentation. Our gift bag features a "peek-a-boo" window bordered with festive trims.

CHRISTMAS PRETZELS

- 1 tablespoon red coarse decorating sugar
- 1 tablespoon green coarse decorating sugar
- 1 tablespoon white coarse decorating sugar
- 18 ounces vanilla candy coating, cut into pieces
- 1 package (10 ounces) 3-inch-wide Bavarian-style pretzels

In a small bowl, combine red, green, and white decorating sugars. Stirring frequently, melt candy coating in a heavy medium saucepan over low heat. Remove from heat. Working with pretzels at a time, dip each pretzel into candy coating. Transfer pretzels to waxed paper. Sprinkle pretzels with sugar mixture before coating hardens. Store in an airtight container in a cool place.

Yield: about 2 dozen pretzels

FESTIVE GIFT BAG

You will need a medium-size gift bag, 1/4 yd each of 2 ribbons and 1 yd of a third ribbon for bow, 19" of decorative braid, gold cord to replace bag handles (optional), 4 gold buttons,

scrap paper, clear cellophane, craft knife and small cutting mat or folded newspaper, and glue.

1. For window in bag, cut a $3^{1}/_{2}$" x 6" piece of scrap paper for pattern. Draw around pattern at center front of bag. Place cutting mat inside front of bag and use craft knife to cut out window along drawn lines.
2. Cut a piece of cellophane about 1" larger on all sides than window.
3. Center cellophane over window on inside of bag; glue in place.
4. Cut 9" from 1 yd ribbon length. Follow Step 1 of *Making a Bow*, page 112, to make bow from remaining ribbon lengths; tie bow with 9" ribbon length at center to secure.
5. Glue braid along edges of window, buttons at corners, and bow at top.
6. If desired, remove handles from bag and replace with gold cord.

FOUR CHIPS FUDGE

What sweeter way to offer happy holiday greetings than with gifts of fabulous Four Chips Fudge! The nut-filled confection is created with semisweet chocolate, milk chocolate, peanut butter, and butterscotch chips. For a presentation with flair, the rich, creamy bites are packed in ribbon-tied gold boxes.

FOUR CHIPS FUDGE

- $3/4$ cup butter or margarine
- 1 can (14 ounces) sweetened condensed milk
- 3 tablespoons milk
- 1 package (12 ounces) semisweet chocolate chips
- 1 package ($11^1/2$ ounces) milk chocolate chips
- 1 package (10 ounces) peanut butter chips
- 1 cup butterscotch chips
- 1 jar (7 ounces) marshmallow creme
- $1^1/2$ teaspoons vanilla extract
- 1 teaspoon almond extract
- 4 cups coarsely chopped walnuts

Line a $10^1/2$ x $15^1/2$-inch jellyroll pan with aluminum foil, extending foil over ends of pan; grease foil. Melt butter in a heavy Dutch oven over low heat; stir in sweetened condensed milk and milk. Add semisweet, milk chocolate, peanut butter, and butterscotch chips; stir until smooth. Remove from heat; stir in marshmallow creme and extracts. Stir i walnuts. Spread mixture into prepared pan. Chill 1 hour.

Use ends of foil to lift fudge from pan. Cut into 1-inch pieces. Store in an airtight container in refrigerator.

Yield: about 12 dozen pieces fudge

CAPPUCCINO NUT CRUNCH

You can "espress" your sentiments to that special someone with our Cappuccino Nut Crunch. For an elegant presentation, wrap the treats in cellophane and place in a beribboned cone made from a dinner napkin.

CAPPUCCINO NUT CRUNCH

    2   tablespoons hot water
$^1/_2$ teaspoon espresso powder
$^3/_4$ cups whole almonds, toasted
$^3/_4$ cup flaked coconut
    1   cup plus 2 tablespoons sugar
$^1/_3$ cup whipping cream
$^1/_4$ cup butter
    2   teaspoons light corn syrup
$^1/_2$ teaspoon ground cinnamon
$^1/_2$ teaspoon salt

In a small bowl, combine water and espresso powder; set aside. In another small bowl, combine almonds and coconut. Spread in a single layer in greased $10^1/_2$ x $15^1/_2$-inch jellyroll pan. Butter sides of a heavy medium saucepan. Combine sugar, whipping cream, butter, corn syrup, cinnamon, salt, and espresso mixture in saucepan. Stirring constantly, cook over medium-low heat until sugar dissolves. Using pastry brush dipped in hot water, wash down any sugar crystals on sides of pan. Attach a candy thermometer to pan, making sure thermometer does not touch bottom of pan. Increase heat to medium and bring to a boil. Cook, without stirring, until mixture reaches 290 degrees. Test about $^1/_2$ teaspoon

mixture in ice water. Mixture will form hard threads in ice water but will soften when removed from water. Pour mixture in a thin stream over nut mixture; do not stir. Let cool; break into pieces. Store in an airtight container.

Yield: about $1^1/_2$ pounds candy

NAPKIN GIFT CONE

You will need 18" each of $2^1/_4$"w wired ribbon and gold cord, 20" square fabric napkin, $1^1/_4$" dia. button, 5" x 12" clear cellophane bag, $3^1/_4$" x 4" piece of card stock, and gold and silver permanent fine-point markers.

1. Tie ribbon into a bow.
2. Matching wrong sides, fold napkin in half from top to bottom and again from left to right.
3. With finished edges of napkin at top and overlapping edges at front, shape napkin into a cone. Centering button on bow, sew button and bow to front of cone to secure shape.
4. Place cellophane bag in cone. Place gift in bag. Tie cord into a bow around top of bag.
5. For tag, match short ends and fold card stock in half. Use gold marker to write message and draw leaves and berries on tag. Use silver marker to add details to leaves.

PISTACHIO FUDGE

O Christmas tree, O Christmas tree, how tasty are your branches! This Pistachio Fudge is holiday "greenery" at its best. Deliver your gift in a tree-shaped papier-mâché box that has been painted green, decorated with swirl ornaments, and topped with a wooden star.

PISTACHIO FUDGE

$1^1/_2$ cups sugar

1 package (3.4 ounces) pistachio instant pudding mix

$^2/_3$ cup evaporated milk

2 tablespoons butter or margarine

$^1/_4$ teaspoon salt

2 cups miniature marshmallows

$1^1/_2$ cups white baking chips

1 teaspoon vanilla extract

$^1/_2$ cup chopped pistachios, divided

Line a 9-inch square baking pan with aluminum foil, extending foil over 2 sides of pan; grease foil. In a heavy large saucepan, combine sugar, pudding mix, evaporated milk, butter, and salt. Stirring constantly, bring mixture to a boil over medium heat; boil 5 minutes. Remove from heat. Stir in marshmallows, baking chips, and vanilla until smooth. Reserving 2 tablespoons pistachios, stir in remaining nuts. Spread mixture into prepared pan. Sprinkle reserved nuts on top. Chill 2 hours or until firm.

Use ends of foil to lift fudge from pan. Cut into 1-inch squares. Store in an airtight container.

Yield: about 5 dozen pieces fudge

PAINTED TREE BOX

You will need a papier-mâché box with lid (we used a 6" x 6" tree-shaped box with a cellophane window in lid); gold, green, and dark green acrylic paint; paintbrushes; household sponge; gold fine-point paint pen; 2"w wooden star; black permanent fine-point marker; and a hot glue gun.

1. Paint lid dark green. Follow *Sponge Painting*, page 112, to lightly paint top of lid green. Allow paint to dry after each application.

2. Use gold pen to paint swirls and dots on top of lid.

3. Using acrylic paint, paint wooden star gold. Use marker to write message on star; glue star to lid.

CHUNKY CHOCOLATE CANDIES

Traditional candy canes take on a new twist in this cheery offering. The temptingly rich Chunky Chocolate Candies are formed in cane-shaped cookie cutters, wrapped in cellophane, and embellished with curling ribbon.

CHUNKY CHOCOLATE CANDIES

3 candy bars (7 ounces each) milk chocolate with almonds
1/3 cup flaked coconut
1/3 cup miniature marshmallows
1/3 cup finely chopped candied cherries
1/4 cup raisins

In a heavy medium saucepan, melt chocolate bars over low heat. Stir in coconut, marshmallows, cherries, and raisins until well blended. Remove from heat. Spoon into fourteen 1 1/4 x 3 1/4-inch candy cane-shaped plastic cookie cutters that have been placed on a waxed paper-lined baking sheet. Chill 1 hour or until firm. Store in an airtight container in refrigerator.

Yield: 14 candies

COOKIE CUTTER CANDY BAGS

For each bag, you will need a 3" x 9" clear cellophane bag, two 20" lengths each of red and green curling ribbon, curling ribbon shredder, hot glue gun, 1" dia. white pom-pom, Christmas motif sticker 2" high or smaller, 2 1/2" x 4" piece of white card stock, red and green permanent fine-point markers, and a hole punch.

1. Place candy-filled cookie cutter in cellophane bag; knot ribbons around top of bag.
2. Curl ribbon ends. Following manufacturer's instructions, use ribbon shredder to shred streamers.

3. Glue pom-pom to knot of ribbon.
4. For tag, apply sticker to left side of card stock. Trim left side of tag along sticker shape. Use red marker to draw design along edges of tag and green marker to write message on tag. Punch hole in tag. Use a ribbon streamer to tie tag to bag.

EASY PEANUT PATTIES

our friends will think these
delicious Easy Peanut Patties came
from the candy store! Evaporated
milk and pudding mix give the
nutty confections an extra-rich
taste. Dressed up with evergreen
appliqués, our fabric-covered Shaker
boxes make festive gift containers.

EASY PEANUT PATTIES

1/2 cups sugar
1 package (3 ounces) vanilla
     pudding and pie filling mix
3/4 cup evaporated milk
1 teaspoon vanilla extract
2 cups Spanish peanuts

Combine sugar, pudding mix, and
evaporated milk in a heavy medium
saucepan over medium-high heat.
Stirring frequently, bring mixture to a
boil. Reduce heat to medium and boil
minutes. Remove from heat. Stir in
vanilla. Beat 3 minutes or until candy
thickens. Stir in peanuts. Drop by
tablespoonfuls onto waxed paper. Allow
candy to harden. Store in an airtight
container.

Yield: about 2 dozen candies

CHRISTMAS TREE SHAKER BOXES

For each box, you will need a Shaker
box, fabrics to cover box lid and for
appliqués, polyester bonded batting,
paper-backed fusible web, ribbon to
cover side of box lid, dimensional paints
in squeeze bottles and spray paint to
coordinate with fabrics, Design Master®
glossy wood tone spray (available at
craft stores), spring-type clothespins,
and craft glue.

1. Spray paint box; allow to dry. Lightly
spray box with wood tone spray; allow
to dry.
2. To cover lid, draw around lid on
wrong side of fabric. Cut out fabric
1/2" outside pencil line. At 1/2" intervals,
clip edge of fabric to 1/8" from line. Use
top of lid as a pattern to cut a piece of
batting. Glue batting to lid; allow to
dry. Center fabric piece right side up on
lid. Alternating sides and pulling fabric
taut, glue clipped edges of fabric to side
of lid; secure with clothespins until glue
is dry. If necessary, trim edges of fabric
even with bottom edge of lid.
3. To cover a lid with 2 fabrics, cut a
second fabric piece desired size to cover
part of lid, allowing 1/2" on all sides
for finishing. Press top edge of fabric
piece 1/2" to wrong side. Position fabric
on fabric-covered lid as desired; glue

pressed edge in place. Allow to dry. At
1/2" intervals, clip raw edge of fabric to
1/8" from lid. Pulling fabric taut, glue
clipped edges of fabric to side of lid;
secure with clothespins until glue is dry.
If necessary, trim edges of fabric even
with bottom edge of lid.
4. Use desired patterns and follow
Making Appliqués, page 112, to
make appliqués to fit on box lid. For
tree trunks, follow manufacturer's
instructions to fuse web to wrong side
of fabric. Cut an approx. 1/2"w desired
length strip from fabric for each trunk.
Remove paper backing from appliqués
and arrange on lid, overlapping
appliqués as necessary; fuse in place.
5. Measure around side of lid; add
1/2". Cut a length from ribbon the
determined measurement. Glue ribbon
to side of lid; secure with clothespins
until glue is dry.
6. Use dimensional paints to paint dots
on trees and to paint dots along center
of ribbon on side of lid. Allow to dry.

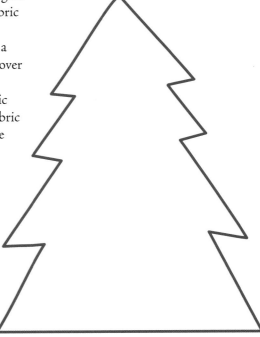

EASY TRUFFLES

These taste-tempting truffles will quickly become holiday stars. By melting the chocolate and butterscotch chips in the microwave, you can make rich confections for all the sweets lovers on your list, and still have time for entertaining! Wrap a star-shaped plate of truffles with cellophane and tie with ribbon and an ornament for a dazzling delivery.

EASY TRUFFLES

  1 package (6 ounces) semisweet
      chocolate chips
  1 cup butterscotch chips
$^3/_4$ cup confectioners sugar
$^1/_2$ cup sour cream
  2 teaspoons grated orange zest
$^1/_4$ teaspoon salt
  1 package (11 ounces) vanilla
      wafers, finely crushed
      Confectioners sugar

In a medium microwave-safe bowl, microwave chips on medium power (50%) until chips soften, stirring frequently until smooth. Stir in $^3/_4$ cup confectioners sugar, sour cream, orange zest, salt, and wafer crumbs. Shape mixture into 1-inch balls. Roll in confectioners sugar. Store in an airtight container in refrigerator.

Yield: about 5 dozen balls

STARRY PLATES

For each plate, you will need an 8"w decorative plate (we used a silver star-shaped plate), 30" square of clear cellophane, 24" each of $^5/_8$"w red satin and $^7/_8$"w white sheer ribbon, two 24" lengths of silver cord, white and red card stock, decorative-edge craft scissors, spray adhesive, red permanent fine-point marker, hole punch, and an ornament with hanger.

1. Arrange truffles on plate. Place plate on center of cellophane. Gather cellophane over top of plate; tie ribbons and one length of cord into a bow around gathers.

2. For tag, cut a $1^3/_4$" x $2^1/_2$" piece from red card stock. Use craft scissors to cut a $1^1/_4$" x 2" piece from white card stock. Apply spray adhesive to one side of white card stock; smooth white card stock onto red card stock.

3. Use marker to write message on tag. Punch a hole in one corner of tag. Use remaining length of cord to tie tag and ornament to gift.

IRRESISTIBLE PRALINES

Simple to whip up using pudding mix, Easy-But-Rich Pralines are irresistible sweets! Package small batches in handcrafted nutcracker bags created from brown paper sacks and scraps of craft materials. They make great gifts for surprise holiday visitors.

EASY-BUT-RICH PRALINES

1 cup firmly packed brown sugar
1/2 cup granulated sugar
1 package (3 ounces) vanilla
    pudding mix
1 can (5 ounces) evaporated milk
1 tablespoon butter or margarine
1/2 cups chopped pecans

In a heavy large saucepan, combine sugars, pudding mix, evaporated milk, and butter. Stirring frequently, bring to boil over medium heat; stir in pecans. Attach a candy thermometer to pan, making sure thermometer does not touch bottom of pan. Cook, stirring occasionally, until mixture reaches 234 degrees. Test about 1/2 teaspoon mixture in ice water. Mixture will easily form a ball in ice water but will flatten when removed from water. Remove from heat; beat 2 to 3 minutes or until mixture begins to thicken. Working quickly, drop tablespoonfuls of candy onto waxed paper; let cool. Store in an airtight container.

Yield: about 2 dozen pralines

NUTCRACKER GIFT BAG

You will need a lunch-size brown paper bag; 2¹/₂"w ribbon; low-temperature glue gun; tracing paper; peach, red, and blue craft foam; white artificial fur; red permanent medium-point marker; ³/₄" x 1¹/₈" piece of white poster board; two ⁵/₈" dia. black buttons; and a ³/₄" dia. yellow button.

1. Measure width of front of bag. Cut a length of ribbon the determined measurement. Glue ribbon across bottom on front of bag.
2. Trace patterns, page 115, onto tracing paper; cut out. Using patterns, cut nose from peach craft foam, crown and two cheeks from red craft foam, and hatband from blue craft foam. Cutting through fabric backing only, cut mustache, beard, and two eyebrows from fur. Use marker to draw teeth on poster board piece.
3. Fold top of bag 1¹/₂" to back. Overlapping as necessary, arrange and glue foam shapes, fur shapes, and teeth on bag. Glue black buttons to bag for eyes and yellow button to top of crown.
4. Unfold top of bag. Place gift in bag. Refold top of bag; glue to secure.

PEPPERMINT BRITTLE

A new twist on an old favorite, our innovative Peppermint Brittle is a refreshingly different holiday treat. Candy cane pieces are a delicious (and colorful!) addition to the crunchy brittle. Our merry Santa, cleverly crafted from a paper bag and fabric scraps, makes a cheerful carrier for your gift.

PEPPERMINT BRITTLE

10 6-inch candy canes, broken into small pieces
 3 cups granulated sugar
 1 cup light corn syrup
$1/2$ cup water
 3 tablespoons butter or margarine
 1 teaspoon salt
 2 teaspoons baking soda

Spread candy cane pieces evenly on a large piece of greased aluminum foil.

Grease sides of a large stockpot. Combine next 3 ingredients over medium-low heat, stirring constantly until sugar dissolves. Syrup will become clear. Using a pastry brush dipped in hot water, wash down any sugar crystals on sides of pan. Attach candy thermometer to pan, making sure thermometer does not touch bottom of pan. Increase heat to medium and bring to a boil. Do not stir while syrup is boiling. Continue to cook syrup until it reaches hard crack stage (approximately 300 to 310 degrees) and turns golden brown. Test about $1/2$ teaspoon syrup in ice water. Syrup will form brittle threads in ice water and remain brittle when removed from the water. Remove from heat and add butter and salt; stir until butter melts. Add soda (syrup will foam); stir until soda dissolves. Pour syrup over candy cane pieces. Cool completely on foil. Break into pieces. Store in an airtight container.

Yield: about 2 pounds candy

SANTA BAG

You will need a lunch-size brown paper bag, fabric for hat, artificial lamb fleece for hat trim, muslin for beard, thread to match muslin, 12" of 3-ply jute, $3/4$" dia. shank button with shank removed for nose, black felt-tip pen, 9" of cotton yarn, a $1/2$" dia. jingle bell, and craft glue.

1. Trim top of bag straight across.
2. For hat, measure height of bag and divide measurement in half; measure width of front of bag. Cut a piece of fabric the determined measurements. Matching edges, glue fabric piece to top front of bag.
3. For hat trim, cut a 1"w strip of fleece 2" longer than width of front of bag. Fold each end of strip 1" to wrong side; glue to secure. Overlapping bottom edge of hat fabric piece $1/2$", glue trim strip to front of bag.
4. For beard, cut a piece of muslin the same height and 1" wider than front of bag. Center jute between short edges of muslin. Using a medium width zigzag stitch with a medium stitch length, sew jute along center of muslin. Trim ends of jute even with edges of muslin.
5. Matching short edges, fold muslin in half with jute on inside. At approximately $3/4$" intervals, clip $1/4$" into short edges of muslin (Fig. 1). At each clip, tear fabric up to zigzag-stitched line.

Fig. 1

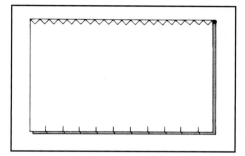

6. Glue folded edge of beard to front of bag. Trim beard to desired length. Glue button to bag for nose. Use pen to draw eyes.
7. Place a plastic bag of candy in bag. To fold top of bag for hat, fold top right corner of bag diagonally to back of bag; fold top left corner of bag straight down to front of bag. Tie cotton yarn into a bow. Glue bow and jingle bell to point of hat. Allow to dry.

COOKIES & BARS

More than a dozen crispy, chewy, nutty, awesomely good cookies and bars await your discovery on the following pages—some are even made without baking! We've included easy instructions for a variety of gift-giving ideas, so you can make seasonal treats for everyone you know.

EASY FRUITCAKE COOKIES

Fruitcake has been a Christmas tradition for generations. Now it's even easier to carry on the custom with our Easy Fruitcake Cookies. Using a package of refrigerated cookie dough, the chewy treats can be made in a snap. Place them in a Christmas-motif gift bag that you've tied with curling ribbon, and they're ready to give.

EASY FRUITCAKE COOKIES

    1 package (1 pound, 2 ounces)
         refrigerated sugar cookie dough
 $^1/_4$ cup all-purpose flour
 $^1/_2$ teaspoon ground allspice
    1 container (4 ounces) red candied
         cherries, chopped
    1 container (4 ounces) green
         candied cherries, chopped
 $^1/_2$ cup chopped walnuts

Allow dough to sit at room temperature 15 minutes. Preheat oven to 350 degrees. In a small bowl, combine flour and allspice. Break up dough in a large bowl. Sprinkle flour mixture over dough; stir until flour is incorporated. Stir in cherries and walnuts. Drop teaspoonfuls of dough 2 inches apart onto a greased baking sheet. Bake 9 to 11 minutes or until edges are lightly browned. Transfer cookies to a wire rack to cool. Store in an airtight container.

Yield: about 4 $^1/_2$ dozen cookies

"MERRY CHRISTMAS" BAGS

For each bag, you will need a lunch-size Christmas-motif gift bag, hole punch, two 21" lengths of gold cord, assorted colors of curling ribbon, tracing paper, gold card stock, black permanent fine-point marker, and a hot glue gun.

1. Place cookies in bag. Fold top of bag 1 $^1/_2$" to back. At each side of bag, punch a hole in folded portion of bag. Thread one length of cord and several lengths of ribbon through hole; tie into a bow. Curl ribbon ends.
2. For tag, trace pattern onto tracing paper; cut out. Using pattern, cut star from card stock. Use marker to write message on tag. Glue tag to bag.

CINNAMON COOKIES

Share the flavor of Christmas with a batch of snowflake-frosted Cinnamon Cookies. An ordinary basket becomes a wintry friend with the addition of a craft foam nose and colorful earmuffs made from juice can lids.

CINNAMON COOKIES

COOKIES

- 1 1/2 cups vegetable shortening
- 3 1/2 cups sugar
- 2 eggs
- 1/2 cup water
- 1 teaspoon vanilla extract
- 5 cups all-purpose flour
- 1 tablespoon ground cinnamon
- 2 teaspoons baking powder
- 1 teaspoon salt

ICING

- 3/4 cup vegetable shortening
- 4 1/4 cups confectioners sugar
- 1 teaspoon vanilla extract
- 4 to 5 tablespoons milk

Preheat oven to 375 degrees. For cookies, cream shortening and sugar in a large bowl until fluffy. Add eggs, water, and vanilla; beat until smooth. In a large bowl, combine flour, cinnamon, baking powder, and salt. Add dry ingredients to creamed mixture; stir until a soft dough forms. Shape dough into 1-inch balls and place 2 inches apart on a greased baking sheet; flatten balls into 2-inch-diameter cookies with bottom of a glass dipped in sugar. Bake 7 to 9 minutes or until bottoms are lightly browned. Transfer cookies to a wire rack to cool.

For icing, combine shortening, confectioners sugar, vanilla, and milk in a large bowl; beat until smooth. Spoon icing into a pastry bag fitted with a small star tip. Pipe snowflake design onto each cookie. Let icing harden. Store in an airtight container.

Yield: about 9 dozen cookies

SNOWMAN BASKET

You will need white spray paint, 7 1/2" dia. basket, two lids from large frozen juice cans, red felt, red embroidery floss, hot glue gun, polyester fiberfill, orange and black craft foam, tracing paper, brown permanent medium-point marker, two black chenille stems, and two 5/8" dia. black buttons for eyes.

1. Spray paint basket white; allow to dry.

2. For each earmuff, draw around lid on felt; cut out circle 1 1/2" outside drawn line. Using floss, work *Running Stitches*, page 113, along edge of circle. Glue a small amount of fiberfill to one side of lid. Center lid fiberfill side down on felt circle. Pulling floss ends, gather felt over lid; knot ends together to secure.

3. For handle, cut a 3/4" x 14" strip from black foam. Glue ends of strip to basket to form handle. Glue earmuffs over ends of handle.

4. Trace pattern onto tracing paper; cut out. Using pattern, cut nose from orange foam. Use marker to draw detail lines on nose.

5. Shape one chenille stem into a wavy smile; position and glue on basket. Cut two 1 1/2" pieces from remaining stem; glue one piece to each end of smile. Glue eyes and nose to basket.

STAR COOKIES

Simple, melt-in-your-mouth Star Cookies are a stellar holiday idea! Baked to crispy perfection, these classic delicacies are gathered in easy-to-make felt drawstring bags. Handmade tree ornaments add pizzazz to your gift.

STAR COOKIES

$3/4$ cup butter or margarine, softened
$1/2$ cup sugar
1 egg
1 teaspoon vanilla extract
$1 3/4$ cups all-purpose flour
3 tablespoons cornstarch
$1/2$ teaspoon baking powder
$1/8$ teaspoon salt

Preheat oven to 350 degrees. In a medium bowl, cream butter and sugar until fluffy. Add egg and vanilla; beat until smooth. In a small bowl, combine flour, cornstarch, baking powder, and salt. Add dry ingredients to creamed mixture; stir until a soft dough forms. On a lightly floured surface, use a floured rolling pin to roll out dough to $1/8$-inch thickness. Use a $2 3/4$-inch-wide scalloped-edge star-shaped cookie cutter to cut out cookies. Transfer to a greased baking sheet. Bake 7 to 9 minutes or until bottoms are lightly browned. Transfer cookies to a wire rack to cool. Store in an airtight container.

Yield: about 4 dozen cookies

FELT GIFT BAGS

For each bag, you will need two 9" x 12" felt pieces; embroidery floss; pinking shears; tracing paper; white, red, and green felt scraps; glue; 7mm jingle bell; and 18" of satin cord.

For each gift tag, you will *also* need colored pencils, photocopy of tag design (page 114), red permanent fine-point marker, green paper, and a hole punch.

1. Matching edges, place 9" x 12" felt pieces together.
2. Using floss and *Running Stitch*, page 113, sew felt pieces together along one short and two long edges. Use pinking shears to trim edges of bag.
3. Trace small, medium, and large star patterns, page 116, onto tracing paper; cut out. Use small star pattern to cut one star from felt scrap. Use patterns and pinking shears to cut one large star and one medium star from felt scraps.

4. Stacking stars from largest to smallest, glue stars together. Glue bell to center of small star.
5. For hanger, cut a $1/4$" x 2" felt piece. Glue short ends together. Glue ends of hanger to back of large star.
6. For gift tag, use pencils to color tag design; cut out. Use marker to write message on tag. Glue tag to green paper. Leaving a $1/8$" border, cut out tag. Punch hole in corner of tag.
7. Place cookies in bag. Thread cord through hanger and hole in gift tag. Tie cord into a bow around top of bag; knot ends.

PECAN MERINGUE COOKIES

Enchant the ladies in your women's club with gifts of airy Pecan Meringue Cookies. The delicate confections are baked with a generous portion of toasted chopped pecans folded into a vanilla-flavored meringue. Packaged in plastic bags and tied with ribbon, your heartwarming surprises are ready for delivery when tucked in these festive canvas totes. The totes are embellished with fused-on fabric appliqués and heart-shaped paper tags.

PECAN MERINGUE COOKIES

$^1/_2$ cup firmly packed brown sugar, divided
$^1/_2$ cup all-purpose flour
$^1/_4$ teaspoon salt
4 egg whites
$^1/_2$ teaspoon vanilla extract
$^3/_4$ cup granulated sugar
3 cups chopped pecans, toasted

Preheat oven to 325 degrees. In a medium bowl, combine $^1/_4$ cup brown sugar, flour, and salt; set aside. In another medium bowl, beat egg whites until soft peaks form; add vanilla. Gradually add granulated sugar and remaining $^1/_4$ cup brown sugar; beat until stiff peaks form. Gently fold flour mixture into egg white mixture. Fold in pecans. Drop teaspoonfuls of mixture onto a baking sheet lined with parchment paper. Bake 7 to 9 minutes or until bottoms are lightly browned. Transfer to a wire rack to cool. Store in an airtight container.

Yield: about 8 dozen cookies

CHRISTMAS TOTES

For each tote, you will need a 4$^1/_2$" x 6" canvas tote, fabric for background, Christmas-motif fabric for appliqué, fusible web, 6" of $^1/_8$"w and $^1/_3$ yd of $^3/_8$"w ribbon, cream and a second color of paper, black felt-tip pen, tracing paper, and a hole punch.

1. Fuse web to wrong sides of fabrics and cream paper.
2. Cut a 3$^1/_2$" x 4$^1/_2$" piece from background fabric. Center and fuse fabric piece to front of tote.
3. Cut a motif from appliqué fabric.

Center and fuse motif to background fabric. (Our appliqué fabric has printed blanket stitches along edges of motifs. If your fabric does not have printed stitches, use black pen to draw stitches.)
4. For tag, trace heart pattern onto tracing paper; cut out. Use pattern to cut heart from cream paper. Fuse heart to remaining paper. Cutting close to heart, cut heart from paper. Use pen to draw stitches and write name on tag.
5. Punch a hole in tag. Thread narrow ribbon through hole and tie tag to handle of tote. Tie wide ribbon into a bow around handle above tag.

hese lavishly decorated "gingerbread" houses look good nough to eat—and they are! Easily eated with decorating icing and urchased graham crackers, the dible cottages feature ornate trims cake decorations, candies, gum, nd other tasty treats. You'll have n making one of these sweet tle homes (or a whole village!) r a friend.

"GINGERBREAD" HOUSES

or each house, you will need graham ackers, purchased white decorating ing, and items to decorate house ve used hard candies, purchased cake ecorations, bubble gum, licorice, jelly ans, candy-coated chocolate pieces, nocolate bar pieces, mints, butterscotch nips, stick gum, and candy corn).

(*Note:* Use scissors to cut crackers. se icing to "glue" cracker pieces gether.) For front wall of house, refer Fig. 1 and cut corners from 1 cracker lf. Repeat for back wall.

g. 1

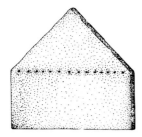

2. Refer to Fig. 2 to glue front and back walls to 1 cracker half (base). Use props to hold walls upright until side walls are added.

Fig. 2

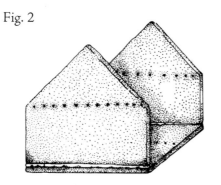

3. For side walls, glue 2 cracker quarters to base and front and back walls (Fig. 3). Allow icing to harden slightly.

Fig. 3

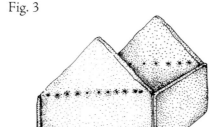

4. For roof, apply icing to top edges of walls. Refer to Fig. 4 to place 2 cracker halves on top of house. Apply icing along peak of roof (Fig. 4). Allow icing to harden for several hours or overnight before decorating house.

Fig. 4

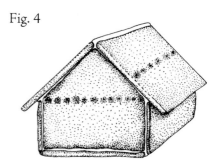

5. Use icing to attach candies and decorative items to house for doors, windows, shutters, chimneys, fences, shrubbery, and roof. Allow icing to harden.
6. Store house in an airtight container until ready to present.

LEMON LACE COOKIES

Spread season's greetings with our light and crispy Lemon Lace Cookies! These delectable confections have a delicate lemon flavor that's just right. Present the sweet sensations in a gold basket accented with white tulle and a pretty poinsettia.

LEMON LACE COOKIES

    2 cups butter or margarine, softened
1¹/₄ cups sugar
    1 tablespoon grated lemon zest
    1 teaspoon lemon extract
    1 teaspoon vanilla extract
    3 cups quick-cooking oats
    2 cups all-purpose flour
 ¹/₂ teaspoon salt
       Confectioners sugar

In a large bowl, cream butter and sugar until fluffy. Beat in lemon zest and extracts. In a medium bowl, combine oats, flour, and salt. Add dry ingredients to creamed mixture; stir until a soft dough forms. Cover and chill 30 minutes.

Preheat oven to 350 degrees. Shape dough into 1-inch balls; place about 2 inches apart on an ungreased baking sheet. Flatten balls with bottom of glass dipped in confectioners sugar. Bake 9 to 11 minutes or until edges are lightly browned. Cool cookies on baking sheet 1 minute; transfer to a wire rack to cool completely. Store in an airtight container.

Yield: about 8 dozen cookies

WHITE POINSETTIA BASKET
You will need two 6" x 30" strips of white tulle, 7" dia. gold basket, hot glue gun, and a large artificial white-flocked poinsettia.

1. Arrange strips of tulle on a flat surface to form a cross (Fig. 1).

Fig. 1

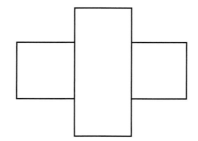

2. Place basket at center of crossed strips of tulle.
3. Place gift in basket.
4. Knot ends of tulle over basket.
5. Glue poinsettia to knot of tulle.

HEAVENLY BARS

If angels indulged in sweets, surely they would nibble on our Heavenly Bars! The chocolaty layered squares are delivered in a gilded tin that's embellished with stickers and gold paint. Netting, starry ribbon, and an easy-to-make tag complete the package.

HEAVENLY BARS

72 butter-flavored rectangular crackers (half of a 16-ounce package), divided
1 cup butter or margarine
1/2 cup milk
2 cups graham cracker crumbs
1 cup firmly packed brown sugar
1/3 cup granulated sugar
1/3 cup smooth peanut butter
1/2 cup milk chocolate chips
1/2 cup semisweet chocolate chips

Line a 9 x 13-inch baking pan with aluminum foil, extending foil over ends of pan; grease foil. Place a layer of crackers in bottom of pan. Melt butter in a heavy medium saucepan over medium-high heat. Stir in milk, graham cracker crumbs, and sugars. Bring mixture to a boil. Reduce heat to medium. Stirring constantly, boil minutes. Remove from heat. Spread half of sugar mixture over crackers. Place another layer of 24 crackers in pan. Spread remaining sugar mixture over crackers. Top with another layer of crackers. In a small saucepan, combine peanut butter and chocolate chips. Stirring frequently, cook over low heat until mixture is smooth. Spread chocolate mixture over crackers. Cover and chill about 4 hours or until firm.

Lift from pan using ends of foil. Cut into 1 1/2-inch squares. Store in an airtight container in refrigerator.

Yield: about 4 dozen squares

ANGEL TIN

You will need a 6 1/2" dia. tin with lid, a 6" x 27" strip of white netting, 1/2 yd of 1 1/2"w wired ribbon, angel stickers, metallic gold spray paint, metallic gold and dark gold liquid acrylic paint, small natural sponge pieces, matte clear acrylic spray, and cream paper for tag.

1. Spray paint tin gold.
2. For tag, fold a piece of cream paper in half.
3. Apply stickers to tag and lid of tin.
4. Using sponge pieces and metallic gold and dark gold paint, follow *Sponge Painting,* page 112, to sponge-paint tin and tag.
5. Apply 2 coats of acrylic spray to tin.
6. Knot netting strip around tin. Tie ribbon into a bow around ends of netting; trim ends of ribbon.

ur cheerfully decorated ingerbread Cookie Rounds ombine traditional Christmas flavor ith a hint of mocha. A fitting gift om one family to another, the spicy ookies are delivered in a sweetly mbellished "gingerbread" box. The olorful container is covered with sed-on fabric and topped with virls and dots of dimensional aint. A matching gift tag ompletes your surprise.

INGERBREAD COOKIE ROUNDS

OOKIES

- 1/2 cup butter or margarine, softened
- 1/2 cup firmly packed brown sugar
- 1/2 cup granulated sugar
- 1/2 cup molasses
- 1/4 cup strongly brewed coffee
- 1 egg
- 1 teaspoon vanilla extract
- 3 cups all-purpose flour
- 1/4 cup cocoa
- 1/2 teaspoons ground ginger
- 1 teaspoon ground cinnamon
- 1 teaspoon baking soda
- 1/4 teaspoon ground cloves
- 1/4 teaspoon salt

ING

- 1/2 cup sifted confectioners sugar
- 1 tablespoon vegetable shortening
- 1 tablespoon butter or margarine, softened
- 1 to 2 teaspoons water
- 1/4 teaspoon vanilla extract

For cookies, cream butter and sugars in a large bowl until fluffy. Add molasses, coffee, egg, and vanilla; beat until smooth. In a medium bowl, combine flour, cocoa, ginger, cinnamon, baking soda, cloves, and salt. Add dry ingredients to creamed mixture; stir until a soft dough forms. Cover and chill 1 hour.

Preheat oven to 350 degrees. On a lightly floured surface, use a floured rolling pin to roll out dough to 1/8-inch thickness. Use a floured 3-inch-diameter fluted-edge cookie cutter to cut out cookies. Transfer to a greased baking sheet. Bake 6 to 8 minutes or until bottoms are lightly browned. Transfer to a wire rack to cool completely.

For icing, beat confectioners sugar, shortening, butter, water, and vanilla in a small bowl until smooth. Spoon icing into a pastry bag fitted with a small round tip. Pipe decorations onto cookies. Let icing harden. Store in an airtight container.

Yield: about 3 1/2 dozen cookies

"GINGERBREAD" BOX

You will need a 6"w hexagon-shaped papier-mâché box; fabric to cover box; fusible web; white, red, and green dimensional paint; brown acrylic paint; paintbrush; 1 yd each of 3 different narrow ribbons; tracing paper; graphite transfer paper; glue; and colored paper and a gift label for tag.

1. Remove lid from box. To cover sides of box, fuse web to wrong side of fabric. Measure height of box; add 1/2". Measure around box; add 1". Cut a fabric strip the determined measurements.

2. Press 1 end of fabric strip 1/2" to wrong side. Beginning with unpressed end and matching 1 long edge of strip to top edge of box, fuse fabric strip around box. Glue fabric at overlap to secure. At bottom of box, clip fabric at each corner to about 1/8" from bottom of box. Fuse clipped edges of fabric to bottom of box.

3. To cover bottom of box, use a pencil to draw around bottom of box on fabric. Cut out fabric shape about 1/8" inside drawn lines. Center and fuse fabric shape to bottom of box.

4. For lid, paint lid brown. Trace pattern, page 117, onto tracing paper. Use transfer paper to transfer pattern to center top of lid.

5. Use white paint to paint over lines and dots indicated in grey on pattern. Use red and green paint to paint remaining dots as indicated on pattern.

6. Place gift in box and replace lid. Tie ribbons together into a bow around box; trim ends. If using curling ribbon, curl ends.

7. For tag, apply label to paper piece. Cutting around label, cut tag shape from paper. Write greeting on tag. Tuck tag under ribbons on box.

MINTY CHOCOLATE COOKIES

Chocoholics will agree—our Chocolate-Mint Sandwich Cookies are a dreamy treat! Rich chocolate coating covers icing-filled crackers to make the doubly sweet delights. Place the cookies inside a painted coffee can laced with old Christmas cards for a resourceful presentation.

CHOCOLATE-MINT SANDWICH COOKIES

$1^1/_2$ packages (12 ounces each) round butter-flavored crackers

1 container (16 ounces) chocolate ready-to-spread frosting

1 package (1 pound, 8 ounces) chocolate candy coating, chopped

2 packages (10 ounces each) mint chocolate chips

Place half of crackers (about 84 crackers) on waxed paper. Spoon frosting into a pastry bag fitted with a large round tip. Pipe about 1 teaspoon frosting onto each cracker. Place remaining crackers on top of frosting and press lightly. In a heavy large saucepan, melt candy coating and chocolate chips over low heat. Remove from heat. Dip each cracker sandwich into chocolate. Place on waxed paper and let chocolate harden. Store in an airtight container in a cool place.

Yield: about 7 dozen cookies

"RECYCLED" CARD CAN

You will need red and green spray paint, clean dry can with lid (we used a $6^3/_4$"h x 6" dia. can), assorted Christmas cards, hole punch, $^1/_8$"w red satin ribbon, glue, $2^1/_2$"w red and white stripe wired ribbon, floral wire, and wire cutters.

1. Spray paint outside of can green and top and sides of lid red.
2. Trim cards to fit side of can. Punch two holes in top and bottom edges of each card.
3. Measure around can; add 8". Cut tw[o] lengths of $^1/_8$"w ribbon the determine[d] measurement. Lace one ribbon length through holes at top of cards. Repeat for bottom of cards.
4. Spacing cards evenly around can; spot glue cards to can to secure. Tie ribbons into a bow around can.
5. Use wired ribbon and follow *Makin[g] a Bow,* page 112, to make a bow to fit lid of can. Tie two lengths of $^1/_8$"w ribbon into a bow around knot. Cente[r] and glue bow to top of lid.

SLICE-AND-BAKE COOKIE KIT

Kids love baking and decorating their own Christmas cookies, especially when you pack everything they need to make them into one fun carrier! Complete with purchased icing, sprinkles, and a nifty kid-size apron, our cookie kit will provide hours of fun. Don't forget to tuck in the most important ingredient— a roll of made-ahead Slice-and-Bake Cookie dough!

SLICE-AND-BAKE COOKIES

$3/4$ cup butter or margarine, softened
$1/4$ cups sugar
1 egg
1 teaspoon vanilla extract
2 cups all-purpose flour
$1/2$ teaspoon salt

In a large bowl, cream butter and sugar until fluffy. Add egg and vanilla; beat until smooth. In a small bowl, combine flour and salt. Add dry ingredients to creamed mixture; stir until a soft dough forms. Divide dough in half. Place each half on plastic wrap. Use plastic wrap to shape dough into two 8-inch-long rolls. Chill 3 hours or until firm (if rolls have flattened, reshape into a round shape). Give with baking instructions.

To bake: Preheat oven to 375 degrees. Cut dough into $1/4$-inch slices. Place 1 inch apart on a lightly greased baking sheet. Bake 6 to 8 minutes or until bottoms are lightly browned. Transfer cookies to a wire rack to cool. Store in an airtight container.

Yield: about $2^{1/2}$ dozen cookies in each roll

COOKIE KIT

You will need a six-pack beverage carrier, red spray paint, Christmas-motif wrapping paper, spray adhesive, assorted cookie baking supplies (sprinkles, decorating icing tubes with tips, and apron), two 5" x 10" cellophane bags, and curling ribbon.

For gift tag, you will *also* need decorative-edge craft scissors, white paper, glue, hole punch, and a red permanent medium-point marker.

1. Spray paint carrier red.
2. Measure around carrier; add $1/2$". Measure height of carrier sides. Cut a piece of wrapping paper the determined measurements. Apply spray adhesive to wrong side of wrapping paper. Overlapping ends at one side edge, glue wrapping paper around carrier.
3. Place desired baking supplies in cellophane bags. Tie several lengths of ribbon into a bow around top of each bag; curl ends. Place bags and remaining supplies in separate sections of carrier.
4. For tag, use craft scissors to cut a $1^{1/4}$" x $3^{3/4}$" piece from white paper. Punch hole in corner of tag.
5. Cut one motif from wrapping paper; glue to tag. Use marker to write message on tag. Thread curling ribbon through hole in tag; tie tag to gift. Curl ribbon ends.

...he aromas and flavors of ...pices naturally accompany the ...olidays, and desserts are no ...xception! Chocolate-Orange-...pice Cookie Mix is a sweet ...hortcut for busy folks. Give ...e easy-to-make mix in a ...aid flannel bag accented ...ith a felt reindeer and cookie ...tter to make their baking festive.

CHOCOLATE-ORANGE-SPICE COOKIE MIX

- 8 cups all-purpose flour
- 1/2 cups granulated sugar
- 1/2 cups firmly packed brown sugar
- 1 cup cocoa
- 1 tablespoon dried orange peel
- 2 teaspoons ground cinnamon
- 2 teaspoons ground ginger
- 1/2 teaspoons baking soda
- 1 teaspoon salt
- 3/4 cups chilled butter or margarine, cut into pieces

In a very large bowl, combine flour, sugars, cocoa, orange peel, cinnamon, ginger, baking soda, and salt. Using a pastry blender or 2 knives, cut in butter until mixture resembles coarse meal. Divide mix evenly into 4 resealable plastic bags (about 4 1/2 to 5 cups mix per bag). Store in refrigerator. Give with baking instructions.

Yield: about 18 cups cookie mix

To bake: Bring cookie mix to room temperature before mixing. Preheat oven to 375 degrees. In a medium bowl, combine cookie mix, 1 egg, 2 tablespoons milk, and 2 teaspoons vanilla extract; beat with an electric mixer until a soft dough forms. Divide dough in half. On a heavily floured surface, use a floured rolling pin to roll out half of dough to slightly less than 1/8-inch thickness. Use a 4-inch-wide x 3 1/2-inch-high reindeer-shaped cookie cutter to cut out cookies. Transfer to a lightly greased baking sheet. Bake 4 to 6 minutes or until bottoms are lightly browned. Transfer cookies to a wire rack to cool. Repeat with remaining dough. Store in an airtight container.

Yield: about 5 dozen cookies

FLANNEL GIFT BAG

You will need a 10 1/2" x 25" piece of plaid flannel fabric, 3 1/2"h x 4"w reindeer cookie cutter, 5" square white felt, glue, 23" length each of red and black 1/4"w grosgrain ribbon, one 6" length and two 23" lengths of jute twine, artificial greenery (we used a stem of holly leaves with berries) and two 1" dia. jingle bells.

1. Matching right sides and short edges, fold fabric in half. Using a 1/4" seam allowance, sew sides of bag together. Turn bag right side out. Fringe top edge of bag.
2. Draw around cookie cutter on felt; cut out shape. Glue shape to bag front.
3. Place a bag of cookie mix in gift bag.
4. Tie ribbons and 23" lengths of jute into a bow around top of bag. Insert greenery into knot of bow; glue to secure.
5. Thread two jute streamers through shank of one jingle bell; knot ends together. Repeat for remaining bell and streamers.
6. Thread remaining length of jute through cookie cutter; tie to bag.

A yummy filling of vanilla frosting and colorful candy-coated chocolates is sandwiched between two layers of marshmallow cereal squares for these Crispy-Crunchy Candy Bars. Individually wrapped in cellophane, the lip-smacking snacks make great party favors for your "deerest" friends. The cute reindeer pins are fashioned from crafting foam and can be worn throughout the holidays.

CRISPY-CRUNCHY CANDY BARS

2 1/2 cups red and green candy-coated mini chocolate pieces
1 can (16 ounces) vanilla-flavored ready-to-spread frosting
1/2 cup butter or margarine, divided
10 cups miniature marshmallows, divided
1 cup creamy peanut butter, divided
1/2 cup light corn syrup, divided
10 cups crispy rice cereal, divided

In a small bowl, stir together chocolate pieces and frosting; set aside.

Microwave 1/4 cup butter in a large microwave-safe bowl on high power (100%) 40 seconds or until butter melts. Stir in 5 cups marshmallows and microwave on high power about 1 minute or until marshmallows begin to soften; stir until marshmallows melt. Add 1/2 cup peanut butter and 1/4 cup corn syrup. Stir in 5 cups cereal until well blended. With greased hands, press half of cereal mixture into each of 2 greased 7 x 11-inch baking dishes. Spread cereal layers with frosting mixture. Make a second batch of cereal mixture using remaining 1/4 cup butter, 5 cups marshmallows, 1/2 cup peanut butter, 1/4 cup corn syrup, and 5 cups cereal. Carefully press second batch of cereal mixture over frosting layers in both pans. Cover and chill 30 minutes or until mixture is firm. Cut into 2-inch squares. Store in an airtight container.

Yield: about 2 1/2 dozen bars

REINDEER PIN FAVORS

For each favor, you will need tan and brown 1/16" thick crafting foam, two 10mm oval wiggle eyes, a 12mm red pom-pom for nose, 1 pin back, either small sharp scissors or craft knife and cutting mat (for cutting foam), 6" of 3/8"w ribbon for bow tie, liquid fray preventative, tracing paper, hot glue gun, glue sticks, a small cellophane gift bag, and desired ribbons to tie around top of bag.

1. Trace patterns onto tracing paper; cut out. Use a pencil to draw around antler and muzzle patterns on tan foam and head pattern on brown foam; cut out shapes along drawn lines.

2. For bow tie, tie 3/8"w ribbon into a bow; trim ends. Apply fray preventative to ribbon ends; allow to dry.
3. Glue bow tie, muzzle, antlers, eyes, and pom-pom to reindeer head. Glue pin back to back of reindeer head.
4. Place 1 candy bar in bag. Tie ribbons together into a bow around top of bag; trim ends. Pin reindeer to bow.

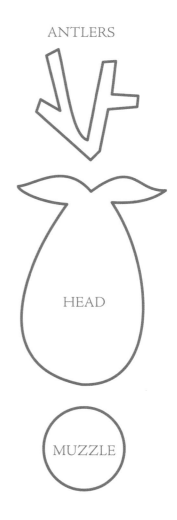

ANTLERS

HEAD

MUZZLE

SUGAR COOKIE "BURGERS"

Boggle their eyes and delight their taste buds with these creative hamburger look-alikes! Filled with tinted coconut and chocolate frosting, our Sugar Cookie "Burgers" are a merry treat that everyone will enjoy. Small snackers who are always on the go will especially like the scrumptious sweets in a "take-out" bag straight from the North Pole!

SUGAR COOKIE "BURGERS"

Cookies are best when given the day they are made.

- 1 package (18 ounces) refrigerated sugar cookie dough
- $1/4$ cup chopped peanuts
- $1^1/2$ cups flaked coconut
  Green liquid food coloring
- 1 container (16 ounces) chocolate ready-to-spread frosting

Preheat oven to 350 degrees. Cut cookie dough into $1/4$-inch slices. Place 2 inches apart on an ungreased baking sheet; shape into rounds. On half of cookies, press $1/2$ teaspoon peanuts into each cookie. Bake 8 to 10 minutes or until tops are lightly browned. Transfer cookies to a wire rack to cool.

Place coconut in a resealable plastic bag. Add 5 to 6 drops food coloring. Shake coconut until evenly tinted; set aside. Spread 1 tablespoon frosting over flat side of each plain cookie; sprinkle about $1^1/2$ tablespoons coconut over frosting. Spread 1 teaspoon frosting over flat side of each peanut cookie. Place peanut cookies on coconut-covered cookies; gently squeeze cookies together. Store in an airtight container.

Yield: about 16 cookie "burgers"

MERRY MEAL BAGS

For each bag, you will need a 6" x 11" gift bag, hole punch, two 24" lengths each of two colors of curling ribbon, photocopy of tag design (page 114) on white card stock, craft glue stick, and one $4^3/4$" x 6" sheet of self-adhesive stickers.

1. Place gift in bag. Fold top of bag 2" to back. At each side of bag, punch a hole through center folded portion of bag. Thread one ribbon of each color through hole; tie together into a bow. Curl ribbon ends.

2. Cut out tag; glue at top center front of bag. Glue corners of sticker sheet to front of bag.

CHRISTMAS LIGHT COOKIES

These Christmas Light Cookies will be a bright surprise for your special friends. Imagine how their faces will light up when they discover what's packed inside the cleverly disguised gift box! The mint-flavored treats are easy to make and fun to decorate with icing in traditional tree light colors.

CHRISTMAS LIGHT COOKIES

COOKIES

$^3/_4$ cup butter or margarine, softened
$^1/_3$ cup granulated sugar
$^1/_3$ cup firmly packed brown sugar
 1 egg
 1 teaspoon mint extract
 2 cups all-purpose flour
$^3/_4$ teaspoon baking soda
$^1/_3$ cup finely ground walnuts

ICING

 5 cups confectioners sugar
$^1/_2$ cup plus 1 tablespoon milk
    Green, red, orange, and blue paste
    food coloring

For cookies, cream butter and sugars in a large bowl until fluffy. Add egg and mint extract, beating until smooth. In another large bowl, sift together flour and baking soda. Stir flour mixture and nuts into creamed mixture, mixing until a soft dough forms. Cover and chill 1 hour.

Preheat oven to 350 degrees. On a lightly floured surface, use a floured rolling pin to roll out dough to $^1/_4$-inch thickness. For pattern, use a black permanent marker to draw pattern on clear acetate; cut out. Place pattern on dough and use a sharp knife to cut out cookies. Transfer to a greased baking sheet. Use a drinking straw to make a hole at the bottom of each cookie. Bake 8 to 10 minutes or until cookies are light brown. Cool completely on a wire rack.

For icing, beat sugar and milk in a large bowl until smooth. Divide icing evenly into 5 small bowls. Leaving 1 bowl white, tint remaining bowls green, red, orange, and blue. Referring to photo, spread icing on cookies. Allow icing to harden. Store in an airtight container.

Yield: about 2 dozen cookies

CHRISTMAS LIGHTS BOX

You will need a box with lid, white paper, red paper, desired lettering stencil, stencil brush, paper towels, removable tape (optional), black acrylic paint, glue stick, and tissue paper to line box.

1. For box label, follow Step 3 of *Stenciling*, page 112, to stencil "CHRISTMAS LIGHTS" on white paper. Cut label desired size.
2. Cut a piece of red paper $^1/_4$" larger on all sides than label. Center label on red paper; glue to secure.
3. Position label on box; glue to secure.
4. Line box with tissue paper.

CHRISTMAS CAKES & PIES

Christmas cakes of every kind and perfectly scrumptious pies—gifts that tantalize the taste buds are welcomed by everyone. Create these velvety-rich desserts and their pretty packaging for all your friends and neighbors.

FUN CHRISTMAS TREES

We'll let you decide which is more fun—making these jolly Christmas tree treats or eating them! Created using a packaged cake mix, the "trees" are glazed with green icing and then trimmed with red "garlands" and candy sprinkles. Peppermint sticks form the "trunks."

FUN CHRISTMAS TREES

CAKE
1 package (18^1/$_4$ ounces) white cake mix with pudding in the mix and ingredients to prepare cake
Green paste food coloring

GREEN ICING
4 cups confectioners sugar
5 to 6 tablespoons half and half
1 teaspoon vanilla extract
Green paste food coloring

RED ICING
1 cup confectioners sugar
1 to 2 tablespoons half and half
^{1}/$_2$ teaspoon vanilla extract
Red paste food coloring
Multicolored non-pareils
Peppermint candy sticks or candy canes

Trace pattern onto stencil plastic; cut out. Preheat oven to 350 degrees. For cake, grease a 10^1/$_2$ by 15^1/$_2$-inch jellyroll pan. Line bottom with waxed paper; grease waxed paper. Mix cake according to package directions; tint batter green. Pour into prepared pan. Bake 18 to 20 minutes or until a toothpick inserted in center of cake comes out clean. Cool in pan. Invert cake onto a large cutting board. Cut cake lengthwise into thirds (each piece should measure about 3^1/$_4$ x 14 inches). Use pattern to cut 9 tree-shaped cakes from each section. Place cakes on a wire rack with waxed paper underneath.

For green icing, combine confectioners sugar, half and half, and vanilla in a medium bowl; stir until smooth. Tint green.

For red icing, combine confectioners sugar, half and half, and vanilla in a small bowl; stir until smooth. Tint red. Spoon icing into a pastry bag fitted with a small round tip.

To decorate cakes, spoon green icing over tops of cakes. While icing is still wet, pipe red "garland" onto cakes. Sprinkle some of the cakes with non-pareils. Let icing harden. Store in an airtight container in a single layer. When ready to give, insert a peppermint stick into bottom of each cake for "tree trunk."

Yield: 27 cakes

COCONUT POUND CAKES

Drizzled with a snowy glaze and sprinkled with flakes of coconut, our Coconut Pound Cakes are simply delicious! To create these rich confections, simply enhance purchased cake mix with sour cream and coconut extract. The recipe yields six miniature cakes, so you can treat several friends and co-workers.

COCONUT POUND CAKES

1 package (16 ounces) pound cake mix
1 cup sour cream
2 eggs
1 teaspoon coconut extract
1 cup frozen shredded coconut, divided
1/2 cups sifted confectioners sugar
2 tablespoons milk

Preheat oven to 325 degrees. Combine cake mix, sour cream, eggs, and coconut extract in a medium bowl; beat until well blended. Stir in 1/4 cup coconut. Spoon into greased and floured cups of a 6-mold fluted tube pan. Bake 35 to 40 minutes or until a toothpick inserted in center of cake comes out clean. Cool in pan minutes; invert cakes onto a wire rack with waxed paper underneath. Combine confectioners sugar and milk; stir until smooth. Drizzle glaze over warm cakes. Sprinkle with remaining 1/4 cup coconut. Allow glaze to harden. Store in an airtight container.

Yield: six 4-inch cakes

GERMAN CHOCOLATE CHEESECAKE

A very Merry Christmas from the Prathers!

...eat family friends to
...e temptingly rich flavor of
...ecadent German Chocolate
...heesecake. A crunchy topping
...layered over a smooth filling
...d homemade crust—makes
...is cheesecake irresistible!
...esent your gift in a cake box
...vered with holiday gift wrap
...d tied with a pretty bow.

GERMAN CHOCOLATE CHEESECAKE

CRUST
1 1/2 cups chocolate graham cracker crumbs
6 tablespoons butter or margarine, melted
1/4 cup sugar

FILLING
3 packages (8 ounces each) cream cheese, softened
1 1/4 cups sugar
2 tablespoons all-purpose flour
4 eggs
1 package (4 ounces) German baking chocolate, melted
1/4 cup whipping cream
1 teaspoon vanilla extract

TOPPING
3/4 cup sugar
3/4 cup whipping cream
2 egg yolks
6 tablespoons butter or margarine
1 cup flaked coconut
1 cup chopped pecans

Preheat oven to 325 degrees. For crust, combine cracker crumbs, melted butter, and sugar in a small bowl. Firmly press into bottom and 1/2 inch up sides of a lightly greased 9-inch springform pan.

For filling, beat cream cheese and sugar in a large bowl until fluffy. Beat in flour. Beat in eggs, 1 at a time, just until combined. Stir in melted chocolate, whipping cream, and vanilla. Pour over crust. Bake 1 hour or until center is almost set. Cool in pan 1 hour. Loosen and remove sides of pan. Cool completely.

For topping, whisk sugar, whipping cream, and egg yolks in a medium saucepan until well blended. Whisking constantly, add butter and cook over medium heat until mixture is thickened and bubbly. Reduce heat to low; cook 2 minutes longer. Remove from heat and stir in coconut and pecans. Transfer topping to a heat-proof bowl. Let cool 20 minutes or until thick enough to spread on cooled cheesecake. Store in an airtight container in refrigerator.

Yield: about 16 servings

HOLLY CAKE BOX
You will need a 10" square x 4"h cake box, wrapping paper, spray adhesive, craft knife, cutting mat, 2 2/3 yds. of 2 1/2"w wired ribbon, 6" of floral wire, black permanent fine-point marker, and a purchased gift tag.

1. Unfold box. Cut piece from wrapping paper 1" larger on all sides than box. Place paper wrong side up on a flat surface. Apply spray adhesive to outside of box. Center unfolded box adhesive side down on paper; press firmly to secure.
2. Use craft knife to cut paper even with edges of box. If box has slits, use craft knife to cut through slits from inside of box; reassemble box.
3. Place cake in box.
4. Knot a 32" length of ribbon around box. Use remaining ribbon and follow *Making a Bow*, page 112, to make a bow with a 3" center loop, six 7" loops, and two 8" streamers. Wire bow over knot of ribbon on top of box.
5. Use marker to write message on tag.

PARTY CUPCAKE CONES

Kids will love these novel party favors, and you won't have to worry about the "ice cream" melting—it's really frosting atop cupcakes baked right in the cones! Given in a cup wrapped in cellophane and tied with a festive bow, the cones make sweet tokens of "confection!"

PARTY CUPCAKE CONES

These should be given the day they are made for maximum freshness of cones.

CUPCAKES

- 1 package (18¼ ounces) white cake mix and ingredients to prepare cake
- 1 tablespoon *each* green and red sprinkles
- 25 small flat-bottom ice-cream cones

ICING

- 5 cups confectioners sugar
- ¾ cup vegetable shortening
- ½ cup butter or margarine, softened
- 2½ to 3 tablespoons milk
- 1¼ teaspoons clear vanilla extract
  Peppermint candies

Preheat oven to 350 degrees. For cupcakes, prepare cake mix according to package directions, stirring in sprinkles. Fill each cone with about 2½ tablespoons batter. Place cones about 3 inches apart on an ungreased baking sheet. Bake 25 to 30 minutes or until a toothpick inserted in center of cupcake comes out clean. Cool completely.

For icing, combine confectioners sugar, shortening, butter, milk, and vanilla in a medium bowl; beat until smooth. Ice cupcakes. Place a candy on each cupcake. Let icing harden. Loosely cover with waxed paper.

Yield: 25 cupcakes

PARTY CUPCAKE BAGS

For each bag, you will need 22" of 1⅝"w red mesh ribbon, one white and one green chenille stem, two wrapped peppermint candies, 8-oz. clear plastic cup, and a 21" square of clear cellophane.

1. Fold mesh ribbon into a bow; twist green chenille stem around center of bow to secure. Twist green chenille stem around center of white chenille stem. Wrap each green stem end around a candy; curl green ends.
2. Place cone in cup; center cup on cellophane. Gather cellophane over cup; secure gathers with white stem.

RED VELVET CUPCAKES

When the colorful batter is baked, our Red Velvet Cupcakes take on a crimson hue and a velvety texture. Topped with rich cream cheese icing and packed in a ribbon-tied cupcake container, these delectable confections will make a special someone's day.

RED VELVET CUPCAKES

CAKE

- 2/3 cup butter or margarine, softened
- 2/3 cups sugar
- 2 eggs, separated
- 1 bottle (1 ounce) red liquid food coloring
- 2 tablespoons vanilla extract
- 1/4 cups sifted cake flour
- 1/4 cup cocoa
- 1 teaspoon baking soda
- 3/4 teaspoon salt
- 1 cup plus 2 tablespoons buttermilk
- 2 teaspoons white vinegar

ICING

- 4 ounces cream cheese, softened
- 1/3 cup vegetable shortening
- 1/3 cup butter or margarine, softened
- 1/2 teaspoons clear vanilla extract
- 1/3 cups sifted confectioners sugar
- 1 tablespoon water
- Crushed red and green peppermint candies to decorate

Preheat oven to 350 degrees. For cake, cream butter and sugar in a large bowl until fluffy. Add egg yolks, food coloring, and vanilla; beat until smooth. In a medium bowl, combine cake flour, cocoa, baking soda, and salt. In a small bowl, combine buttermilk and vinegar.

Alternately beat dry ingredients and buttermilk mixture into creamed mixture, beating until well blended. Beat egg whites in a small bowl until stiff peaks form; fold into batter. Fill paper-lined muffin cups about two-thirds full. Bake 15 to 17 minutes or until a toothpick inserted in center of cupcake comes out clean. Transfer cupcakes to a wire rack to cool.

For icing, beat cream cheese, shortening, butter, and vanilla in a medium bowl until fluffy. Add confectioners sugar and water; beat until smooth. Ice each cupcake with about 1 tablespoon icing. Sprinkle candies on cupcakes. Store in an airtight container.

Yield: about 2 1/2 dozen cupcakes

COCONUT CREAM CAKE

opped with snowy drifts of fluffy osting, our luscious Coconut ream Cake looks like a delightful inter wonderland! To surprise a iend, send a trio of playful papier-âché penguins along with the nowcapped cake. Even when the ake is gone, they'll make adorable it-abouts or ornaments.

COCONUT CREAM CAKE

AKE
- 1 cup butter or margarine, softened
- 2 cups sugar
- 5 eggs
- 1 teaspoon vanilla extract
- 2 cups all-purpose flour
- 1 teaspoon baking soda
- 1/2 teaspoon salt
- 1 cup buttermilk
- 2 cups sweetened shredded coconut
- 1 cup finely chopped pecans

ROSTING
- 2 cups whipping cream
- 1/3 cup sugar
- 1/3 cup sour cream
- 3 cups sweetened shredded coconut, divided

Preheat oven to 350 degrees. For ake, cream butter and sugar in a large owl until fluffy. Add eggs, 1 at a time, eating well after each addition. Stir vanilla. In another large bowl, sift ogether next 3 ingredients. Stir dry ngredients and buttermilk alternately nto creamed mixture. Fold in coconut nd pecans. Pour batter into 3 greased nd floured 9-inch round cake pans.

Bake 30 to 35 minutes or until a toothpick inserted in center comes out clean. Cool in pans 10 minutes; turn onto wire racks to cool completely.

For frosting, whip cream in a chilled large bowl until soft peaks form. Add sugar and sour cream; beat until stiff peaks form. Fold in 2 cups coconut. Spread about 1/3 cup frosting between layers of cake. Spread remaining frosting on sides and top of cake. Sprinkle remaining coconut on top and sides of cake.

Yield: about 20 servings

PENGUIN ORNAMENTS

For each ornament, you will need one 2 1/2" long papier-mâché egg (available at craft stores); white, dk yellow, orange, and black acrylic paint; foam brush; paintbrushes; tracing paper; lightweight cardboard; two 5" squares of red flannel fabric for hat; fabric marking pencil; small crochet hook (for turning fabric); one 1/2" dia. white pom-pom; 2" of 1/4"w red satin ribbon; red thread; hot glue gun; and glue sticks.

1. Paint egg black. Allow to dry.
2. Use a pencil to sketch body pattern onto egg.
3. (*Note:* Allow to dry after each paint color.) Paint shirt and eyes white, buttons black, and nose orange.
4. Trace foot and hat patterns onto tracing paper; cut out.
5. Use foot pattern and cut 2 feet from cardboard. Paint feet dk yellow; allow to dry. Overlapping round ends of feet, glue feet to bottom of egg.

6. For hat, leave bottom edge open and follow *Sewing Shapes*, page 113, to make hat from fabric squares. Press bottom edge 1/4" to wrong side; glue to secure. Glue pom-pom to point of hat. Glue hat to penguin. Fold hat to 1 side; glue in place.
7. For tie, wrap thread around center of ribbon and knot ends together. Cut a V-shaped notch in each end of ribbon. Glue tie to penguin.

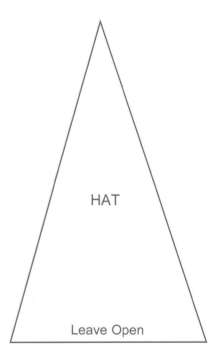

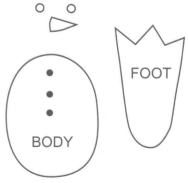

NOEL CAKES

Lighter in texture than traditional fruitcake, ginger-spiced Noel Cakes are laden with dried apricots and cherries, candied pineapple, and pecans. Buttery Orange Sauce, flavored with orange liqueur, makes a delectable topping for the moist cake. For an elegant presentation, place one of the fruitcakes and a bottle of the spirited sauce on a brass tray lined with a festive cloth.

NOEL CAKES WITH ORANGE SAUCE

CAKE

- $^2/_3$ cup chopped dried apricots
- 1 container (4 ounces) candied pineapple
- $^1/_2$ cup all-purpose flour, divided
- 1 cup dried cherries, pitted
- 1 cup orange-flavored liqueur
- 6 tablespoons butter or margarine, softened
- $^1/_4$ cup firmly packed brown sugar
- 2 tablespoons finely chopped crystallized ginger
- $^1/_2$ teaspoon ground cinnamon
- $^1/_4$ teaspoon ground nutmeg
- $^1/_8$ teaspoon ground cloves
- 2 eggs
- 1 cup chopped pecans

ORANGE SAUCE

- 1 cup butter or margarine
- 1 cup firmly packed brown sugar
- 1 cup orange-flavored liqueur

In a food processor fitted with a steel blade, process apricots, pineapple, and 2 teaspoons flour until coarsely chopped. Combine apricot mixture, cherries, and liqueur in a medium saucepan. Cook over medium heat until mixture begins to boil; remove from heat. Drain fruit, reserving liquid for sauce.

Preheat oven to 350 degrees. Place remaining flour and next 6 ingredients in a food processor fitted with a steel blade; process until a soft dough forms. Add eggs; process until smooth. Transfer mixture to a large bowl. Stir in nuts and drained fruit. Pour batter evenly into 2 greased $3^1/_2$ x 5-inch loaf pans. Bake 20 to 25 minutes or until a toothpick inserted in center comes out clean. Cool 10 minutes in pans; turn onto a wire rack to cool completely. Store in an airtight container.

For sauce, combine butter and sugar in a medium saucepan over medium heat. Bring to a boil, stirring constantly until sugar is dissolved. Remove from heat; whisk in reserved liquid and liqueur. Store in an airtight container in refrigerator. Give with instructions to serve.

Serve sauce warm with cake. To reheat, transfer sauce to a medium saucepan. Cook over medium heat 2 to 3 minutes, stirring constantly until heated through.

Yield: 2 cakes

CARAMEL-NUT SPICE CAKE

The next time you're invited to a holiday gathering, surprise the hostess with a Caramel-Nut Spice Cake. This delicious dessert offers bakery-shop taste—but you can make it in no time! Topped with a nutty caramel glaze, our cake uses packaged cake and pudding mixes. A purchased cake box covered with wrapping paper and topped with a fancy bow becomes an elegant container for delivery.

CARAMEL-NUT SPICE CAKE

1 package (18.25 ounces) spice cake mix
1 package (3.5 ounces) butterscotch instant pudding and pie filling mix
4 eggs
$1/4$ cups water
$1/2$ cup vegetable oil
24 caramels (about $1/2$ of a 14-ounce package)
3 tablespoons water
$1/4$ cup chopped walnuts

Preheat oven to 350 degrees. Combine cake mix, pudding mix, eggs, water, and oil in a large bowl; beat until well blended. Pour into a greased -inch fluted tube pan. Bake 43 to minutes or until a toothpick inserted center of cake comes out clean. Allow ke to cool in pan on a wire rack minutes. Invert cake onto a serving ate.

Combine caramels and water in a medium microwave-safe bowl. Microwave on medium-high power (80%) 3 minutes or until caramels melt, stirring after each minute. Stir in walnuts. Drizzle caramel mixture over warm cake. Allow cake to cool completely. Store in an airtight container.

Yield: about 16 servings

CAKE BOX

Follow *Steps 1-3 of Holly Cake Box*, page 43, to cover a purchased cake box. Tie a length of 2"w wired ribbon around box. Follow *Making a Bow*, page 112, to make a bow from another length of wired ribbon. Use florist wire to attach bow to ribbon around box.

GOOD NEIGHBORS' CAKES

These delicious Orange Cakes decorated with a homey motif are the perfect way to show your neighbors how much you appreciate them. A popular old quilt pattern inspired the house design, which is easily created with Christmas red icing. Our recipe makes two of the delicately flavored cakes so you can share this festive holiday greeting with more than one family!

ORANGE CAKES

CAKE

- $^3/_4$ cup butter or margarine, softened
- $1^1/_2$ cups sugar
- 1 tablespoon grated dried orange peel
- 3 eggs
- $2^1/_2$ cups all-purpose flour
- $2^1/_2$ teaspoons baking powder
- $^3/_4$ teaspoon salt
- 1 cup milk
- 2 tablespoons frozen orange juice concentrate, thawed

ICING

- 4 cups confectioners sugar, divided
- 6 tablespoons milk, divided
  Red paste food coloring

Preheat oven to 325 degrees. For cake, cream butter, sugar, and orange peel in a large bowl until fluffy. Add eggs, 1 at a time, beating well after each addition. In another large bowl, sift together next 3 ingredients. Stir dry ingredients alternately with milk and orange juice concentrate into creamed mixture,

beating until smooth after each addition. Pour batter into 2 greased and floured 8-inch square baking pans. Bake 35 to 40 minutes or until a toothpick inserted in center comes out clean. Cool in pans 10 minutes. Turn onto a wire rack to cool completely.

For icing, combine 2 cups confectioners sugar and 3 tablespoons milk in a medium bowl; beat until smooth. Spread icing on sides and top of each cake. Allow icing to harden. To transfer pattern to top of each cake, trace pattern onto tracing paper. Center pattern on top of each cake and use a toothpick to punch holes about $^1/_4$ inch apart through pattern into icing. Remove pattern. Combine remaining sugar and milk in another medium bowl, beating until smooth. Tint with food coloring. Spread icing inside house design. Allow icing to harden. Store in an airtight container.

Yield: 2 cakes

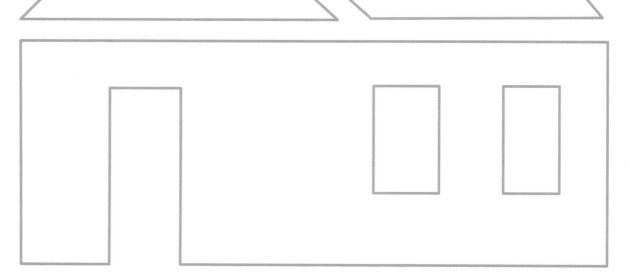

CRANBERRY-ORANGE PIES

If someone on your gift list deserves a special treat, reward them with a Cranberry-Orange Pie. The creamy filling is poured into a ready-made graham cracker crust, so it's extra-easy to prepare. For a sweet delivery, we wrapped a pie in cellophane and decorated it with a striped bow and a handmade ornament.

CRANBERRY-ORANGE PIES

- 1 container (8 ounces) frozen non-dairy whipped topping, thawed and divided
- 1 can (14 ounces) sweetened condensed milk
- 1 can (6 ounces) frozen cranberry juice cocktail concentrate, thawed
- 3/4 cup whole berry cranberry sauce
- 1/4 teaspoon orange extract
- 2 purchased graham cracker pie crusts (6 ounces each)

Place 1 cup whipped topping in a small bowl; set aside. Beat sweetened condensed milk, cranberry juice concentrate, cranberry sauce, and orange extract in a large bowl with an electric mixer until well blended. Fold in remaining whipped topping. Spoon into crusts. Spoon reserved whipped topping into a pastry bag fitted with a large star tip. Pipe topping onto each pie. Cover with plastic lids and store in freezer. Serve chilled.

Yield: 2 pies, 8 servings each

ORANGE SLICE ORNAMENTS

For each ornament, you will need tracing paper, corrugated paper, poster board, hot glue gun, preserved evergreen, cinnamon sticks, dried orange slice, hole punch, and 6" of string.

1. Trace star pattern, page 119, onto tracing paper; cut out. Using pattern, cut one star each from corrugated paper and poster board. Glue corrugated paper star to poster board star. Glue evergreen, cinnamon sticks, and dried orange slice to star.

2. For hanger, punch a hole in top of star. Thread string through hole; knot ends 2" from ornament.

MOCHA BROWNIE PIES

Create swirls of fun with our Mocha Brownie Pies! These tasty treats will always be welcome gifts. A luscious blend of brownie mix, instant coffee, and cream cheese makes up the dessert, and this time-saving recipe will be doubly pleasing because there's enough for two pies. For country charm, wrap up your gift in a fresh kitchen towel and trim it with greenery and a raffia bow.

MOCHA BROWNIE PIES

$1/2$ cup plus 2 tablespoons hot water
$1/2$ tablespoons instant coffee granules
1 package (21.6 ounces) brownie mix
$1/4$ cup vegetable oil
1 egg
2 purchased chocolate graham cracker pie crusts (6 ounces each)
1 package (8 ounces) cream cheese, softened
$1/2$ cup sifted confectioners sugar

Preheat oven to 350 degrees. In a small bowl, combine hot water and coffee granules; set aside. In a large bowl, combine brownie mix, oil, $1/2$ cup coffee mixture, and egg. Mix until dry ingredients are moistened. Spread half of batter in bottom of each pie crust. In a medium bowl, combine cream cheese and confectioners sugar; beat until smooth. Beat in remaining 2 tablespoons coffee mixture. Spoon cream cheese mixture evenly over brownie batter in pans. Carefully swirl with a knife. Bake 28 to 31 minutes (do not overbake). Cool 10 minutes before serving. Serve warm or cool completely on a wire rack. Store in an airtight container in refrigerator.

Yield: 2 pies, about 8 servings each

CHRISTMAS SNACKS & SIPS

When the holiday season arrives, it's nice to have an excuse to slow down and savor the moments. Give your friends a reason to rest awhile with these sweet or salty snacks and a nice variety of blended beverages. Even Fido and Fluffy can enjoy their very own treats.

PEAR WINE

For a Yuletide gift with European flavor, present a bottle of Pear Wine in a ribbon-tied basket. The mellow beverage is easy to make by adding fresh fruit and sugar to white wine, and it's wonderful served with fresh bread sticks or cheese. A simple wax seal gives the bottle a gourmet look.

PEAR WINE

    4 ripe Bartlett pears
    1 bottle (720 ml) dry white wine
$^1/_4$ cup granulated sugar

Wash and core pears; cut into small cubes. Combine pears and remaining ingredients in a large bowl; stir until sugar dissolves. Pour into bottle and chill 3 days to allow flavors to blend. Store in an airtight container in refrigerator.

Yield: about 3 cups wine

WAX BOTTLE SEAL

Follow *Sealing Bottle with Wax* instructions, page 113.

WINE AND CHEESE BASKET

Neatly packaged for two in a holly-trimmed basket, a gift of Cranberry Wine and Cheese Balls brings a classic taste of the holidays to a super couple. Etched wine glasses and a pretty bottle serve up the refreshing spirit, while cheeses blended with marinated cranberries make a delicious topper for crackers.

CRANBERRY WINE

> 1 package (6 ounces) sweetened dried cranberries
> ¹/₂ cup water
> 1 bottle (750 ml) white wine

For wine, combine cranberries and water in a small saucepan over medium heat. Bring to a boil; boil 1 minute. Remove from heat and cool. In a half-gallon container, combine cranberry mixture and wine. Cover and chill _ days.

Strain wine (we used a paper coffee filter), reserving cranberries for Cranberry Cheese Balls. Return wine to wine bottle; cork and store in refrigerator.

Yield: about 3¹/₂ cups wine

CRANBERRY CHEESE BALLS

> 2 packages (8 ounces each) cream cheese, softened
> 2 cups (8 ounces) shredded sharp Cheddar cheese
> 1 cup reserved cranberries from Cranberry Wine, chopped
> 1¹/₂ cups chopped pecans, toasted, coarsely ground, and divided
> Crackers to give

In a large bowl, beat cheeses until well blended. Stir in cranberries and ¹/₄ cup pecans. Shape into 2 balls; roll in remaining pecans. Wrap in plastic wrap and store in refrigerator. Give with crackers.

Yield: 2 cheese balls (about 2 cups each)

FESTIVE STEMWARE AND BASKET

You will need wine glasses (we used glasses with a 2³/₄" dia. base), self-adhesive stars, glass etching cream, rubber gloves, 42" of holly garland, 10" square basket with handle, glue, 1³/₈ yds of 1¹/₄"w wired ribbon, and Christmas-motif napkin for basket liner.

1. For each glass, apply stars to outside of glass and top of glass base as desired.
2. Follow manufacturer's instructions to apply etching cream to outside of glass and top of glass base.
3. Remove etching cream and stars.
4. Arrange garland around rim of basket; glue in place.
5. Tie ribbon into a bow around handle. Arrange streamers as desired.
6. Place napkin in basket. Place glasses and gifts in basket.

PEPPERMINT-CREAM LIQUEUR

Let it snow! On a cold, blustery day, your friends can stay inside and enjoy smooth Peppermint-Cream Liqueur. The spirited beverage mixes up quickly with schnapps and vodka. Our appliquéd tote will remind folks to serve the creamy drink chilled.

PEPPERMINT-CREAM LIQUEUR

1¹/₂ cups whipping cream
1 can (14 ounces) sweetened condensed milk
¹/₂ cup peppermint schnapps
¹/₄ cup vodka
1 teaspoon vanilla extract

In a large bowl, combine whipping cream, sweetened condensed milk, peppermint schnapps, vodka, and vanilla. Beat at low speed of an electric mixer until blended. Pour into gift bottles. Store in refrigerator. Serve chilled.

Yield: about 3³/₄ cups liqueur

SNOWMAN CANVAS BAG

You will need white, orange, red, and black felt; paper-backed fusible web; two coordinating fabrics; pinking shears; canvas bag (we used a 7¹/₂" x 13" canvas bag with handles); hot glue gun; four ¹/₂" dia. wooden buttons; one ¹/₄" dia. black pom-pom; five ³/₈" dia. white buttons; two 5mm black cabochons for eyes; 1" of black embroidery floss for mouth; two ³/₈" dia. green buttons; black permanent fine-point marker; and green raffia.

1. Using patterns, page 116, follow *Making Appliqués*, page 112, to make snowman from white felt, nose from orange felt, brim from red felt, and hat from black felt. Make one 5¹/₄" x 7" background and one 6" x 8" border appliqué from coordinating fabrics. Trim border edges with pinking shears.
2. Fuse border to bag; fuse background to border. Arrange and fuse snowman appliqués on background. Glue wooden buttons to corners of background.
3. For scarf, cut one ¹/₄" x 7" strip from fabric. Cut a 2" piece from strip. Trimming to fit, glue 2" piece to neck. Tie a knot in center of remaining piece; glue knot to scarf.
4. Glue pom-pom to hat, white buttons along brim, eyes and mouth to face, and green buttons to front of snowman.
5. Use marker to write "Let it Snow!" across top of bag. Tie several lengths of raffia together into a bow; glue to bag.

ALMOND COCOA MIX

Help friends take the chill off winter by presenting them with a jar of Almond Cocoa Mix. An ideal treat for anyone who enjoys warming up with a cup of hot cocoa, the delectable drink gets its creamy goodness from vanilla ice cream. Place a fabric-topped jar in a cheery mug for a quick, heartwarming gift.

ALMOND COCOA MIX

- 1 cup butter
- 1 cup granulated sugar
- 1 cup firmly packed brown sugar
- 2/3 cup cocoa
- 2 cups softened vanilla ice cream
- 1/2 teaspoons almond extract

In a medium saucepan, combine butter, sugars, and cocoa over low heat. Stirring frequently, cook until butter melts. Transfer mixture to a medium bowl. Add ice cream and almond extract; beat until smooth. Store in an airtight container in refrigerator. Give with storage and serving instructions.

Yield: about 4 cups cocoa mix

To serve: Store cocoa mix in refrigerator until ready to serve. Pour 3/4 cup boiling water or hot coffee over 1/4 cup cocoa mix; stir until well blended.

HOLIDAY JAR LID COVER

You will need a jar with lid, fabric, pinking shears, rubber band, green raffia, and an artificial holly sprig with berries.

1. Draw around jar lid on wrong side of fabric. Using pinking shears, cut out circle 2" outside drawn line.

2. Center fabric circle over jar lid; secure with rubber band. Knot several lengths of raffia around lid, covering rubber band. Insert holly under knot.

CREAMY FRUIT SPREAD

Whipping up a fun, fruity spread is a great way for people on the go to say "Merry Christmas!" Just mix the ingredients in a bowl and refrigerate, and the creamy delight is ready to give. Bursting with blueberries and oranges, the fluffy cream cheese topping is a luscious treat. Present a jar of it in a star-studded basket along with some store-bought cookies, and you've got a gift that's sure to be appreciated.

BLUEBERRY-ORANGE FRUIT SPREAD

 1 can (15 ounces) blueberries in heavy syrup
11 ounces cream cheese (one 8-ounce and one 3-ounce package), softened
$^1/_4$ cup sifted confectioners sugar
$^1/_2$ teaspoon vanilla extract
 1 can (11 ounces) mandarin oranges, drained
   Shortbread cookies or vanilla wafers to serve

Drain blueberries, reserving $^1/_4$ cup syrup. Beat cream cheese, confectioners sugar, reserved blueberry syrup, and vanilla with an electric mixer until well blended and smooth. Add blueberries and oranges; beat at low speed until fruit is broken into coarse pieces. Store in an airtight container in refrigerator. Serve chilled with shortbread cookies or vanilla wafers.

Yield: about 3 cups spread

WINE-TIME CHEESE SPREAD

Offer a special couple on your list this delightful appetizer basket. Our cheese spread is layered with flavor, as well as visual appeal. Include a jar of the spread, crackers, and Christmas goblets for a "vintage" gift.

WINE-TIME CHEESE SPREAD

- 1 package (8 ounces) cream cheese, softened
- 2 cups (8 ounces) shredded sharp Cheddar cheese
- /2 cup sour cream
- 1 teaspoon dried Italian seasoning
- /2 teaspoon hot pepper sauce
- 4 ounces Genoa salami, finely chopped
- 1 jar (5 ounces) pimiento-stuffed green olives, drained and finely chopped
   Crackers to serve

In a medium bowl, beat cream cheese til fluffy. Add Cheddar cheese, sour eam, Italian seasoning, and pepper uce; beat until well blended. Layer lami and olives between layers of eese mixture in 2 pint-size jars. Cover d chill 24 hours to let flavors blend. rve with crackers.

eld: about 4 cups cheese spread

WINE GOBLET BASKET

You will need 30" of 1¹/₂"w wire-edged ribbon, 4" dia. airtight jar with knobbed lid, artificial greenery (we used a sprig of holly leaves with berries), oval basket (we used a 10" x 14" oval basket), white shredded paper, and two decorative goblets.

1. Tie ribbon into a bow around knob on jar lid. Insert ends of greenery under knot of bow.
2. Line basket with shredded paper. Arrange goblets, a bag of crackers, and gift jar in basket.

CREAMY CURRY DIP

A heartwarming change from the usual holiday snack fare, Creamy Curry Dip served with fresh veggies is delicious and oh-so-easy to prepare. An assortment of pre-cut vegetables from the grocer's salad bar or produce aisle makes a tasteful addition to your gift. For delivery, tuck everything in a cheery gift basket lined with homey fabrics and trims.

CREAMY CURRY DIP

- 1 cup mayonnaise
- 1 cup sour cream
- 1 tablespoon curry powder
- 1 teaspoon Worcestershire sauce
- $^3/_4$ teaspoon rice vinegar
- $^1/_4$ teaspoon garlic powder
- $^1/_4$ teaspoon minced dried onion
- $^1/_4$ teaspoon salt
- $^1/_4$ teaspoon ground red pepper

Combine all ingredients in a medium bowl; whisk until well blended. Store in an airtight container in refrigerator. Serve with fresh vegetables.

Yield: about 2 cups dip

BRIE DIP

It's hard to believe that such a simple recipe makes an appetizer that tastes this good! Brie Dip is an irresistible gourmet delicacy that you can share, complete with ready-to-eat breadsticks, in a gift basket tied with a holiday bow.

BRIE DIP

    8 ounces Brie cheese
$^1/_4$ cup finely chopped green onions
    2 cloves garlic, minced
    2 tablespoons vegetable oil
    1 tablespoon Dijon mustard
$^1/_8$ teaspoon ground red pepper
    1 cup mayonnaise
      Purchased breadsticks to give

Remove rind from cheese; cut cheese into several pieces. In a medium skillet, sauté green onions and garlic in oil over medium heat until tender. Reduce heat to medium low. Stirring constantly, add cheese, mustard, and red pepper; stir until cheese melts. Remove from heat and stir in mayonnaise. Transfer to a microwave-safe container. Cover and store in refrigerator. Give with serving instructions and breadsticks.

Yield: about $1^3/_4$ cups dip

To serve: Cover and microwave on medium power (50%) 5 minutes or until softened, stirring every 2 minutes. Serve with breadsticks.

DECORATED BASKET WITH BOW

You will need a basket with an open weave around center (we used a white $1^1/_2$" x $10^1/_2$" oval basket), $1^1/_4$"w wire-edged ribbon, floral wire, wire cutters,

artificial greenery (we used two sprigs of holly leaves with berries), red shredded paper, piece of clear cellophane (large enough to wrap bowl), clear cellophane bag, and two 19" lengths of $^5/_8$"w green satin ribbon.

For gift tag, you will *also* need green and red colored pencils, photocopy of tag design (page 114), and a black permanent medium-point marker.

1. Measure around basket; add 3". Cut a length of wire-edged ribbon the determined measurement. Weave ribbon around basket.
2. Use wire-edged ribbon and follow *Making a Bow*, page 112, to make a bow with six 6" loops and two 4" streamers. Use wire at back of bow to secure bow to basket. Glue greenery to center of bow. Place shredded paper in basket.
3. Place bowl of dip at center of cellophane. Gather cellophane over top of bowl. Tie satin ribbon into a bow around gathers. Place breadsticks in bag. Tie remaining ribbon length around top of bag; place bowl and bag in basket.
4. For gift tag, use pencils to color tag. Use marker to write baking instructions on tag. Glue tag to red paper. Leaving a $^1/_8$" red border, cut out tag.

ORIENTAL MIXED NUTS

...ass along this good-luck surprise
... a special friend. A crunchy
...lternative to traditional snack mix,
...riental Mixed Nuts features two
...mple ingredients—chow mein
...oodles and nuts—flavored with
...tir-fry seasoning. For a clever gift
...ea, tuck a batch of the munchable
...ixture inside a painted flowerpot.
...rimmed with a bow inscribed
...ith Chinese symbols for good
...ck, this package is sure to deliver
...appiness and prosperity!

ORIENTAL MIXED NUTS

1   can (22 ounces) mixed nuts
2   cans (5 ounces each) chow mein
     noodles
1   package (1.5 ounces) dry stir-
     fry seasoning
3   tablespoons vegetable oil

Preheat oven to 250 degrees.
...ombine nuts and noodles in a large
...asting pan. In a small bowl, combine
...asoning and oil. Pour oil mixture over
...t mixture; stir until well coated. Bake
... minutes, stirring after 15 minutes.
...llow to cool. Store in an airtight
...ontainer.
...ield: about 10 cups snack mix

"GOOD LUCK" CONTAINER

You will need a 5¹/₄"h clay pot, red spray
paint, metallic gold acrylic paint, two
22" lengths and one 30" length of 1¹/₂"w
double-faced black satin ribbon, metallic
gold paint pen, 2 rubber bands, two
1-yd lengths of gold curling ribbon,
2 glass ball ornaments, a 24" square of
clear cellophane, small sponge piece,
tracing paper, transfer paper, and tissue
paper or newspaper (if needed).

1. Spray paint pot red; allow to dry. Use
damp sponge to lightly stamp gold paint
onto pot; allow to dry.
2. For gift bundle, place mixed nuts
at center of cellophane. Bring edges of
cellophane together over nuts. Wrap
1 rubber band around cellophane.
Place bundle in pot. If necessary, place
crumpled tissue paper in bottom of pot
to raise height of bundle.

3. Overlap centers of 22" ribbon
lengths to form an "X." Place pot
over ribbon centers. Bring ends of
ribbon up over pot and gather around
gathered cellophane. Wrap remaining
rubber band around ribbon ends and
cellophane to hold ribbons in place.
4. Trace good luck symbols onto tracing
paper. Transfer design 2" from each
end of 30" ribbon length. Use paint pen
to paint over transferred design; allow
to dry. Tie ribbon into a bow around
cellophane, covering rubber bands and
ribbon ends; trim ends.
5. Thread ornaments onto curling
ribbon lengths. Tie ribbon lengths
together into a bow around cellophane
below black ribbon bow. Curl
ribbon ends.

SHOPPING SURVIVAL KIT

Help a friend through the hectic holiday shopping season with our clever survival kit! Apricot Cider is a delicious way to unwind after a long day at the mall, and it's great whether served warm or over ice. You'll also want to include a few shopping "necessities" such as a note pad, emergency snacks, and pain relievers. For a quick, festive finish, tie on a seasonal bow and a handmade tag.

APRICOT CIDER

- 2 quarts apple cider
- 2 cans (11$\frac{1}{2}$ ounces each) apricot nectar
- 2 cups apricot brandy
- 1 tablespoon freshly squeezed lemon juice

In a 1-gallon container, combine apple cider, apricot nectar, apricot brandy, and lemon juice. Store in an airtight container in refrigerator. Serve warm or over ice with a lemon slice.

Yield: about 12$\frac{1}{2}$ cups apricot cider

CHRISTMAS SHOPPER GIFT TAG

You will need a photocopy of tag design (page 117), green paper, red marker, decorative-edge craft scissors, black permanent felt-tip pen, and glue.

1. Use red marker to color tag design. Use pen to write message on tag. Cut out tag.
2. Glue tag to green paper. Leaving a $\frac{1}{4}$" green border, use craft scissors to cut out gift tag.

CHOCOLATE RICE BITES

Santa can't compete with these sensational sweets! Our Chocolate Rice Bites are "snow-capped" treasures that combine the tantalizing taste of chocolate with a crunch that's out of this world! Make a co-worker's day by delivering the munchables in a bright red gift bag topped off with a jolly Santa.

CHOCOLATE RICE BITES

- 1 package (12 ounces) square rice cereal
- 1 package (12 ounces) semisweet chocolate chips
- 1/4 cup butter or margarine
- 2 tablespoons chocolate syrup
- 1 teaspoon vanilla extract
- 3 1/2 cups confectioners sugar, divided

Place cereal in a very large lightly greased bowl. In a medium saucepan, combine chocolate chips, butter, and chocolate syrup. Stirring constantly, cook over low heat until chocolate chips melt and mixture is smooth. Stir in vanilla. Pour over cereal in bowl; stir to evenly coat. In a 2-gallon resealable bag, combine 2 1/2 cups confectioners sugar and coated cereal. Seal and shake bag to evenly coat cereal with sugar. Spread on aluminum foil; let stand 30 minutes. Return cereal to bag with remaining cup confectioners sugar. Seal and shake bag to coat cereal again. Store in an airtight container.

Yield: about 15 cups snack mix

SANTA LABEL BAG

You will need a 5" x 7" gift bag, stapler, 8" of 1"w grosgrain ribbon, hot glue gun, colored pencils, photocopy of label design (page 117) on white card stock, and a red permanent fine-point marker.

1. Place gift in bag. Fold top of bag 1" to front twice; staple through center folded portion to secure.

2. Fold ribbon into a "V" shape; staple at top of bag.

3. Use pencils to color label. Use marker to write message on label. Leaving a 1/8" border, cut out label. Glue label at top of bag.

SPECIAL CHOCOLATE EGGNOG

Add pizzazz to plain eggnog just by stirring in crème de cacao and chocolate syrup. Mixed in minutes, it's a smooth and creamy concoction that's sure to lift someone's spirits! For the holidays, present a bottle of your special beverage in a paper bag that's embellished with a personalized label. The tag is easy to make using a photocopied design and colored pencils.

SPECIAL CHOCOLATE EGGNOG

    1   quart prepared eggnog
    1   cup crème de cacao liqueur
 1/4   cup chocolate-flavored syrup

   In a 1/2-gallon pitcher, combine all ingredients. Store in refrigerator. Serve hot or cold.

Yield: about six 6-ounce servings

BOTTLE GIFT SACK

The illustration we used for our label is from the Dover Clip-Art Series® Old-fashioned Christmas Illustrations, but any black-and-white label illustration can be used.

You will need a brown paper sack to hold bottle, white paper, a black-and-white label illustration, colored pencils, Design Master® glossy wood tone spray (available at craft stores), spray adhesive, black felt-tip pen with fine point, and red raffia.

1. Photocopy label illustration onto white paper. Use colored pencils to color label. Use black pen to write your name and "Special Chocolate Eggnog" on label. Lightly spray label with wood tone spray. Allow to dry. Cut out label.
2. Use spray adhesive to adhere label to sack.
3. Place bottle in sack. Tie raffia into a bow around top of sack.

The design on this page is copyright-free and may be photocopied for personal use.

HOLIDAY WINE PUNCH

Tart and tangy, Holiday Wine Punch is laced with Christmas cheer! A delicious blend of white wine, cranberry juice, and citrus flavors, the spirited beverage is great for holiday celebrations. A starry yo-yo jar topper and a raffia bow add heartwarming appeal to this sweet offering, and the tag provides easy instructions for stirring up a batch of the merry mixture.

HOLIDAY WINE PUNCH

- 1 bottle (1.5 liters) white wine
- 1 bottle (32 ounces) cranberry juice cocktail
- 1 can (12 ounces) frozen pineapple juice concentrate
- 1 can (12 ounces) frozen pink lemonade concentrate

In a large container, combine wine, cranberry juice cocktail, and concentrates; cover and chill. Give with serving instructions.

Yield: 13 cups wine mixture

To serve: For each 6¹/₂ cups of wine mixture, combine chilled wine mixture and 3 cups chilled lemon-lime soda.

Yield: about twelve 6-ounce servings

YO-YO JAR

You will need a jar with round lid; fabrics for yo-yo, star, and tag; thread; paper-backed fusible web; white poster board; cream-colored heavy paper; a ¹/₂" dia. button; raffia; green felt-tip pen with fine point; drawing compass; hole punch; tracing paper; craft glue; hot glue gun; and glue sticks.

1. Draw around top of jar lid on poster board. Cut out circle along drawn line.
2. Measure diameter of poster board circle; double measurement. Using determined measurement as diameter, use compass to draw a circle on yo-yo fabric. Cut out circle along drawn line.
3. Use a double strand of thread to baste ¹/₈" from edge of fabric circle. Place poster board circle at center on wrong side of fabric circle. Pull ends of threads to tightly gather fabric circle over poster board circle; knot thread and trim ends.
4. For star, follow manufacturer's instructions to fuse web to wrong side of star fabric. Fuse fabric to poster board. Trace star pattern onto tracing paper; cut out. Use pattern to cut star from fabric-covered poster board. Hot glue star to center of yo-yo, covering raw edges of fabric. Hot glue button to center of star. Tie a small bow from several lengths of raffia; trim ends. Hot glue bow to star below button.
5. Hot glue yo-yo to jar lid. Tie several lengths of raffia into a bow around lid; trim ends.
6. For tag, follow manufacturer's instructions to fuse web to wrong side of tag fabric. Fuse fabric to poster board. Cut a piece of heavy paper. Use craft glue to glue paper piece to fabric-covered poster board; allow to dry. Cutting approx. ¹/₄" from paper piece, cut out paper piece. Use green pen to write "Holiday Wine Punch" and serving instructions on tag. Punch a hole in tag. Thread tag onto 1 raffia streamer.

FAVORITE PETS' SNACK MIXES

Santa doesn't forget his four-legged friends at Christmastime, and neither should you! Simply combine a variety of dry pet foods with dog or cat treats to make doggone good or "purr-fectly" delicious snack mixes. Packaged in clear bags, the gifts are presented with new pet toys and food dishes that are festively decorated with paint pens.

FAVORITE PETS' SNACK MIXES

DOG SNACK MIX
Combine a variety of dry dog food and dog treats to yield 6 cups. Store in an airtight container.

CAT SNACK MIX
Combine a variety of dry cat food and cat treats to yield 6 cups. Store in an airtight container.

SAUCES, SEASONINGS, & MIXES

Spice up someone's life with these favorite sauces
and mixes from the kitchen. Almost two dozen easy
recipes and plenty of packaging ideas will help
you stir up flavorful gifts in a hurry!

DRIED BEAN SOUP MIX

Deliver an abundance of Christmas wishes with this "soup-er" gift. The colorful Dried Bean Soup Mix is made with six types of beans to symbolize the blessings of health and prosperity. Layered inside a glass jar, the beans will make an appealing counter top accent—and a hearty soup when they're prepared with the spicy seasoning mix and soup recipe that you provide.

DRIED BEAN SOUP MIX AND SEASONING

DRIED BEAN MIX

$1/2$ cup of *each* of the following:
kidney beans, split yellow peas, black beans, red lentils, small red beans, and split green peas

SEASONING MIX

1 tablespoon dried sweet pepper flakes
2 teaspoons chicken bouillon granules
2 teaspoons dried minced onion
$1^1/2$ teaspoons salt
1 teaspoon dried parsley flakes
$1/2$ teaspoon ground black pepper
$1/2$ teaspoon garlic powder
$1/2$ teaspoon celery seed

For dried bean mix, layer each type of bean in a clear gift container.

For seasoning mix, combine all ingredients. Store in a resealable plastic bag. Give with recipe for Seasoned Bean Soup.

Yield: about 3 cups dried bean mix and about $1/4$ cup seasoning mix

SEASONED BEAN SOUP

Dried Bean Mix (3 cups)
2 cans ($14^1/2$ ounces each) stewed tomatoes
Seasoning Mix ($1/4$ cup)

Rinse beans and place in a large Dutch oven. Pour 4 cups boiling water over beans; cover and let soak overnight.

Drain beans and return to Dutch oven. Add 6 cups water, cover, and bring to a boil over high heat. Reduce heat to low and simmer 1 to $1^1/2$ hours or until beans are almost tender. Add tomatoes and seasoning mix. Stirring occasionally, cover and simmer 30 minutes. Uncover beans and continue to simmer about 1 hour longer or until beans are tender and soup thickens. Serve warm.

Yield: about 10 cups soup

CURRY SOUP MIX

A steaming pot of home-cooked soup made with our spicy Curry Soup Mix is a flavorful way to warm up on a cold winter's day. To share the warmth with a friend, give the dry mix—a blend of rice, nuts, and seasonings—along with instructions for making the soup. Your friend can add cooked chicken or shrimp to make a hearty one-dish meal. A pretty basket trimmed with ribbon and greenery makes a nice container for a bag of the mix and a pair of soup mugs. When the soup is gone, the basket can be used to display Christmas cards or other holiday accents.

CURRY SOUP MIX

2 cups uncooked instant rice
$^1/_2$ cup raisins
$^1/_3$ cup chopped walnuts
$^1/_4$ cup dried minced onions
2 tablespoons salt
1 tablespoon curry powder
1 tablespoon granulated sugar
2 teaspoons paprika
$^1/_2$ teaspoons dried dill weed
1 teaspoon dry mustard
1 teaspoon ground coriander
1 teaspoon garlic powder
$^1/_2$ teaspoon ground cardamom

In a large bowl, combine all ingredients, stirring until well blended. Store in an airtight container. Give with instructions for making soup.

To make soup, bring 10 cups water to a boil in a large stockpot over high heat; add soup mix. Cover and reduce heat to medium. Stirring occasionally, simmer 20 to 25 minutes or until rice is tender. Stir in about 2 cups shredded cooked chicken or cooked peeled shrimp; cook until heated through. Serve immediately. Store in an airtight container in refrigerator.

Yield: 6 to 8 servings

FABRIC BAG

Cut a 7" x 30" piece of fabric. Matching right sides and short edges, fold fabric in half. Leaving a $^1/_4$" seam allowance, sew sides of bag together. Turn right side out. Press top edge of bag 3" to wrong side. Place a plastic bag of soup mix in bag. Tie a 20" length of ribbon into a bow around top of bag. Tuck a sprig of artificial holly behind bow.

thing can beat a bowl
steaming soup on a cold
inter day! Our Lentil Soup Mix
akes a welcome gift during the
usy holidays—your friends can
njoy a hot, hearty meal
ithout a lot of fuss. Deliver the
ecret" seasoning mix, lentils,
nd cooking directions in a
ecorated basket that includes
pair of festive bowls!

LENTIL SOUP MIX

- 2 cups dried lentils
- 1 tablespoon chicken bouillon granules
- 1 tablespoon onion powder
- 1 teaspoon ground cumin
- 1 teaspoon celery salt
- $^3/_4$ teaspoon salt
- $^1/_2$ teaspoon garlic powder
- $^1/_2$ teaspoon dried thyme leaves
- $^1/_2$ teaspoon ground black pepper
- $^1/_4$ teaspoon dried lemon peel
- 1 bay leaf

Place lentils in a resealable plastic bag. In a small bowl, combine chicken bouillon, onion powder, cumin, celery salt, salt, garlic powder, thyme, pepper, lemon peel, and bay leaf. Transfer seasoning mixture to a small cellophane bag. Give with serving instructions.

Yield: about 3 tablespoons seasoning mix

To serve: Rinse lentils. In a Dutch oven, cover lentils with 2 quarts water. Bring to a boil over medium-high heat. Reduce heat to medium low. Stirring occasionally, cover and simmer 15 minutes or until lentils are barely tender. Stir in seasoning mix. Cover and simmer 30 minutes longer or until lentils are tender. Serve warm.

Yield: about 7 cups soup

SOUP BOWL BASKET

You will need a $6^1/_2$" x 22" piece of fabric, pinking shears, 12" of 1"w ribbon, 7" of $^1/_4$"w ribbon, white card stock, black permanent fine-point marker, hole punch, two 5" lengths of $^1/_{16}$"w satin ribbon, fabric for card, paper-backed fusible web, 3" x 5" plain index cards, hot glue gun, artificial berry garland, 10" dia. basket, natural excelsior, and two decorative soup bowls.

1. For fabric bag, matching right sides and short edges, fold fabric in half. Leaving a $^1/_4$" seam allowance, sew sides of bag. Turn bag right side out. Trim top of bag with pinking shears. Place bag of lentils in fabric bag. Tie 1"w ribbon into a bow around top of bag.
2. Tie $^1/_4$"w ribbon into a bow around top of seasoning mix bag.
3. For tags, cut two $1^1/_2$" x 2" pieces from card stock. Use marker to write message on tags. Punch hole in corner of each tag; use $^1/_{16}$"w ribbon to attach tags to bows.
4. For instruction card, cut one 1" x 3" piece each from fabric and web. Fuse web to fabric; fuse fabric to left side of index card. Use marker to write serving instructions on card.
5. Glue garland around rim of basket. Line basket with excelsior and place bags and bowls in basket.

'is the "season" to be
lly, so here are six savory
lends to help you serve up
hristmas cheer to several
iends! Packaged individually
ribbon-tied cellophane bags,
iese flavor enhancers will
ring out the natural goodness
f seafood, poultry, vegetables,
nd much more. When sharing
iese gifts, be sure to include
easoning suggestions.

AY SEAFOOD SEASONING

1 tablespoon crushed bay leaves
1/2 teaspoons celery salt
1/2 teaspoons dry mustard
1/2 teaspoons ground black pepper
3/4 teaspoon ground nutmeg
1/2 teaspoon ground cloves
1/2 teaspoon ground ginger
1/2 teaspoon paprika
1/2 teaspoon ground red pepper
1/4 teaspoon ground mace
1/4 teaspoon ground cardamom

Process all ingredients in a food
rocessor until well blended. Store in an
rtight container. Use seasoning with
eafood or chicken.

ield: about 1/4 cup seasoning

CREOLE SEASONING

1 tablespoon salt
1 1/2 teaspoons garlic powder
1 1/2 teaspoons onion powder
1 1/2 teaspoons paprika
1 1/4 teaspoons dried thyme leaves
1 teaspoon ground red pepper
3/4 teaspoon ground black pepper
3/4 teaspoon dried oregano leaves
1/2 teaspoon crushed bay leaf
1/4 teaspoon chili powder

Process all ingredients in a food
processor until well blended. Store in an
airtight container. Use seasoning with
seafood, chicken, beef, or vegetables.

Yield: about 1/4 cup seasoning

GREEK SEASONING

2 teaspoons salt
2 teaspoons ground oregano
1 1/2 teaspoons onion powder
1 1/2 teaspoons garlic powder
1 teaspoon cornstarch
1 teaspoon ground black pepper
1 teaspoon beef bouillon granules
1 teaspoon dried parsley flakes
1/2 teaspoon ground cinnamon
1/2 teaspoon ground nutmeg

Process all ingredients in a food
processor until well blended. Store in an
airtight container. Use seasoning with
steaks, pork chops, chicken, or fish.

Yield: about 1/4 cup seasoning

GROUND SEASONING

2 tablespoons celery seed
1 tablespoon onion powder
1 tablespoon salt

Process all ingredients in a food
processor until well blended. Store in
an airtight container. Use seasoning in
stews, chowders, or sandwich spreads.

Yield: about 1/4 cup seasoning

FIVE-SPICE POWDER

2 teaspoons anise seeds, crushed
2 teaspoons ground black pepper
2 teaspoons fennel seeds, crushed
2 teaspoons ground cloves
2 teaspoons ground cinnamon
1 1/2 teaspoons ground ginger
1/2 teaspoon ground allspice

Combine all ingredients; store in an
airtight container. Use with fish or pork.

Yield: about 1/4 cup seasoning

HERBS SEASONING

1 tablespoon ground thyme
1 tablespoon dried oregano leaves
2 teaspoons rubbed sage
1 teaspoon dried rosemary leaves
1 teaspoon dried marjoram leaves
1 teaspoon dried basil leaves
1 teaspoon dried parsley flakes

Process all ingredients in a food
processor until well blended. Store in
an airtight container. Use seasoning
in omelets or with fish, vegetables, or
chicken.

Yield: about 1/4 cup seasoning

Photocopy tag, page 118, and color
with colored pencils. Glue tag to red
cardstock and leaving an 1/8" border; cut
out tag.

APPLE CRISP KIT

An apple a day keeps the doctor away, and an Apple Crisp Kit will keep the holiday stress at bay! Your friends can toss this simple dessert together in minutes using the crumbly homemade topping and purchased apple pie filling. Create a sponge-painted holly wreath bag to present the tasty kit, and you'll have a super gift idea for a special family.

APPLE CRISP KIT

     2 cups all-purpose flour
     1 cup firmly packed brown sugar
     1 cup old-fashioned oats
 $^1/_2$ teaspoon ground cinnamon
 $^1/_2$ teaspoon salt
 $^1/_4$ teaspoon ground nutmeg
     1 cup chilled butter or margarine
     1 cup chopped pecans
     4 cans (21 ounces each) apple pie filling to give

In a large bowl, combine flour, brown sugar, oats, cinnamon, salt, and nutmeg. Using a pastry blender or 2 knives, cut in butter until mixture resembles coarse meal. Stir in pecans. Divide topping into 2 resealable plastic bags; store in refrigerator. Give each bag of topping with 2 cans apple pie filling and serving instructions.

Yield: about 7 cups topping

To serve: Spread 2 cans apple pie filling in a lightly greased 9 x 13-inch baking dish. Sprinkle topping over apples. Bake in a 400-degree oven 19 to 21 minutes or until filling bubbles and topping is golden brown. Serve warm.

Yield: about 12 servings

HOLLY WREATH GIFT BAG

You will need tracing paper, compressed craft sponge, green and dark green acrylic paint, 10"w x 13"h red gift bag, black fine-point permanent marker, fifteen white buttons, glue, and a 28" length of 1¹/₂"w wired ribbon.

1. Trace leaf pattern onto tracing paper; cut out. Use pattern to cut leaf from sponge.

2. Follow *Sponge Painting,* page 112, to paint green and dark green leaves in a round wreath design on bag front. Use marker to outline and add detail lines on leaves.

3. For berries, glue five clusters of three buttons each on wreath.

4. Tie ribbon length into a bow. Glue bow at top of bag.

DOUBLE CHIP COOKIE MIX

Share the joy of holiday baking with our Double Chip Cookie Mix! A combination of white and chocolate chips makes the cookies twice as nice. Layer the ingredients in a jar, top with a doily, and tuck into a coordinating bag. Don't forget to include the directions!

DOUBLE CHIP COOKIE MIX

- 1 cup plus 2 tablespoons all-purpose flour
- $^1/_4$ teaspoon baking powder
- $^1/_8$ teaspoon salt
- $^1/_2$ cup chopped pecans
- $^1/_2$ cup white chocolate baking chips
- $^1/_2$ cup semisweet chocolate chips
- 6 tablespoons firmly packed brown sugar
- 6 tablespoons granulated sugar

In a small bowl, combine flour, baking powder, and salt; stir until well blended. Spoon flour mixture into wide-mouth 1-quart jar with lid. Layer pecans, white chocolate chips, semisweet chocolate chips, brown sugar, and granulated sugar in jar. Cover with lid. Give with baking instructions.

Yield: about 3$^1/_2$ cups cookie mix

To bake: Preheat oven to 350 degrees. Pour cookie mix into a medium bowl and stir until ingredients are well blended. In a small bowl, combine $^1/_4$ cup vegetable oil, 1 egg, 2 tablespoons milk, and $^1/_2$ teaspoon vanilla extract; beat until blended. Add oil mixture to dry ingredients; stir until soft dough forms. Drop rounded teaspoonfuls of dough 2 inches apart

onto a greased baking sheet. Bake 8 to 10 minutes or until edges are lightly browned. Transfer to a wire rack to cool. Store in an airtight container.

Yield: about 3 dozen cookies

DOILY-WRAPPED BAG AND JAR

You will need a quart-size jar with lid, fabric, pinking shears, rubber band, two 11" dia. doilies, two 28" lengths of $^3/_8$"w grosgrain ribbon, 6" x 11" brown paper bag, paper-backed fusible web, hole punch, and kraft paper.

1. For jar lid cover, draw around lid on wrong side of fabric. Using pinking shears, cut out circle 3" outside drawn line. Center circle over lid; secure with rubber band.

2. Place one doily over lid. Thread one ribbon length through openings in doily along lid edge. Pull ribbon ends to gather doily around lid; tie into a bow to secure.

3. For bag, cut one 6" x 11" piece each from fabric and fusible web. Fuse web to wrong side of fabric; fuse fabric to front of bag.

4. Place gift in bag. Fold top of bag 1$^1/_2$" to back. Punch two holes 1" apart in center of folded portion of bag. Place remaining doily over top of bag. Thread remaining ribbon length through doily and holes from back to front; tie ribbon ends into a bow.

5. For tag, cut one 3" x 4$^1/_2$" piece each from kraft paper, fabric, and fusible web. Fuse web to wrong side of fabric; fuse fabric to paper. Matching short edges, fold tag in half.

STIR FRY!

your gift list includes some folks who like to stir things up, surprise them with a batch of our spicy Stir-Fry Sauce. It's great in a variety of dishes, such as our Stir-Fry Chicken. Turn your gift into an authentic Oriental dinner by including the recipe, chow mein noodles, fortune cookies, green tea, and chopsticks.

STIR-FRY SAUCE

Include chow mein noodles, fortune cookies, green tea, and chopsticks with sauce.

- 1/4 cup soy sauce
- 1/4 cup oyster sauce (in Oriental section of supermarket)
- 2 tablespoons freshly squeezed lime juice
- 1 tablespoon freshly grated gingerroot
- 1 tablespoon sugar
- 1/2 teaspoon crushed red pepper flakes

In a small bowl, combine soy sauce, oyster sauce, lime juice, gingerroot, sugar, and red pepper flakes. Store in an airtight container in refrigerator. Give sauce with purchased items and recipe for Stir-Fry Chicken.

Yield: about 2/3 cup sauce

STIR-FRY CHICKEN

Stir-Fry Sauce
- 1 pound skinless, boneless chicken breasts, cut into bite-size pieces
- 3 tablespoons dark sesame oil, divided
- 3 carrots, peeled and cut into thin diagonal slices
- 1 large green pepper, thinly sliced
- 1 large sweet red pepper, thinly sliced
- 1 large onion, thinly sliced
- 1 package (8 ounces) fresh mushrooms, sliced
- 4 cups cooked rice to serve

Pour Stir-Fry Sauce over chicken in a shallow dish. Cover and refrigerate 30 minutes, stirring after 15 minutes.

Drain chicken, reserving sauce. In a large skillet or wok, heat 2 tablespoons sesame oil over medium-high heat. Stirring constantly, cook chicken 5 minutes or until chicken is tender. Remove chicken and set aside. Add remaining tablespoon sesame oil to skillet. Add carrots, peppers, and onion. Stir fry on medium high 5 minutes or until vegetables are crisp tender. Stir in chicken, mushrooms, and reserved sauce. Bring sauce to a boil; cook about 2 minutes or until mushrooms are tender. Serve warm over rice with chow mein noodles on top.

Yield: 6 to 8 servings

STIR-FRY SAUCE LABEL

You will need tracing paper, transfer paper, 1 1/2" square of white card stock, black permanent fine-point marker, craft glue, and a jar with lid.

1. Trace pattern onto tracing paper. Use transfer paper to transfer pattern to center of card stock.
2. Use marker to trace over words.
3. Glue label to jar.

SAVORY HERB BAGEL MIX

Give your favorite bagel lover something to smile about this Christmas. A package of Savory Herb Bagel Mix, when blended with softened cream cheese, will add flavor to the holidays. Fuse cheery checked fabric to poster board to create the wraparound packet; finish by tying on a handy cheese spreader.

SAVORY HERB BAGEL MIX

   1 cup dried parsley flakes
 1/3 cup dried dill weed
 2 1/2 tablespoons dried oregano
         leaves
 2 1/2 tablespoons dried thyme leaves
   2 tablespoons salt
   4 teaspoons dried rosemary leaves
   4 teaspoons dried marjoram leaves
   2 teaspoons paprika

Combine all ingredients in a resealable plastic bag. Give with serving instructions.

Yield: about 2 cups mix

To serve: Process 2 teaspoons mix with one 8-ounce package softened cream cheese in a food processor until smooth. Transfer to an airtight container. Chill 2 hours to let flavors blend. Serve spread on bagel slices.

Yield: about 1 cup spread

BAGEL SPREAD PACKETS

For each packet, you will need one 6" x 15" piece each of white poster board, fabric, and paper-backed fusible web; stapler; hole punch; two 15" lengths of 1/4"w grosgrain ribbon; hot glue gun; decorative spreader; photocopy of label design (page 118) on white card stock; spray adhesive; and green card stock.

1. Fuse fabric to poster board.
2. Fold one end of poster board 6 1/2" to wrong side. Staple bag of seasoning mix to wrong side of folded end. For flap, fold opposite end of poster board 2" to wrong side. Punch two holes 1/2" apart in center of flap. Thread ribbons through holes. Fold packet and glue flap to secure.
3. Tie ribbons into a bow around spreader.
4. For label, cut out label design. Apply spray adhesive to wrong side of label design; smooth onto green card stock. Leaving a 1/8" green border, cut out label. Apply spray adhesive to wrong side of label; center and smooth onto packet.

BAYOU POPCORN SPICE

Perk up plain popcorn with our Bayou Popcorn Spice! This Cajun sensation can be concocted in seconds: simply blend all the sassy spices together and pack with a bag of microwave popcorn. Add a handmade label and then "pop" in on friends— everyone will love the zesty taste.

BAYOU POPCORN SPICE

3 tablespoons paprika
1 tablespoon garlic powder
2 teaspoons onion powder
1/2 teaspoons ground red pepper
1 teaspoon dried thyme leaves
1 teaspoon dried oregano leaves
1 teaspoon brown sugar
1 teaspoon ground black pepper
1/2 teaspoon ground nutmeg
   Microwave popcorn to give

In a small bowl, combine all ingredients until well blended. Store in an airtight container. Give with popcorn and serving instructions.

Yield: about 7 tablespoons mix

To serve: Microwave a 3 1/2-ounce bag of microwave popcorn according to package directions. Open bag carefully to avoid steam. Sprinkle 1/2 to 1 teaspoon seasoning mix, or more to taste, over popcorn. Hold top of bag closed and shake until popcorn is coated.

POPCORN SEASONING BAG

You will need a brown lunch-size paper bag, craft glue stick, decorative-edge craft scissors, stapler, colored pencils, and a photocopy of label design (page 119) on ecru card stock.

1. With bag folded, glue bottom of bag in place. Use craft scissors to trim top of bag. Place popcorn and seasoning mix in bag. Fold top of bag 1 1/2" to front; staple through center folded portion to secure.

2. Use pencils to color label. Leaving a 1/2"w border, use craft scissors to cut out label. Glue label to bag.

CHRISTMAS BARBECUE SAUCE

Rustle up a batch of Christmas Barbecue Sauce for a cowpoke who hankers for zesty holiday grub! Made with a passel of fresh red and green peppers, this sassy sauce wakes up the taste of poultry, pork, or beef. A red bandanna tied with rope and accented with a sprig of holly will outfit your gift jar with cowboy cheer.

CHRISTMAS BARBECUE SAUCE

- 1 cup chopped sweet red pepper
- 1 cup chopped green pepper
- 4 cups ketchup
- $1/2$ cup firmly packed brown sugar
- $1/3$ cup apple cider vinegar
- $1/3$ cup Dijon-style mustard
- 2 tablespoons dried minced onion
- 1 teaspoon Creole seasoning

Place red and green peppers in a large microwave-safe bowl and cover with microwave-safe plastic wrap. Microwave on high power (100%) 4 minutes or until peppers are almost tender, stirring after 2 minutes. Add remaining ingredients; stir until well blended. Cover with plastic wrap and microwave on medium-high power (80%) 10 minutes, stirring after 5 minutes. Cool and store in an airtight container in refrigerator.

Yield: about 6 cups sauce

COVERED JAR

Place jar at center of a bandanna. Gather edges of bandanna over jar. Wrap a rubber band around bandanna close to jar. Fold a 20" length of rope in half. Wrap rope around bandanna, covering rubber band; slip ends of rope through loop formed at fold of rope and tighten. Hot glue an artificial holly sprig with berries to rope.

CHILI SEASONING MIX

Give the gift of warmth this winter! Wrapped in beribboned plaid bags, this Chili Seasoning Mix is perfect for friends on the go. By adding ground beef and a few canned items to this mix, even a "non-cook" can create a hearty meal.

CHILI SEASONING MIX

$^1/_2$ cup chili powder
$^1/_4$ cup dried minced onions
2 tablespoons dried minced garlic
2 tablespoons ground cumin
2 tablespoons cornstarch
2 tablespoons salt
1 tablespoon sweet pepper flakes
1 tablespoon ground coriander
1 tablespoon ground black pepper
1 tablespoon dried cilantro
1 teaspoon dried oregano leaves
$^1/_2$ teaspoon ground red pepper
$^1/_8$ teaspoon ground cloves

In a small bowl, combine all ingredients; stir until well blended. Store in an airtight container. Give $^1/_4$ cup seasoning mix with Chili recipe.
Yield: about $1^1/_4$ cups seasoning mix

CHILI

2 pounds ground beef
2 cans (8 ounces each) tomato sauce
1 can (16 ounces) pinto beans, undrained
1 can ($14^1/_2$ ounces) diced tomatoes, undrained
$^1/_4$ cup Chili Seasoning Mix

In a large skillet, cook beef over medium heat until brown; drain meat. Stir in tomato sauce, beans, tomatoes, and chili seasoning mix. Reduce heat to low. Stirring occasionally, cover and simmer 30 minutes. Serve warm.
Yield: about 7 cups chili

CHILI BAGS

For each bag, you will need a brown paper bag (we used 4" x 8" bags), paper-backed fusible web, fabric, photocopy of tag design (page 118) on ecru card stock, colored pencils, black permanent fine-point marker, spray adhesive, hole punch, and a 16" length of $^5/_8$"w wired ribbon.

1. Draw around front of bag on paper side of web. Fuse web to wrong side of fabric; cut out along drawn line. Follow manufacturer's instructions to fuse fabric piece to front of bag.

2. With tag design at center, draw a 3" x 5" rectangle around tag; cut out along drawn lines. Use colored pencils to color tag. Use marker to write name on tag. Apply spray adhesive to wrong side of tag; smooth onto front of bag.

3. Place gift in bag. Fold top of bag $1^1/_2$" to back. Punch two holes 1" apart through center folded portion of bag. Thread ribbon through holes in folded portion of bag; tie into a bow at front of bag.

FRUITY TEA MIX

Chilly Yuletide weather is no match for the warming appeal of Fruity Tea Mix! This whimsical gift is prepared with fun-flavored drink mixes and fruit-shaped candies. For a lighthearted delivery, pack the tea in a gift box adorned with candy, greenery, and a cheery ribbon. A hand-lettered label announces your gift.

FRUITY TEA MIX

- 1 cup sweetened powdered instant tea mix with lemon flavor
- $^1/_2$ cup sugar
- 1 package (0.16 ounce) unsweetened punch-flavored soft drink mix
- 1 package ($7^1/_2$ ounces) fruit-shaped fruit-flavored candy

In a medium bowl, combine tea, sugar, soft drink mix, and candy. Store in an airtight container. Give with serving instructions.

Yield: about 2 cups mix

To serve: Pour 8 ounces hot or cold water over 2 tablespoons tea mix; stir until well blended.

FRUITY WREATH BOX

You will need an oval papier-mâché box with lid (our box measures about 5" x $6^1/_2$"), silk greenery, fruit-shaped candy, 1 yd of $1^1/_2$"w wired ribbon, green paper, black felt-tip calligraphy pen, serrated-cut craft scissors, wire cutters, and glue.

1. Draw around lid on green paper. Use craft scissors to cut out shape about 1" inside drawn line. Use pen to write "Fruity Tea Mix" on shape. Glue shape to center of lid.
2. Glue greenery along edge of lid. Glue candy pieces to greenery.
3. Place gift in box. Place lid on box. Tie ribbon into a bow around lid; trim ends. If necessary, glue ribbon to secure.

FLAVORFUL MIXES

Friends who enjoy sampling a variety of tastes will savor these flavorful mixes. Used in place of curry powder, Caribbean Spice Mix brings a hint of the islands to recipes. Buttermilk Dressing, a true Southern specialty, is tasty served on salads or as a vegetable dip. Finish each bag of mix with a colorful label and a wooden spoon for a clever delivery.

CARIBBEAN SPICE MIX

$^1/_4$ cup ground turmeric
  2 tablespoons ground coriander
  1 tablespoon ground cumin
  1 tablespoon ground cinnamon
$^1/_4$ teaspoons ground ginger
$^1/_4$ teaspoons garlic powder
  1 teaspoon ground black pepper
$^1/_2$ teaspoon ground cloves

Combine all ingredients in a small bowl; stir until well blended. Store in an airtight container. Substitute for curry powder in recipes.

Yield: about $^1/_2$ cup spice mix

BUTTERMILK DRESSING MIX

  2 tablespoons dried thyme leaves
$^1/_2$ tablespoons dried parsley flakes
  1 tablespoon lemon pepper
  2 teaspoons salt
  1 teaspoon dried sage leaves
  1 teaspoon garlic powder
  1 teaspoon ground black pepper

Process all ingredients in a small food processor until well blended. Store in an airtight container. Give with serving instructions.

Yield: about $^1/_4$ cup dressing mix

To serve: For salad dressing, combine $1^1/_2$ teaspoons dressing mix, $^1/_2$ cup buttermilk, and $^1/_2$ cup mayonnaise; stir until blended. Cover and chill 1 hour to allow flavors to blend.

For dip, combine $1^1/_2$ teaspoons dressing mix, $^1/_2$ cup sour cream, and $^1/_2$ cup mayonnaise; stir until blended. Cover and chill 1 hour to allow flavors to blend.

SPOON-TOPPED GIFT SACKS

For each sack, you will need a small gift sack (ours measure 3" x $6^1/_2$"), $^3/_8$ yd of $^1/_4$"w grosgrain ribbon, wooden spoon, small glass ball ornament, white paper, black felt-tip pen, colored pencils, a stapler, and glue.

1. For label, use pen to trace desired design, page 114, onto white paper. Use colored pencils to color label; cut out.
2. Place gift in sack. Fold top of sack about $1^3/_4$" to back and staple twice about 1" from fold. Glue label to top front of sack. Slide handle of spoon between fold and staples.
3. Thread ornament onto ribbon. Tie ribbon into a bow around spoon.

WAFFLE AND SYRUP

Start that special someone's day off with an eye-opening breakfast treat. Ideal for the coffee amorist, our Cappuccino Waffle Mix with Coffee Syrup is sure to provide a morning boost. A decorated lunch bag filled with waffle mix and accompanied by a bottle of syrup can be given in a plastic crate that will come in handy later. Be sure to send along the serving instructions!

CAPPUCCINO WAFFLE MIX WITH COFFEE SYRUP

CAPPUCCINO WAFFLES
- $1/2$ cup butter or margarine, softened
- 1 cup sugar
- 1 teaspoon vanilla extract
- $1^1/3$ cups all-purpose flour
- $1/3$ cup nonfat dry milk
- $1/4$ cup non-dairy powdered creamer
- 2 tablespoons instant coffee granules
- 2 teaspoons baking powder
- $1/4$ teaspoon salt
- $1/4$ teaspoon ground cinnamon

COFFEE SYRUP
- 1 cup strongly brewed coffee
- 2 cups sugar

For cappuccino waffles, cream butter, sugar, and vanilla in a medium bowl until fluffy. In a small bowl, combine remaining ingredients. On low speed of an electric mixer, beat dry ingredients into creamed mixture (mixture will be crumbly). Transfer to a resealable plastic bag; store in refrigerator. Give with serving instructions.

For coffee syrup, combine coffee and sugar in a heavy medium saucepan. Stirring constantly over medium-high heat, cook mixture until sugar dissolves. Without stirring, bring mixture to a boil; boil 2 minutes. Remove from heat; cool to room temperature. Store in an airtight container in refrigerator.

Yield: about 4 cups waffle mix and $1^3/4$ cups syrup

To serve: Preheat waffle iron. Transfer bag of waffle mix into a medium bowl. Add $3/4$ cup water and 2 eggs; stir just until blended. For each waffle, pour about $2/3$ cup batter into waffle iron. Bake 3 to 5 minutes or according to manufacturer's instructions. Serve hot waffles with coffee syrup.

Yield: about five 8-inch waffles

BREAKFAST GIFT BAG

You will need silver spray paint, lunch-size white paper bag, craft glue, Christmas card, hole punch, and red and green $1/4$"w curling ribbons.

1. Spray paint front of bag silver; allow to dry.
2. Glue Christmas card to front of bag; allow to dry. Place gift in bag.
3. Fold top of bag 1" to front twice. Punch two holes 1" apart in center of folded portion of bag.
4. Thread ribbons through holes and ti into a bow at front of bag. Curl ribbon ends.

CRANBERRY MUFFINS

A happy Noel is close at hand when you deliver the ingredients for our Christmas Cranberry Muffins along with instructions for making them. All the recipient has to do is add sour cream and bake! Tuck a bag of mix in an embroidered pot holder for a cheery presentation.

CHRISTMAS CRANBERRY MUFFINS

   2 cups all-purpose flour
   1 cup sugar
   1 teaspoon baking soda
   1/2 teaspoon salt
   1/2 cup chilled butter, cut into pieces
   1 cup sweetened dried cranberries, chopped
   1/2 cup chopped pecans, toasted
   1/2 teaspoons grated orange zest

In a medium bowl, combine flour, sugar, baking soda, and salt. Using pastry blender, cut butter into dry ingredients until mixture resembles coarse meal. Stir in cranberries, pecans, and orange zest. Divide mix into 2 resealable plastic bags. Store in refrigerator. Give with baking instructions.

Yield: 2 bags muffin mix, about 1/2 cups each

To bake: In a medium bowl, combine cup sour cream and 1 bag muffin mix (1/2 cups); stir just until moistened. Fill paper-lined muffin cups full. Sprinkle with granulated sugar. Bake in a 400-degree oven 18 to 20 minutes or until a toothpick inserted in center of muffin comes out clean and tops are golden brown.

Yield: about 6 muffins

"NOEL" POT HOLDER

You will need tracing paper; pot holder with pocket; red, green, and brown embroidery floss; one 3/4" dia. button; 6" x 22" piece of fabric; pinking shears; several 12" lengths of natural raffia; fabric for card; paper-backed fusible web; 3" x 5" piece of ecru card stock; and a black permanent fine-point marker.

Refer to Embroidery Stitches, page 113, before beginning project.

1. Trace pattern, page 118, onto tracing paper. Pin pattern to pot holder. Stitch design through paper using four strands of green floss to work *Stem Stitches* for holly, six strands of red floss to work *French Knots* for berries, and six strands of brown floss to work *Straight Stitches* for letters. Carefully tear away paper. Use floss to sew button in place for the "O" in NOEL.
2. For bag, matching right sides and short edges, fold fabric in half. Use a 1/4" seam allowance to sew sides of bag. Turn bag right side out. Trim top of bag with pinking shears. Place gift in bag. Tie raffia into a bow around top of bag.
3. For card, cut one 1/2" x 5" strip each from fabric and web. Fuse web to fabric; fuse fabric along top edge of card stock. Use marker to write baking instructions on card.
4. Place bag and card in pocket of pot holder.

MARINATED FRUIT MEDLEY

Oranges, kiwis, and cherries make a colorful showing in this Marinated Fruit Medley. Great for spooning over ice cream or cake, the mixture gets its deliciously different taste from orange liqueur and anise seed. The cute no-sew stocking cap on our gift jar is easy to make from an ordinary red crew sock.

MARINATED FRUIT MEDLEY

5 small oranges, peeled, seeded, and sliced
2 kiwis, peeled and sliced
1 jar (6 ounces) maraschino cherries, drained
1 cup orange-flavored liqueur
1 teaspoon anise seed
$^1/_2$ cup granulated sugar

Combine all ingredients in a large bowl. Stir until sugar dissolves. Cover and chill 8 hours or overnight to allow flavors to blend. Store in an airtight container in refrigerator. Serve alone or with ice cream or shortcake.

Yield: about 3 cups fruit

STOCKING CAP JAR TOPPER

For a topper to fit a regular canning jar, you will need a women's crew-style sock, a cotton ball or small piece of polyester fiberfill, 8" of $^1/_8$"w ribbon, and a $^1/_2$" dia. jingle bell.

1. Place cotton ball inside toe of sock. Knot ribbon around sock just above cotton ball. Thread jingle bell onto one ribbon end; tie ribbon ends into a bow.
2. Fold cuff in half; fold in half again. Place cap over jar lid.

CHERRIES JUBILEE SAUCE

For a sweet, spirited surprise in very little time, whip up a batch of our Cherries Jubilee Sauce. A fruity topping splashed with cherry-flavored liqueur, it's wonderful over ice cream or pound cake. A basket lined with gilded mesh ribbon and trimmed with silk poinsettias is a delightful gift carrier for a jar of the dessert sauce. Make your present even more special by adding a sundae glass and an ice-cream scoop.

CHERRIES JUBILEE SAUCE

2 cans (15 ounces each) red pitted cherries in heavy syrup

/2 cups sugar

/2 cup kirsch (cherry liqueur)

Drain cherries, reserving syrup. In a rge saucepan, combine cherry syrup d sugar over medium heat; stir until gar dissolves. Increase heat to medium gh and bring to a boil. Stirring nstantly, boil 4 minutes; remove m heat. Stir in cherries and kirsch. rve warm or chilled as a dessert pping. Store in an airtight container in frigerator.

eld: about 6^1/2 cups sauce

BREADS & SPREADS

Nothing is better than fresh-baked—unless it's that same bread with a sweet or savory topping. This Christmas, share loaves, muffins, and pastries with everyone you know, and include one or two delicious spreads for a little something extra.

CINNAMON ROLL BREAD

A swirl of sugar, cinnamon, and toasted pecans makes this bread a tasty breakfast treat! Our Cinnamon Roll Bread would make a splendid gift for that special friend or co-worker who brightens your life throughout the year. Present the flavorful gift (along with your warmest wishes) in an appliquéd canvas bag.

CINNAMON ROLL BREAD

 1 loaf (16 ounces) frozen white yeast dough, thawed in refrigerator overnight
 $1/2$ cup butter or margarine, softened
 $1/2$ cup granulated sugar
 $1/4$ cup chopped pecans, toasted
 2 teaspoons ground cinnamon
   Vegetable oil cooking spray
 1 cup confectioners sugar
 $1^1/2$ tablespoons milk
 $1/2$ teaspoon vanilla extract

Let dough stand at room temperature 30 minutes. On a lightly floured surface, use a floured rolling pin to roll dough into a 10 x 12-inch rectangle. Spread butter over dough. In a small bowl, combine granulated sugar, pecans, and cinnamon. Sprinkle sugar mixture over butter to within 1 inch of edges. Beginning at 1 short edge, roll up dough jellyroll style. Pinch seam to seal. Place, seam side down, in a greased $4^1/2$ x $8^1/2$-inch loaf pan, turning ends under. Spray top of dough with cooking spray, cover, and let rise in a warm place (80 to 85 degrees) about 30 minutes or until almost doubled in size.

Preheat oven to 350 degrees. Cut 5 slashes in top of loaf. Bake 30 to 35 minutes or until golden brown. Cool in pan 5 minutes. Transfer to a wire rack with waxed paper underneath. In a small bowl, combine confectioners sugar, milk, and vanilla; stir until smooth. Drizzle icing over warm loaf. Serve warm or cool completely. Store in an airtight container.

Yield: 1 loaf bread

CANVAS MITTEN BAG

You will need paper-backed fusible web, assorted fabrics for appliqués, canvas bag (we used a 10" x 5" x $4^1/2$" bag with handles), hot glue gun, two $5/8$" dia. buttons for each pair of mittens, black permanent fine-point marker, and tissue paper.

1. For each pair of mittens, use pattern and follow *Making Appliqués*, page 11, to make two (one in reverse) mitten appliqués from fabrics.
2. Arrange and fuse mittens on bag. Glue one button at outer corner of each mitten at wrist. Use marker to draw a squiggly line to connect mittens.
3. Line bag with tissue paper. Place gift in bag.

CRANBERRY-NUT MUFFINS

Take a batch of fruity Cranberry-Nut Muffins to a mom who's too busy for holiday baking. She's sure to appreciate the moist homemade treats, especially when they're spread with lightly sweet Orange Butter. A basket lined with holiday fabric makes a cheery presentation, and a handmade gift tag lends a personal touch.

CRANBERRY-NUT MUFFINS WITH ORANGE BUTTER

MUFFINS

2 cups all-purpose flour
2/3 cup sugar
2 teaspoons baking powder
1 teaspoon salt
1/2 teaspoon baking soda
1/2 teaspoon ground cinnamon
1/2 cup orange juice
1/2 cup orange marmalade
1/4 cup buttermilk
1/4 cup vegetable oil
1 egg
1 cup coarsely chopped fresh cranberries
3/4 cup chopped walnuts

ORANGE BUTTER

1/2 cup butter, softened
2 tablespoons orange marmalade

Preheat oven to 375 degrees. For muffins, combine flour, sugar, baking powder, salt, baking soda, and cinnamon in a large bowl. In a small bowl, combine orange juice, orange marmalade, buttermilk, oil, and egg. Make a well in center of dry ingredients.

Add orange juice mixture, cranberries, and walnuts; stir just until moistened. Fill paper-lined muffin cups about two-thirds full. Bake 17 to 22 minutes or until muffins are golden brown. Serve warm or transfer to a wire rack to cool. Store in an airtight container.

For orange butter, combine butter and orange marmalade in a small bowl. Store in an airtight container in refrigerator.

Yield: about 1 1/2 dozen muffins and about 3/4 cup orange butter

GINGERBREAD MAN TAG

Trace gingerbread man pattern onto tracing paper; cut out. Use pattern to cut shape from tan paper. Use a black felt-tip pen to draw eyes and mouth and a red colored pencil to color cheeks. Glue to green paper. Cutting close to gingerbread man, cut shape from green paper. Cut a 2 1/2" x 1 1/2" piece of white paper. Glue white paper piece to red paper. Leaving a red border, cut out. Glue to gingerbread man. Use a red pen to write name on tag.

How does Mrs. Claus reward Santa's reindeer on Christmas morning? With gifts of her homemade Sweet and Savory Spiral Rolls, of course! And you can deliver those same treats on Christmas Eve as next-morning nibbles for special families on your holiday list. The basic yeast dough recipe makes three pans of rolls, which can each be prepared with one of our three sweet or savory fillings. Wrap the rolls in cellophane and tie on a festive reindeer ornament for an eye-opening offering.

SWEET AND SAVORY SPIRAL ROLLS

YEAST DOUGH
- 1 package quick-acting dry yeast
- 1/4 cup plus 1 teaspoon sugar, divided
- 1/4 cup warm water
- 3/4 cups milk
- 1/3 cup butter or margarine
- 1 teaspoon salt
- 5 to 6 cups all-purpose flour, divided
- 1 egg
- Vegetable cooking spray

PARMESAN-HERB FILLING
- 3 tablespoons butter or margarine
- 2 cloves garlic, minced
- 2 teaspoons dried Italian seasoning
- 1/4 cup freshly grated Parmesan cheese

CINNAMON-PECAN FILLING
- 1/3 cup firmly packed brown sugar
- 2 teaspoons ground cinnamon
- 4 tablespoons butter or margarine, softened
- 1/2 cup chopped pecans

APRICOT-ALMOND FILLING
- 1/2 cup apricot preserves
- 1/4 cup sugar
- 1/2 cup sliced almonds

VANILLA GLAZE
- 1/2 cup sifted confectioners sugar
- 2 teaspoons water
- 1/2 teaspoon vanilla extract

ALMOND GLAZE
- 1/2 cup sifted confectioners sugar
- 2 teaspoons water
- 1/2 teaspoon almond extract

In a small bowl, dissolve yeast and teaspoon sugar in 1/4 cup warm water. In a small saucepan, heat milk, butter, remaining 1/4 cup sugar, and salt over medium heat until butter melts; remove from heat. In a large bowl, combine cups flour and milk mixture. Beat in east mixture and egg; beat until well ended. Add 3 cups flour, 1 cup at a time; stir until a soft dough forms. Turn onto a lightly floured surface. Knead about 5 minutes or until dough becomes smooth and elastic, using additional flour as necessary. Place in a large bowl sprayed with cooking spray, turning once to coat top of dough. Cover and let rise in a warm place (80 to 85 degrees) 1 1/4 hours or until doubled in size.

Turn dough onto a lightly floured surface and punch down. Divide dough into thirds. Roll each third into a 10 x 14-inch rectangle. Spread each rectangle with 1 of the following fillings:

For Parmesan-herb filling, combine butter, garlic, and Italian seasoning in a small microwave-safe bowl. Microwave on medium power (50%) 1 minute; stir until butter melts. Cover and allow to stand 10 minutes for flavors to blend. Brush dough with herb butter mixture. Sprinkle Parmesan cheese over dough.

For cinnamon-pecan filling, combine brown sugar and cinnamon in a small bowl. Spread butter on dough. Sprinkle with brown sugar mixture. Sprinkle with pecans.

For apricot-almond filling, combine apricot preserves and sugar in a small bowl; stir until well blended. Spread apricot mixture on dough. Sprinkle with almonds.

Beginning at 1 short edge, roll up each rectangle jellyroll style. Pinch seams to seal. Cut dough into 1-inch slices. Place each type of roll, cut side down, in a greased 8-inch round cake pan. Spray rolls with cooking spray, cover, and let rise in a warm place about 40 minutes or until doubled in size.

Preheat oven to 350 degrees. Bake 20 to 27 minutes or until golden brown. Cool in pans 10 minutes. Remove rolls from pans. Serve Parmesan-herb rolls warm or cool completely.

For vanilla glaze, combine confectioners sugar, water, and vanilla in a small bowl; stir until smooth. Drizzle glaze over warm cinnamon-pecan rolls. Serve warm or cool completely.

For almond glaze, combine confectioners sugar, water, and almond extract in a small bowl; stir until smooth. Drizzle glaze over warm apricot-almond rolls. Serve warm or cool completely.

Yield: 3 pans, 10 rolls each

REINDEER ORNAMENT
You will need one 6" square each of red fabric, muslin, and low-loft cotton batting; fusible web; 6" of 1/4"w ribbon for hanger; red, green, tan, and metallic gold acrylic paint; stencil brushes; small paintbrush; acetate for stencils; black permanent felt-tip pen with fine point; craft knife and cutting mat; tracing paper; graphite transfer paper; pressing cloth; and glue.

1. Fuse web to wrong sides of fabric squares. Fuse red fabric to batting. Do not remove paper backing from muslin.
2. To stencil reindeer on muslin, use pattern, page 119, and follow *Stenciling,* page 112, to stencil head, antlers, and bow tie.
3. Trace detail lines of pattern (shown in grey) onto tracing paper. Use transfer paper to transfer detail lines to reindeer. Use pen to outline stenciled shapes, draw over transferred detail lines, and color eyes. Paint nose and beads red.
4. Cutting close to design, cut reindeer from muslin square. Using pressing cloth, fuse reindeer to center of red fabric square. Cutting about 1/4" from reindeer, cut reindeer from red fabric.
5. For hanger, fold ribbon in half and glue ends to top back of reindeer.

CUMIN BREAD

Your friends will say "Olé!" when you deliver this spicy holiday treat! Presented in a basket with a festive fabric liner, our Cumin Bread lends a Southwestern taste to the Yuletide celebration. For extra South-of-the-Border style, send along a cactus all decked out for Christmas!

CUMIN BREAD

    3 cups all-purpose flour
$^1/_4$ cup granulated sugar
    2 tablespoons baking powder
    4 teaspoons ground cumin
    2 teaspoons salt
    1 teaspoon cumin seed, crushed
$^1/_2$ teaspoon dry mustard
    3 eggs
$1^1/_2$ cups milk
$^1/_3$ cup vegetable oil
    3 tablespoons picante sauce

Preheat oven to 350 degrees. In a large bowl, combine first 7 ingredients. In a medium bowl, whisk together remaining ingredients. Add egg mixture to dry ingredients; stir just until batter is moist. Pour batter evenly into 3 greased 3 x 5$^1/_2$-inch loaf pans. Bake 25 to 30 minutes or until a toothpick inserted in center comes out clean. Cool in pans 10 minutes; remove from pans and place on wire racks to cool completely. Store in an airtight container. Give with serving instructions.

Yield: 3 loaves bread

To serve: Bread may be served at room temperature or warm. To reheat, preheat oven to 350 degrees. Bake uncovered on an ungreased baking shee 3 to 5 minutes or until heated through

LUSCIOUS LEMON-NUT BREAD

Share this moist, nutty loaf with your best coffee-break pal. Packed with homemade goodness, Lemon-Nut Bread is easy to make with items you probably have on hand. While the bread is baking, you can whip up a cheery no-sew gift bag and matching tag using cute print fabric and fusible web.

LEMON-NUT BREAD

$3/4$ cup butter or margarine, softened
$1^1/2$ cups sugar
3 eggs
$2^1/4$ cups all-purpose flour
$1/4$ teaspoon salt
$1/4$ teaspoon baking soda
$1/4$ cup buttermilk
$3/4$ cup chopped pecans
Grated zest of 1 lemon
$3/4$ cup sifted confectioners sugar
6 tablespoons freshly squeezed lemon juice

Preheat oven to 325 degrees. Grease and flour a 5 x 9-inch loaf pan. In a large bowl, cream butter and sugar until fluffy. Add eggs; beat until smooth. In a medium bowl, combine flour, salt, and baking soda. Alternately add dry ingredients and buttermilk to creamed mixture; stir just until moistened. Stir in pecans and lemon zest. Spoon batter into prepared pan. Bake $1^1/4$ hours or until a toothpick inserted in center of loaf comes out clean. Cool in pan 15 minutes. Remove from pan and place on a wire rack with waxed paper underneath. In a small bowl, combine confectioners sugar and lemon juice. Use a toothpick to punch holes in top of warm bread; pour glaze over bread. Cool bread completely. Store in an airtight container.

Yield: 1 loaf bread

SNOWMAN FABRIC BAG AND TAG

You will need snowman-motif fabric, $3/4$ yd of $7/8$"w wired ribbon, $3/8$ yd of $1/16$"w ribbon, $1/2$"w fusible web tape, fusible web, poster board, tracing paper, and hole punch.

1. For bag, cut a $9^1/2$" x 35" fabric piece. Match right sides and short edges and press fabric piece in half (fold is bottom of bag). Unfold fabric piece and fuse web tape along each long edge on right side. Refold fabric piece and fuse edges together. Fold top of bag 2" to wrong side and press. Unfold top of bag and fuse web tape along top edge on wrong side. Refold top of bag and fuse in place. Turn bag right side out.
2. Place gift in bag. Tie $7/8$"w ribbon into a bow around top of bag; trim ends.
3. For tag, cut a 3" square from fabric with desired motif at center. Fuse web to wrong side of fabric. Fuse fabric to poster board. Cut out a $2^1/2$" dia. circle. Punch hole in tag. Loop remaining ribbon through hole in tag. Tie tag onto bow on bag.

or a gift that will
atisfy even the most
articular cheese-lover, our
ensational Swiss Cheese
pread is a real palate pleaser.
he zesty spreadable is easy to
ut together using shredded
heese, deviled ham spread,
eam cheese, and a few
easonings. Pack it in a jar
ith a fabric-covered lid and
eliver it in our cute paper
ag featuring a fused-on
bric gingerbread boy. The
edge of cheese he's holding
ovides a clever hint to the
ag's delicious contents!

SWISS CHEESE SPREAD

2 cans (4¹/₄ ounces each) deviled ham
    spread
1 package (8 ounces) shredded
    Swiss cheese
1 package (3 ounces) cream cheese,
    softened
2 teaspoons Dijon-style mustard
1 teaspoon dried minced onion
¹/₂ teaspoon caraway seed

Place all ingredients in a food
rocessor; process until well blended.
poon into jars with lids. Store in
efrigerator. To serve, let stand at room
mperature 20 to 30 minutes or until
oftened; serve with crackers.

ield: about 2¹/₂ cups spread

GINGERBREAD BOY SACKS

For each sack and jar lid, you will need a paper sack; fabrics for gingerbread boy, bow tie, tag, and jar lid; four 1¹/₄" lengths of white rickrack; black felt-tip pen with fine point; yellow colored pencil; red lipstick; white paper; heavy cream-colored paper; tissue paper; paper-backed fusible web; raffia; ¹/₄" dia. and ¹/₈" dia. hole punches; and craft glue.

1. Follow *Making Appliqués*, page 112, to make gingerbread boy and bow tie appliqués. Remove paper backing. Fuse gingerbread boy and bow tie to sack.
2. For rickrack trim, glue lengths of rickrack to arms and legs of gingerbread boy, trimming to fit; allow to dry.
3. Use black pen to draw eyes and mouth on gingerbread boy. Use lipstick to color cheeks.
4. Trace cheese pattern onto white paper. Use yellow pencil to color cheese. Cut out cheese. Use hole punches to punch holes in cheese. Glue cheese to sack; allow to dry.
5. For tag, fuse web to wrong side of fabric. Fuse fabric to heavy paper. Cut a rectangle from fabric-covered paper. Match short edges and fold tag in half with fabric side out. Punch a hole in corner of tag. Punch 2 holes approx. ¹/₄" apart in sack. Thread a strand of raffia through holes in sack and tag and tie into a bow.
6. Line sack with tissue paper.
7. To cover jar lid, use flat part of a jar lid as a pattern and cut a circle from fabric. Remove band from filled jar. Glue fabric circle to flat part of jar lid. Replace band over lid.

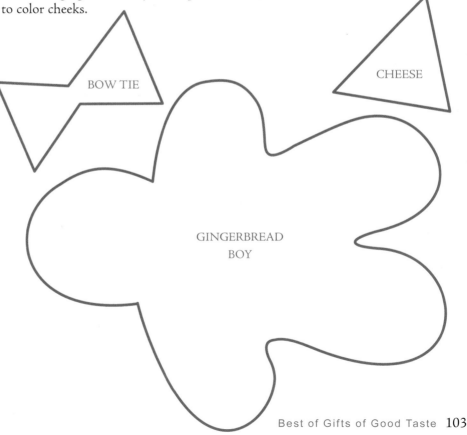

BOW TIE

CHEESE

GINGERBREAD
BOY

BAKED CRAB SPREAD

Bring a taste of summer fun to the holidays with piquant Baked Crab Spread. Spiced with horseradish and hot pepper sauce, this savory appetizer is delicious with crackers. Wrap the dish in clear cellophane and tie on a cute seashell wreath to please a beachcombing friend. Don't forget the serving instructions!

BAKED CRAB SPREAD

- 1 package (8 ounces) cream cheese, softened
- $^1/_2$ cup mayonnaise
- 2 tablespoons freshly squeezed lemon juice
- 1 tablespoon grated onion
- 1 tablespoon prepared horseradish
- $^1/_4$ teaspoon garlic salt
- $^1/_4$ teaspoon ground white pepper
- $^1/_8$ teaspoon hot pepper sauce
- 8 ounces fresh crabmeat or 2 cans crabmeat (6 ounces each), drained
- $^1/_4$ cup finely chopped water chestnuts

In a large bowl, beat cream cheese, mayonnaise, lemon juice, onion, horseradish, garlic salt, white pepper, and pepper sauce until well blended. Fold in crabmeat and water chestnuts. Spoon into a 3-cup baking dish. Cover and store in refrigerator. Give with serving instructions.

Yield: about 2$^1/_2$ cups spread

To serve: Uncover and bake in a 350-degree oven 25 to 30 minutes or until lightly browned around edges. Serve warm with crackers.

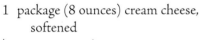

SEASHELL WREATH ORNAMENT

You will need a 4" square of foam core board, $^3/_4$ yd of $^1/_4$"w ribbon, seashells (available at craft stores), tracing paper, craft knife, cutting mat, and glue.

1. For wreath pattern, draw a 3" dia. circle with a 1$^1/_4$" dia. circle in the center; cut out. Draw around pattern on foam core board. Use craft knife to cut out wreath shape.
2. Glue seashells to wreath shape.
3. Cut two 11" lengths from ribbon. Ti ribbon lengths together into a bow; tri ends. Glue bow to top of wreath.
4. For hanger, glue ends of remaining ribbon length to top back of ornament.

CHRISTMAS BREAD

Buttermilk baking mix gives you a head start on making flavorful Christmas Bread! Studded with candied fruit and chopped pecans, the batter is blended with applesauce for extra moistness. For giving, wrap the mini loaves in kitchen towels and decorate them with ribbon and berry sprays.

CHRISTMAS BREAD

$^1/_4$ cup butter or margarine, softened
$^1/_2$ cup granulated sugar
2 eggs
$^1/_3$ cup applesauce
1 teaspoon vanilla extract
2 cups buttermilk baking mix
$1^1/_2$ cups chopped candied pineapple and green and red cherries
$^1/_2$ cup chopped pecans
$^2/_3$ cup sifted confectioners sugar
1 tablespoon milk

Preheat oven to 350 degrees. In a large bowl, cream butter and granulated sugar until fluffy. Add eggs, applesauce, and vanilla; beat until well blended. Add baking mix; stir just until moistened. Stir in candied fruit and pecans. Spoon batter into 4 greased and floured 3 x 5$^1/_2$-inch loaf pans. Bake 25 to 30 minutes or until a toothpick inserted in center of bread comes out clean. Cool in pans 5 minutes. Remove from pans and place on a wire rack with waxed paper underneath.

For glaze, combine confectioners sugar and milk in a small bowl; stir until smooth. Drizzle glaze over warm bread. Allow glaze to harden. Store in an airtight container.

Yield: 4 mini loaves bread

SANTA'S SPICY SPREAD

This Spicy Bean and Tomato Spread has just the right zip to make the taste buds tingle! For a jolly presentation, place a jar of spread and a bag of baguette slices in a Christmas container and tie with a bright bow.

SPICY BEAN AND TOMATO SPREAD

This spread is for garlic lovers!

  1 cup boiling water
$1/2$ cup finely chopped sun-dried tomatoes
  2 cans (15.8 ounces each) great Northern beans
  3 cloves garlic, chopped
  2 tablespoons olive oil
  1 tablespoon freshly squeezed lemon juice
$1/2$ teaspoon ground cumin
$1/2$ teaspoon ground coriander
$1/2$ teaspoon salt
$1/8$ teaspoon ground red pepper
$1/4$ cup finely chopped fresh cilantro
    Baguette slices to serve

In a small heatproof bowl, pour boiling water over tomatoes. Cover and let stand 20 minutes; drain.

Rinse and drain beans. Process beans, garlic, oil, lemon juice, cumin, coriander, salt, and red pepper in a large food processor until smooth. Transfer to a medium bowl; stir in drained tomatoes and cilantro. Cover and chill at least 2 hours to let flavors blend. Serve spread at room temperature on toasted baguette slices.

Yield: about $2^1/2$ cups spread

SMOKED TURKEY SPREAD

During the hectic holiday season, friends will enjoy a relaxing happy-hour at home with this quick-to-fix snack. Our Smoked Turkey Spread is a guaranteed taste bud pleaser! Share a bowl of the savory spread in a white basket adorned with pretty poinsettias. Be sure to include crackers for a crunchy complement!

SMOKED TURKEY SPREAD

- 1 package (8 ounces) cream cheese, softened
- 1 cup chopped smoked turkey
- 1/4 cup mayonnaise
- 2/3 cup chopped pecans, toasted and divided
- 6 tablespoons chopped fresh parsley, divided
- 1/8 teaspoon ground red pepper
  Crackers to serve

Process cream cheese, turkey, and mayonnaise in a food processor until well blended. Add 1/2 cup pecans, 4 tablespoons parsley, and red pepper. Pulse process until blended. Spoon into small bowl; garnish with remaining pecans and 2 tablespoons parsley. Cover and store in refrigerator. Serve with crackers.

Yield: about 2 1/4 cups spread

WHITE BASKET WITH POINSETTIAS

You will need wire cutters, 4" dia. artificial poinsettias, hot glue gun, white basket (we used an 8" x 10 1/2" basket with handle), and tissue paper.

1. Use wire cutters to cut poinsettias and leaves from stems. Glue flowers and leaves around rim of basket.

2. Line basket with tissue paper. Place gift in basket.

PIMIENTO CHEESE SPREAD

Simple to prepare and packed with flavor, this gourmet cheese spread makes an ideal last-minute gift. No one will guess that you created the zesty mixture using only three ingredients! Delivery is easy, too—just dress up a brown bag with paint and a Christmas card.

GOURMET PIMIENTO CHEESE SPREAD

- 1 container (14 ounces) pimiento cheese spread
- 1 cup finely chopped pecans, toasted
- $^1/_2$ cup dill pickle relish *or* $^1/_4$ cup sweet pickle relish
  Crackers to serve

In a medium bowl, combine cheese spread, pecans, and relish. Stir until well blended. Cover and chill 2 hours to let flavors blend. Serve with crackers.

Yield: about $2^1/_4$ cups spread

BROWN BAG WITH CHRISTMAS CARD MOTIF

You will need a Christmas card, craft glue, lunch-size brown paper bag, white and gold acrylic paint, paintbrush, $1^1/_4$"w wooden star, hole punch, green raffia, and a hot glue gun.

1. Cut desired motif from card. Use craft glue to glue card to front of bag; allow to dry.
2. Paint white dots on bag; paint wooden star gold. Allow to dry.

3. Place gift in bag. Fold top of bag $1^1/_2$" to back. Punch two holes 1" apart in center of folded portion of bag.

4. Thread several 15" lengths of raffia through holes and tie into a bow at front of bag. Hot glue star to knot of bow.

FABULOUS FRUIT SPREADS

Give friends a taste of the tropics with these bagel spread mixes. The fruity blends are created in a flash by mixing gelatin and dried fruit. Simply combine with cream cheese and enjoy! To make the nifty packets, fuse fabric to a paper bag, draw on "stitches," and tie on snowman spreaders for wintry fun.

FRUITY BAGEL SPREAD MIXES

Try variations of these mixes using your favorite gelatin and dried fruit.

BERRY BERRY MIX

1 package (3 ounces) raspberry gelatin

1/2 cup dried sweetened cranberries

In a small bowl, combine gelatin and dried fruit. Store in a resealable plastic bag in refrigerator. Give with serving instructions.

Yield: about 3/4 cup mix

TROPICAL FRUIT MIX

1 package (3 ounces) pineapple gelatin

1/2 cup chopped dried pineapple

1/4 cup flaked coconut

In a small bowl, combine gelatin, dried fruit, and coconut. Store in a resealable plastic bag in refrigerator. Give with serving instructions.

Yield: about 1 cup mix

To serve: In a small bowl, beat 3 tablespoons mix into one 8-ounce package softened cream cheese until well blended. Cover and chill 2 hours to let flavors blend. Serve spread on bagels.

Yield: about 1 cup spread

BAGEL MIX GIFT BAGS

For each bag, you will need a 4" x 7 1/2" brown paper bag, hot glue gun, fabric, paper-backed fusible web, permanent medium-point black marker, several 18" lengths of red raffia, and a decorative spreader.

1. Leaving bag folded, glue bottom to secure.

2. Measure height and width of bag; subtract 1/4" from each measurement. Follow *Making Appliqués,* page 112, to make one appliqué using the determined measurements. Fuse appliqué to front of bag.

3. Fold top of bag 2" to front. Use marker to draw "stitches" along sides and bottom of flap.

4. Place bagel spread mix and serving instructions in bag. Knot several lengths of raffia around bag. Tie raffia ends into a bow around spreader.

SMOKED SALMON SPREAD

There's something fishy about this gift basket! It features savory Smoked Salmon Spread and crispy sesame crackers for serving. Designed to delight a fisherman, the basket is wrapped in a "fishnet" and tied with a straw ribbon. The floats are actually red Christmas ornaments that have been dipped in white paint. A catchy tag makes a cute finishing touch.

SMOKED SALMON SPREAD

- 1 package (8 ounces) cream cheese, softened
- 2 teaspoons lime juice
- 6 green onions, finely chopped
- 4 teaspoons finely chopped fresh parsley
- 2 teaspoons ground coriander
- 1/2 teaspoon ground cayenne pepper
- 10 ounces skinless, boneless smoked salmon

In a large bowl, beat cream cheese and lime juice until fluffy using highest speed of an electric mixer. Add next 4 ingredients; beat until well blended. Stir in salmon. Cover and refrigerate 8 hours or overnight to allow flavors to blend. Serve with crackers or bread. Store in an airtight container in refrigerator.

Yield: about 1 1/2 cups spread

FISHERMAN'S BASKET

You will need a 9" dia. basket with handle, a cotton net shopping tote, excelsior, green angel hair ribbon, florist wire, 1 3/4" dia. red glass ball ornaments, ornament hangers, white acrylic paint, glossy clear acrylic spray, ivory paper, hole punch, red felt-tip pen, cotton string, craft glue, canning jar with lid, and one 4" square of each of the following: desired fabric, craft batting, and lightweight cardboard.

1. Place basket in tote. Fold top of tote to inside of basket. Fill basket with excelsior.
2. Tie ribbon into a double-loop bow;
wire bow to handle.
3. For each float ornament, attach hanger to ornament. Dip bottom half of ornament into paint; hang to dry. Apply 1 coat of acrylic spray; let dry. Hang ornaments on basket.
4. Cut tag shape from paper. Use pen write "HOOKED ON FISHING" o tag. Punch hole in pointed end of tag. Use string to tie tag to handle.
5. For jar insert, use flat part of lid as a pattern and cut a circle from fabric, batting, and cardboard. Glue batting t cardboard and edges of fabric circle to batting. Place insert and screw ring on jar.

CHOCOLATE PEANUT BUTTER

Yummy Chocolate Peanut Butter is the ultimate combination of two favorite flavors! Great on cookies, the creamy spread will be irresistible to grownups and children alike. Prancing wooden reindeer cutouts and a bright cloth make an ordinary basket a cute (and inexpensive!) way to deliver your gift.

CHOCOLATE PEANUT BUTTER

$1/2$ cups smooth peanut butter
$1/2$ cup semisweet chocolate chips, melted
$1/4$ cup butter or margarine, softened
$1/4$ cup confectioners sugar

1 teaspoon vanilla extract
1 teaspoon instant coffee granules
1 teaspoon hot water

In a large bowl, combine first 5 ingredients; stir until smooth. Combine coffee granules and water; stir until coffee dissolves. Stir coffee into peanut butter mixture. Serve with cookies or crackers. Store in an airtight container.

Yield: about 2 cups peanut butter

REINDEER BASKET

Hot glue purchased 2"-wide wooden reindeer cutouts around basket rim. Line basket with a fabric square.

GENERAL INSTRUCTIONS

STENCILING

1. (*Note:* These instructions are written for multicolor stencils. For single-color stencils, make 1 stencil for entire design.) For first stencil, cut a piece of acetate 1" larger than entire pattern. Center acetate over pattern and use pen to trace outlines of all areas of first color in stencil cutting key. For placement guidelines, outline remaining colored areas using dashed lines. Using a new piece of acetate for each additional color in stencil cutting key, repeat for remaining stencils.
2. Place each acetate piece on cutting mat and use craft knife to cut out stencil along solid lines, making sure edges are smooth.
3. Hold or tape stencil in place. Use a clean, dry stencil brush or sponge piece. Dip brush or sponge in paint; remove excess paint on a paper towel. Brush or sponge should be almost dry to produce good results. Beginning at edge of cutout area, apply paint in a stamping motion over stencil. If desired, highlight or shade design by stamping a lighter or darker shade of paint in cutout area. Repeat until all areas of first stencil have been painted. Carefully remove stencil and allow paint to dry.
4. Using stencils in order indicated in color key and matching guidelines on stencils to previously stenciled areas, repeat Step 3 for remaining stencils.

MAKING APPLIQUÉS

When tracing patterns for more than one appliqué, leave at least 1" between shapes on web.

To make a reverse appliqué, trace pattern onto tracing paper, turn traced pattern over, and follow all steps using traced pattern.

1. Trace appliqué pattern onto paper side of web. (Some pieces may be given as measurements. Draw shape the measurements given in project instructions on paper side of web.) Cutting about 1/2" outside drawn lines, cut out web shape.
2. Follow manufacturer's instructions to fuse web shape to wrong side of fabric. Cut out shape along drawn lines.

SPONGE PAINTING

Use an assembly-line method when making several sponge-painted projects. Place project on a covered work surface. Practice sponge-painting technique on scrap paper until desired look is achieved. Paint projects with first color and allow to dry before moving to next color. Use a clean sponge for each additional color.

For allover designs, dip a dampened sponge piece into paint; remove excess paint on a paper towel. Use a light stamping motion to paint item.

For painting with sponge shapes, dip a dampened sponge shape into paint; remove excess paint on a paper towel. Lightly press sponge shape onto project. Carefully lift sponge. For a reverse design, turn sponge shape over.

MAKING A BOW

1. For first streamer, measure desired length of streamer from 1 end of ribbon and gather ribbon between fingers (Fig. 1). For first loop, keep right side facing out and fold ribbon over to form desired size loop (Fig. 2). Repeat to form another loop same size as first loop (Fig. 3). Repeat to form desired number of loops. For remaining streamer, trim ribbon to desired length.

Fig. 1   Fig. 2   Fig. 3

2. To secure bow, hold gathered loops tightly. Wrap a length of wire around center. Hold wire ends behind bow, gathering loops forward; twist bow to tighten wire. Arrange loops as desired.
3. For bow center, wrap a 6" length of ribbon around center of bow, covering wire and overlapping ends at back; trim excess. Glue to secure.
4. Trim ribbon ends as desired.

SEALING BOTTLE WITH WAX

You will need paraffin, 20" of cotton string, double boiler, pieces of crayon (to color paraffin), masking tape, and newspaper. *Caution: Do not melt paraffin over an open flame or directly on burner.*

1. Cover work area with newspaper. Melt paraffin to a depth of $2^1/2$" in double boiler over hot water. Melt pieces of crayon in paraffin for desired color.
2. (*Note:* Make sure cork is firmly inserted in bottle or cap is screwed on tightly.) On neck of bottle, center string on front; bring string around bottle to back and twist lengths tightly together (Fig. 1a). Keeping string taut, bring both ends over top of bottle (Fig. 1b); tape ends to front of bottle 4" below top.

Fig. 1a   Fig. 1b

 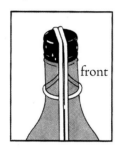

3. Dip approximately 2" of top of bottle in melted paraffin. Allowing paraffin to harden slightly between coats, continue dipping bottle until string is well coated. Remove tape; trim ends of string.
4. To open bottle, pull string up toward top of bottle and unwrap string around bottle, breaking wax.

EMBROIDERY STITCHES
FRENCH KNOT

Bring needle up at 1. Wrap thread once around needle and insert needle at 2, holding thread with non-stitching fingers (Fig. 1). Tighten knot as close to fabric as possible while pulling needle back through fabric.

Fig. 1

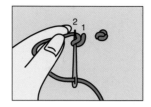

RUNNING STITCH

Make a series of straight stitches with stitch length equal to the space between stitches (Fig. 2).

Fig. 2

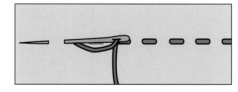

STEM STITCH

Bring needle up at 1; keeping thread below the stitching line, go down at 2 and bring needle up at 3. Take needle down at 4 and bring needle up at 5 (Fig. 3).

Fig. 3

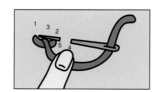

STRAIGHT STITCH

Bring needle up at 1 and go down at 2 (Fig. 4). Length of stitches may be varied as desired.

Fig. 4

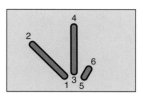

SEWING SHAPES

1. Center pattern on wrong side of 1 fabric piece and use a fabric marking pencil to draw around pattern. DO NOT CUT OUT SHAPE.
2. Place fabric pieces right sides together. Leaving an opening for turning, carefully sew pieces together directly on pencil line.
3. Leaving a $1/4$" seam allowance, cut out shape. Clip seam allowance at curves and corners. Turn shape right side out. Use the rounded end of a small crochet hook to completely turn small areas.
4. If pattern has facial features or detail lines, use fabric marking pencil to lightly mark placement of features or lines.

CHRISTMAS PATTERNS

FELT GIFT BAGS
(Page 22)

buttermilk
dressing
mix

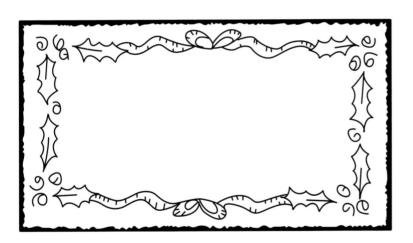

HOLIDAY GIFT TAG
(Page 6)
&
DECORATED BASKET WITH BOW
(Page 63)

caribbean
spice
mix

SPOON-TOPPED GIFT SACKS
(Page 89)

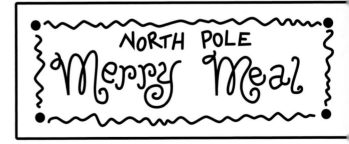

NORTH POLE
Merry Meal

MERRY MEAL BAGS
(Page 36)

NUTCRACKER GIFT BAG
(Page 15)

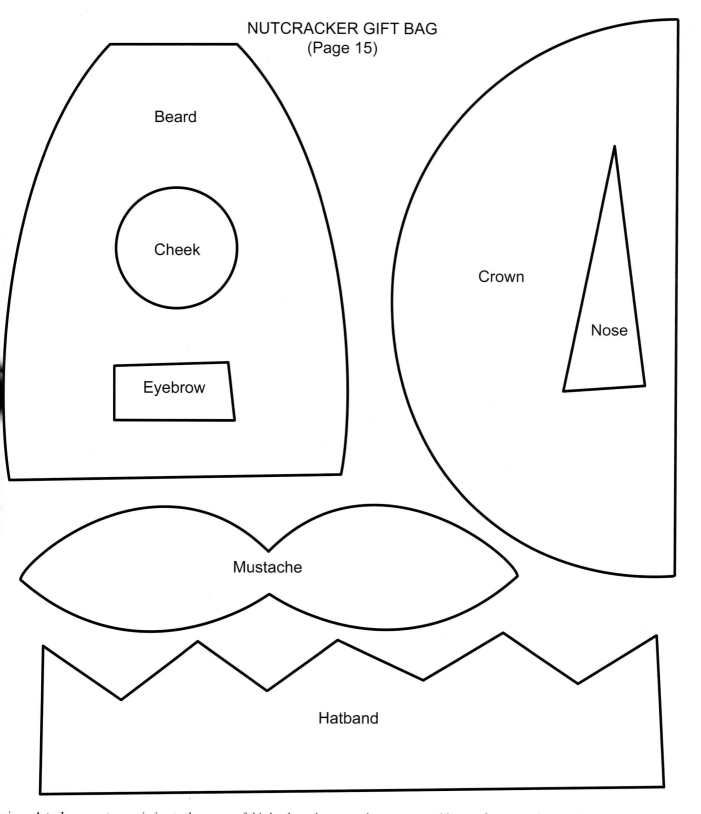

Beard

Cheek

Eyebrow

Crown

Nose

Mustache

Hatband

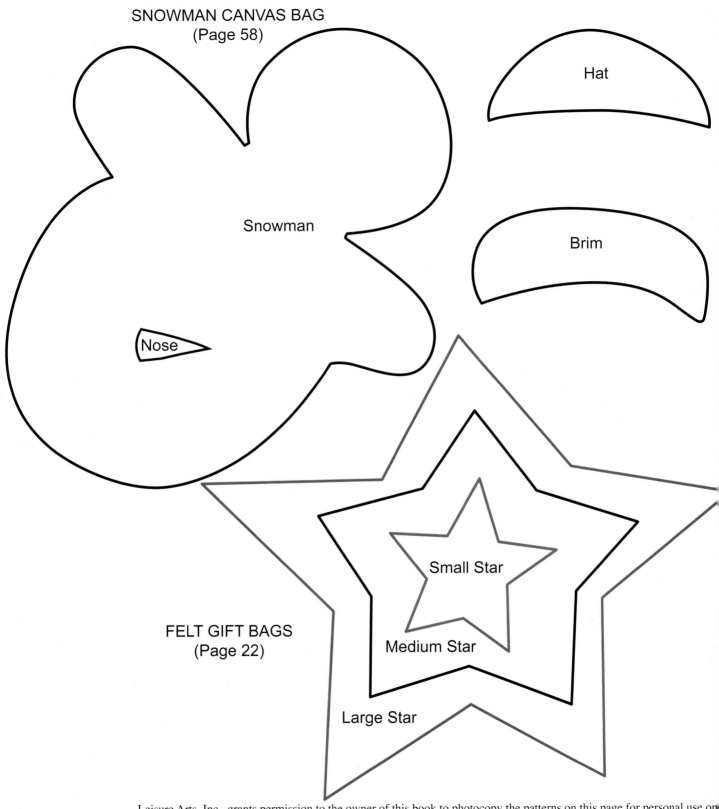

SNOWMAN CANVAS BAG
(Page 58)

Hat

Snowman

Brim

Nose

FELT GIFT BAGS
(Page 22)

Small Star

Medium Star

Large Star

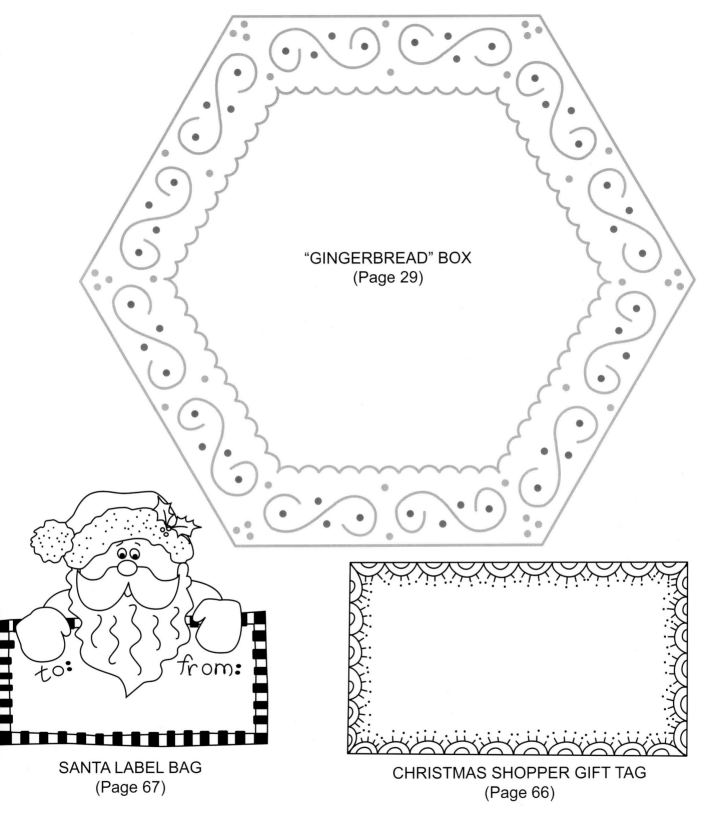

"GINGERBREAD" BOX
(Page 29)

SANTA LABEL BAG
(Page 67)

to: from:

CHRISTMAS SHOPPER GIFT TAG
(Page 66)

'TIS THE "SEASON" TAG
(Page 79)

Savory Herb
BAGEL MIX

To serve: Process 2 teaspoons mix with one 8-ounce package softened cream cheese in a food processor until smooth. Transfer to an airtight container. Chill 2 hours to let flavors blend. Serve spread on bagel slices.

BAGEL SPREAD PACKETS
(Page 84)

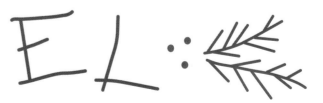

CHILI BAGS
(Page 87)

"NOEL" POT HOLDER
(Page 91)

REINDEER ORNAMENT
(Page 99)

STENCIL CUTTING KEY
Stencil #1
Stencil #2

COLOR KEY
Stencil #1 — tan with gold shading
Stencil #2 — green

POPCORN SEASONING BAG
(Page 85)

Homemade Especially for You!

ORANGE SLICE ORNAMENTS
(Page 52)

Leisure Arts, Inc., grants permission to the owner of this book to photocopy the patterns on this page for personal use only.

CHRISTMAS RECIPE INDEX

best of GIFTS OF GOOD TASTE
EVERYDAY

LEISURE ARTS, INC.
Little Rock, Arkansas

QUICK
GIFTS
4-17

HOLIDAY
GIFTS
32-61

GIFTS BY
THE BAGFUL
82-109

FRIENDSHIP GIFTS
18-31

GIFT BASKETS
62-81

QUICK GIFTS

You need a gift they'll love, and you
need it now! These tempting recipes are
ready-to-relish in minutes. And the fun
presentation ideas are really quick, too.

TROPICAL CRUNCH

Give a friend a taste of the tropics with our Tropical Crunch Snack Mix. With only five ingredients to toss together, you can mix up lots of this delicious, all-natural treat in a minute (or less)! For a sunny presentation, line a child's plastic pail with cellophane and include a plastic toy shovel for serving. So clever, so cute, and so "munch" fun to eat!

TROPICAL CRUNCH SNACK MIX

- 1 can (12 ounces) honey-roasted peanuts
- 1 can (10 ounces) salted cashews
- 10 ounces dried banana chips
- 8 ounces dried pineapple pieces
- 5 ounces coconut chips

Combine all ingredients in a large bowl. Store in an airtight container.

Yield: about 11 cups snack mix

PIMIENTO JACK CHEESE

A delicious twist on the traditional spread, our Pimiento Jack Cheese is perfect for a picnic or sack lunch. Spanish olives offer a tangy contrast to mild Monterey Jack cheese and sweet pimiento peppers, giving the spread a unique flavor. Our special blue pail, lined with checkered napkins, makes a charming carrier. Later, this little "graniteware" bucket will lend an old-timey look to a country kitchen.

PIMIENTO JACK CHEESE

- 4 cups (1 pound) shredded Monterey Jack cheese
- 1 jar (4 ounces) chopped pimiento, drained
- $^1/_2$ cup sliced pimiento-stuffed olives
- 3 tablespoons grated onion
- $^1/_2$ cup mayonnaise
- 3 tablespoons milk
- 1 teaspoon Dijon mustard
- $^1/_4$ teaspoon ground white pepper

In a large bowl, combine cheese, pimiento, olives, and onion. In a small bowl, blend mayonnaise, milk, mustard, and pepper until smooth. Add to cheese mixture, mixing well. Store in an airtight container in refrigerator. Serve with bread or crackers.

Yield: 3 cups of spread

"GRANITEWARE" PAIL

You will need a small metal pail (we bought our 1 qt. pail at a paint store), blue spray paint, white acrylic paint, plastic fork, and matte clear acrylic spray.

1. Spray pail with a light coat of blue paint; allow to dry. Repeat until pail is evenly coated with paint.
2. Use fork dipped in white paint to paint dots; allow to dry.
3. Spray pail with acrylic spray; allow to dry.

COOL MARGARITA PIES

Margarita fans will cheer for this unusual summertime dessert! Nestled in a pretzel crumb crust, the creamy filling for our Margarita Pies is prepared with tequila and purchased drink mixer. The recipe makes two tangy pies, so you can keep one for yourself, too! For a cool presentation, garnish the pie with lime slices and add a clever tag.

MARGARITA PIES

- 2   cups ground pretzels
- 1   cup butter or margarine, melted
- 1   envelope unflavored gelatin
- 1   cup liquid margarita mixer, divided
- 2   cans (14 ounces each) sweetened condensed milk
- $^1/_3$ cup tequila
- 5   tablespoons orange-flavored liqueur
- 2   to 3 drops green food coloring
- 8   ounces frozen non-dairy whipped topping, thawed
    Lime slices to garnish

For crusts, combine pretzel crumbs and butter in a small bowl. Press crumb mixture into bottom and up sides of two 9-inch pie pans. Place in refrigerator to chill.

In a microwave-safe measuring cup, sprinkle unflavored gelatin over $^1/_4$ cup margarita mixer. Let mixture stand 2 minutes. Microwave on high power (100%) 40 seconds; stir thoroughly. Allow to stand 2 minutes or until gelatin is completely dissolved. In a large bowl, combine gelatin mixture, remaining $^3/_4$ cup margarita mixer, condensed milk, tequila, liqueur, and food coloring unt[il] well blended; fold in whipped topping. Divide filling equally between crusts; chill until firm. Garnish with lime slice[s]. Cover and refrigerate.

Yield: two 9-inch pies

KID-PLEASING POPCORN CAKE

Say "Happy Birthday" to a favorite youngster with a colorful Popcorn Cake. A kid-pleasing mixture of popcorn, peanuts, candy-coated chocolate chips, and marshmallows, the "cake" is shaped in a tube pan and decorated with gum ball "balloons" with icing strings. More gum balls are poured in the center hole of the cake to hold an arrangement of real balloons tied to drinking straws. What a fun addition to a party!

POPCORN CAKE

1 package (16 ounces) regular marshmallows
$^1/_2$ cup butter or margarine
$^1/_4$ cup vegetable oil
16 cups popped popcorn
1 can (12 ounces) salted peanuts
$^1/_2$ cup candy-coated mini chocolate chips
Small balloons, plastic drinking straws, gum balls, and purchased decorating icing to decorate

In a large saucepan over medium heat, combine marshmallows, butter, and oil; stir constantly until marshmallows are melted. Place popcorn and peanuts in very large bowl; stir in marshmallow mixture. Add chocolate chips; lightly stir into popcorn mixture. Press popcorn mixture into a greased 10-inch tube pan; pack firmly. Place in refrigerator 30 minutes or until set. Unmold onto a serving plate.

To decorate cake, pipe decorating icing onto cake for balloons strings; place a gum ball at one end of each string. Blow up balloons and tie onto end of straws; place in opening of cake. Fill opening with gum balls.

Yield: about 12 servings

TEX-MEX PECANS

These fiery nuts will leave 'em hankerin' for more! Tex-Mex Pecans are coated with spices and baked for range-riding taste. Tie the nuts in a red bandanna and deliver in a rope-trimmed bucket with a sassy boot-shaped gift tag.

TEX-MEX PECANS

$3^1/_2$ cups pecan halves (about 14 ounces)
1 tablespoon vegetable oil
1 tablespoon ground cumin
1 teaspoon chili powder
$^3/_4$ teaspoon salt
$^1/_8$ teaspoon ground red pepper

Preheat oven to 300 degrees. Place pecans in a lightly greased 9 x 13-inch baking pan. In a small bowl, combine oil, cumin, chili powder, salt, and red pepper. Drizzle oil mixture over pecans; stir to coat. Bake 25 minutes, stirring every 5 minutes. Spread on aluminum foil to cool. Store in an airtight container.

Yield: about 4 cups pecans

BUCKET O' SPICY PECANS

You will need a bucket (we used a $5^1/_2$"h galvanized bucket), $^3/_8$" dia. rope, hot glue gun, bandanna, and 20" of jute twine.

For tag, you will also need photocopy of tag design (page 112) on tan card stock, colored pencils, and $^1/_8$" dia. hole punch.

1. Measure around bucket. Cut a length of rope the determined measurement. Glue rope around bucket.
2. Line bucket with bandanna. Place gift in bucket. Gather bandanna over gift. Tie twine around gathers.

3. For tag, use pencils to color tag. Leaving a $^1/_8$" border, cut out tag. Punch hole in boot loop. Tie one end of twine through hole in tag; knot other end of twine.

LUSCIOUS FRUIT DRESSING

This luscious Lemony Fruit Salad Dressing is wonderful with apples, grapes, and other fresh fruits! It's super-easy to whip up with lemon yogurt and a few ingredients from your pantry. For a presentation that will light up any fruit lover's eyes, place a jar of the creamy dressing in a basket lined with a cheerful cloth and tied with a citrus-trimmed bow. You'll want to add some fresh fruit too, so your friend can enjoy your gift right away.

LEMONY FRUIT SALAD DRESSING

1 can (14 ounces) sweetened condensed milk
2 cups lemon-flavored yogurt
1/4 teaspoon salt
1/8 teaspoon ground white pepper

In a small bowl, combine all ingredients; stir until well blended. Store in an airtight container in refrigerator.

Yield: about 3 cups dressing

JALAPEÑO SNACK MIX

The spicy design that adorns our Jalapeño Snack Mix packages promises that this is one hot gift! To make it, simply pour a zesty combination of butter, peppers, and spices over some of your favorite bite-size snacks and then bake. You're guaranteed a gift that will heat up the holidays!

JALAPEÑO SNACK MIX

- 1 package (16 ounces) cheese snack crackers
- 1 package (10 ounces) small pretzel twists
- 1 package (12 ounces) square corn cereal
- $^1/_2$ cup drained pickled jalapeño pepper slices
- 2 tablespoons Dijon-style mustard
- 3 cloves garlic, coarsely chopped
- 1 teaspoon dried oregano leaves
- 2 teaspoons ground cumin
- $^3/_4$ cup butter or margarine

Preheat oven to 250 degrees. Place crackers, pretzels, and cereal in a large roasting pan. Process jalapeño peppers, mustard, garlic, oregano, and cumin in a small food processor until peppers and garlic are finely chopped. In a medium microwave-safe bowl, combine pepper mixture and butter. Cover and microwave on medium power (50%) until butter melts. Pour over cereal mixture; toss until well coated. Bake $1^1/_4$ hours, stirring every 15 minutes. Spread on aluminum foil to cool. For each gift, place $1^1/_2$ cups in a small cellophane bag; fold and staple top to secure.

Yield: about 22 cups snack mix

HOT PEPPER SLEEVES

For each sleeve, you will need white, yellow, red, and green card stock; decorative-edge craft scissors; tracing paper; $4^1/_2$" x 14" piece of kraft paper; glue stick; black permanent fine-point marker; hole punch; and several 18" lengths of red and natural raffia.

1. Cut a $4^1/_4$" x 5" piece from yellow card stock; cut two $^1/_2$" x $4^1/_4$" strips from green card stock. Using craft scissors, cut two $^1/_2$" x 4" strips from white card stock.
2. Trace patterns, page 113, onto tracing paper; cut out. Using patterns, cut one highlight from white card stock, one stem from green card stock, and one pepper and two pointed strips from red card stock.
3. Arrange and glue shapes and strips on yellow card stock. Glue yellow card stock to kraft paper $^1/_2$" from on short edge.
4. Use marker to write "Hot" and draw swirls and dots on yellow card stock.
5. To form sleeve, fold each end of kraft paper $5^1/_2$" to wrong side. Punch two holes 1" apart at center top of sleeve. Thread raffia through holes and tie into a bow. Place gift in sleeve.

EASY SASSY SALSA!

Ring in the festivities of Cinco de Mayo with our Easy Sassy Salsa! Tortilla chips are the perfect partner for the flavorful dip, and a cute felt sombrero tops the jar for a celebratory finish.

EASY SASSY SALSA

- 1 can (14¹/₂ ounces) Mexican-style stewed tomatoes, undrained
- 1 can (10 ounces) diced tomatoes and green chiles, undrained
- 1 can (4¹/₂ ounces) chopped green chiles, undrained
- /₂ cup chopped fresh cilantro
- 2 tablespoons dried minced onion
- 2 teaspoons ground cumin
- /₂ teaspoons garlic salt
- 1 teaspoon garlic powder
  Tortilla chips to serve

Combine first 3 ingredients in food processor or blender. Add cilantro, onion, cumin, garlic salt, and garlic powder. Pulse process until well blended. Transfer into airtight container and chill hours to let flavors blend. rve with tortilla chips.

eld: about 3¹/₂ cups salsa

OMBREO JAR TOPPER

ou will need a 6" dia. felt witch's hat th a 2³/₄" dia. opening, embroidery ss, ironing board, steam iron, hot glue n, ³/₈"w decorative cord, nine 10mm m-poms, and a jar with a 2³/₄" dia. lid.

Turn hat wrong side out. Tie a length of floss tightly around hat " from tip; tie ends together to secure. rn hat right side out.

2. To curl hat brim, place center of hat brim against edge of pointed end of ironing board; press using steam iron set at medium-high heat. Rotate and press until entire brim is curled.

3. Trimming to fit, glue cord around hat for hatband and outer edge of hat brim.
4. Sew pom-poms to cord at 2" intervals around outer edge of hat brim.
5. Place hat on jar.

Share the summery goodness of peaches any time of the year with luscious Peach Freezer Jam. So much easier to make than traditional jams, this sweet condiment is made with frozen sliced peaches and prepared with the help of a microwave! It keeps for up to a year in the freezer, so you can have it on hand when you need a quick treat. To deliver our surprise, pack the jam jars dressed up with peach-stenciled lids and homespun fabric bows. The lucky recipient of this gourmet gift will think you're a real peach.

EACH FREEZER JAM

making Peachy Jar Lids, store jam in de-mouth canning jars.

1 package (16 ounces) frozen
     peach slices, thawed
1 package (3 ounces)
     peach-flavored gelatin
2 tablespoons lemon juice
/2 teaspoon ascorbic powder
     (used to preserve fruit color)
/2 cups sugar
³/4 cup water
1 package (1³/4 ounces) pectin
     powder

In a food processor, combine peach ces, gelatin, lemon juice, and ascorbic wder; pulse process until peaches are ely chopped. In a large bowl, combine gar and fruit mixture; let stand minutes. In a 1-quart microwave- fe bowl or measuring cup, combine ater and pectin; microwave on high wer (100%) 2 to 2¹/2 minutes or until ixture boils. Microwave another seconds; stir. Microwave 15 seconds nger; stir. Pour hot pectin mixture to fruit mixture; stir 3 minutes. ur into clean jars to within ¹/2 inch tops; wipe off rims of jars. Screw lids. Allow jam to stand at room mperature 24 hours; store in freezer. ace in refrigerator 1 hour before

serving. May be refrozen. Keeps up to 3 weeks in refrigerator or up to 1 year in freezer.

Yield: about 6¹/2 cups jam

PEACHY JAR LIDS

For each canning jar lid insert, you will need cream-colored paper; acetate for stencils (available at craft or art supply stores); craft knife; cutting mat or thick layer of newspapers; peach, coral, dark coral, green, and dark green acrylic paint; small stencil brushes; paper towels; brown permanent felt-tip pen with fine point; and removable tape (optional).

1. Referring to stencil cutting key and color key, follow *Stenciling,* page 110, to stencil peach on cream-colored paper.
2. Use brown pen to draw stem on peach.
3. Center ring of jar lid over stenciled peach and use a pencil to draw around outside of ring; cut out peach just inside drawn line.
4. Place stenciled cutout on flat part of lid and replace ring over jar.

STENCIL CUTTING KEY
■ Stencil #1
■ Stencil #2

COLOR KEY
Stencil #1 (peach half) - peach shaded
     with dark coral
Stencil #1 (leaf half) - dark green
Stencil #2 (peach half) - coral shaded
     with dark coral
Stencil #2 (leaf half) - green

DOUBLE CHOCOLATE TRUFFLES

These sophisticated Double Chocolate Truffles will delight even the pickiest chocolate lover! Displayed in beribboned gift boxes, the rich candies are sure to cause a stir when given as birthday party favors.

DOUBLE CHOCOLATE TRUFFLES

      3 cups semisweet chocolate chips
      1 can (14 ounces) condensed milk
$3^1/_2$ cups chopped pecans, toasted, coarsely ground, and divided
      3 tablespoons chocolate-flavored liqueur
      1 teaspoon vanilla extract

In a medium saucepan, combine chocolate chips and sweetened condensed milk. Stirring constantly, cook over low heat until chocolate chips melt and mixture is smooth. Stir in 1 cup ground pecans, liqueur, and vanilla until well blended. Remove from heat and transfer to a medium bowl. Cover and chill 2 hours or until firm.

Shape mixture into 1-inch balls; roll in remaining ground pecans. Store in an airtight container in refrigerator.

Yield: about 6 dozen truffles

FLOWERED GIFT BOXES

For each box, you will need a $1^1/_2$" x $1^3/_8$" x 10" gift box with clear plastic lid, 1 yd. of $1^3/_8$"w sheer ribbon, hot glue gun, and a silk flower pick.

Place gift in box. Tie ribbon into a bow around box. Position streamers as desired; spot glue to secure. Glue pick to knot of bow.

PRETTY PRETZEL TREATS

Make any occasion extra special with a gift of elegant Raspberry-chocolate Pretzel Treats. Deliciously easy to create, the pretzels are simply dipped in a chocolaty candy coating and drizzled with tinted raspberry-flavored icing. For an eye-catching delivery, package your offering in a pretty jar tied with a colorful ribbon. A handmade tag adds a delightful finishing touch.

RASPBERRY-CHOCOLATE PRETZEL TREATS

14 ounces chocolate-flavored candy coating
1 package (10 ounces) 2¹/₂-inch-wide pretzel knots
1 cup sifted confectioners sugar
2 tablespoons milk
4 drops raspberry-flavored oil
Burgundy paste food coloring

In a heavy medium saucepan, melt candy coating over low heat, stirring frequently. Using a large fork or dipping fork, dip pretzels into chocolate. Transfer to a baking sheet covered with waxed paper. Place in refrigerator to allow coating to harden.

For icing, mix confectioners sugar, milk, and raspberry-flavored oil in a small bowl until smooth. If necessary, icing may be thinned by adding additional milk 1 teaspoon at a time. Divide icing evenly into 2 small bowls. Tint 1 bowl light pink and one bowl dark pink. Place pretzels on a wire rack with waxed paper underneath. Drizzle both colors of icing over pretzels. Allow icing to harden. Store in an airtight container.

Yield: about 25 pretzels

PRETZEL TREATS TAG

Follow manufacturer's instructions to fuse paper-backed fusible web to wrong sides of pink and green fabrics. Cut 3 approx. ¹/₂" dia. circles and 2 approx. 1" long leaf shapes from fabrics. Remove paper backing. Fuse leaves and berries to a 3" x 3³/₄" piece of heavy paper. Use brown felt-tip pen to draw stems on paper. Use pink felt-tip pen to write "raspberry-chocolate pretzel treats" on tag. Punch a hole in tag; thread tag onto ribbon.

FRIENDSHIP GIFTS

Your friends are always there for you. Now you can do the same for them with delicious snacks, soups, casseroles, and baked goods. Whatever the occasion, nourish your friendship with excellent food.

APRICOT-NUT CAKES

The tangy flavor of these moist cakes gets a boost from a "secret" ingredient—baby food! Apricot-Nut Cakes make great neighborhood gifts when they're packaged in market baskets accented with fruit and lined with vibrant fabric.

APRICOT-NUT CAKES

1 package (18¹/₄ ounces) yellow cake mix
4 eggs
³/₄ cup apricot nectar
³/₄ cup vegetable oil
1 jar (4 ounces) apricot baby food
1 cup finely chopped pecans, toasted
1 cup confectioners sugar
¹/₄ cup apricot brandy
4 teaspoons freshly squeezed lemon juice

Preheat oven to 325 degrees. Grease three 3¹/₂ x 7¹/₂-inch loaf pans, line bottoms with waxed paper; grease waxed paper. In a large bowl, combine cake mix, eggs, apricot nectar, oil, and baby food; beat until well blended. Stir in pecans. Pour batter into prepared pans. Bake 40 to 45 minutes or until a toothpick inserted in center of cake comes out clean. Cool in pans 10 minutes on a wire rack. Remove from pans and place on a wire rack with waxed paper underneath.

In a small bowl, combine confectioners sugar, brandy, and lemon juice; stir until smooth. Spoon glaze over warm cakes. Allow cakes to cool completely. Store in an airtight container in refrigerator.

Yield: 3 small cakes

MARKET BASKETS

For each basket, you will need a 6¹/₂" x 8¹/₄" market basket with a ⁷/₈"w handle, ⁷/₈"w and ¹/₄"w grosgrain ribbons, hot glue gun, artificial greenery (we used a stem of leaves with berries), and fabric to line basket.

For gift tag, you will *also* need craft glue, 1¹/₂" x 2³/₈" piece of fabric, 1¹/₂" x 2³/₈" and 1¹/₄" x 2" pieces of light-colored card stock, and a black permanent fine-point marker.

Use hot glue for all gluing unless otherwise indicated.

1. Measure handle of basket; add ¹/₂". Cut one piece from each ribbon the determined measurement. Center and glue ⁷/₈"w ribbon, then ¹/₄"w ribbon along handle.
2. Glue stem of greenery at base of handle.
3. Measure around rim of basket; add ¹/₂". Cut one piece from each ribbon the determined measurement. Overlapping ends at back, glue ⁷/₈"w ribbon, then ¹/₄"w ribbon around rim of basket.
4. Arrange fabric in basket. Tie ¹/₄"w ribbon into a bow around wrapped cake. Place cake in basket.
5. For tag, use craft glue to glue fabric piece to 1¹/₂" x 2³/₈" piece of card stock. Use marker to write message on 1¹/₄" x 2" piece of card stock; center an glue to fabric side of tag.

PEANUT BUTTER DIP

Everybody loves peanut butter, and this creamy dip gives a favorite teacher a rich way to enjoy it! Easy to make with only three ingredients, this delectable snack is great with apple slices. Pack the A⁺ present in a gift basket decorated with clever craft stick "pencils."

PEANUT BUTTER DIP

  1 package (8 ounces) cream cheese, softened
  1 jar (7 ounces) marshmallow creme
$^1/_4$ cup smooth peanut butter
     Fresh fruit to serve

In a small bowl, combine cream cheese, marshmallow creme, and peanut butter. Beat at low speed with an electric mixer until smooth. Store in an airtight container in refrigerator. Serve at room temperature with fresh fruit.

Yield: about $1^3/_4$ cups dip

TEACHER'S BASKET

You will need utility scissors; two jumbo craft sticks; tracing paper; transfer paper; yellow, tan, and metallic silver acrylic paint; paintbrushes; black permanent fine-point marker; hot glue gun; a basket (we used a 9" x $11^3/_4$" x $4^3/_4$"d wire basket); and fabric to line basket.

For jar lid cover, you will *also* need craft glue, jar with a $3^1/_4$" dia. lid, and one $4^3/_8$" dia. circle each of school-motif fabric and poster board.

1. Use utility scissors to cut one end of each craft stick to a point. Trace pencil pattern, page 112, onto tracing paper. Use transfer paper to transfer design to each craft stick. Follow *Painting*

Techniques, page 111, to paint pencils.
3. Use marker to add details to pencils and write message on one pencil. Arrange and glue pencils to basket. Arrange fabric in basket.

4. For jar lid cover, use craft glue to glue fabric circle to poster board circle; allow to dry. Hot glue cover to top of lid.

STRAWBERRY-MINT JAM

If you're "berry" pleased to meet your new neighbors, why not extend a hearty hello with a cheery breakfast basket! Loaded with a jar of luscious Strawberry-Mint Jam, freshly baked biscuits, simple fabric napkins, and easy-to-make napkin rings, this welcome-to-the-neighborhood surprise offers an eye-opening start to a day of unpacking.

STRAWBERRY-MINT JAM

- 2 quarts fresh strawberries, coarsely chopped (about $6^{1}/_{2}$ cups)
- $^{1}/_{4}$ cup coarsely chopped fresh mint leaves
- 1 tablespoon freshly squeezed lemon juice
- 1 package ($1^{3}/_{4}$ ounces) powdered fruit pectin
- 7 cups sugar

In a heavy Dutch oven, combine strawberries, mint leaves, lemon juice, and pectin over medium-high heat. Bring to a rolling boil. Add sugar. Stirring constantly, bring to a rolling boil again and boil 1 minute. Remove from heat; skim off foam. Spoon jam into heat-resistant jars; cover and cool to room temperature. Store in refrigerator.

Yield: about 7 cups jam

BREAKFAST BASKET

You will need a market basket (we used a $6^{1}/_{2}$" x $14^{1}/_{4}$" basket), fabric for trim, two $22^{1}/_{2}$" x 33" kitchen towels, four $2^{3}/_{8}$" long silk strawberries, $1^{1}/_{4}$ yds of silk ivy garland, $1^{1}/_{3}$ yds of $^{3}/_{8}$"w ribbon, wire cutters, wood excelsior, and glue.
For jar lid, you will *also* need one 4" square each of fabric and batting.
For gift tag, you will *also* need red and yellow paper, black permanent felt-tip pen, decorative-edge craft scissors, and ivy leaves.

1. Measure around rim of basket; add 1". Measure width of rim. Tear a fabric strip the determined measurements. Glue fabric strip around rim. Place excelsior in basket.
2. For 4 napkins, cut each towel in half widthwise. Fold raw edge of each towel half $^{1}/_{4}$" to wrong side. Fold $^{1}/_{4}$" to wrong side again and topstitch in place.
3. For 4 napkin rings, use wire cutters to cut ivy garland into four equal lengths; form each length into a circle. Twist ends together to secure.
4. Cut ribbon into four equal lengths. Tie each ribbon length into a bow around twisted ends of circle.
5. Glue one strawberry to each bow.
6. For jar lid, use fabric and batting squares and follow *Jar Lid Finishing,* page 110, to cover lid.
7. For gift tag, cut a 2" x $3^{3}/_{8}$" piece of yellow paper. Glue yellow paper piece red paper. Leaving a $^{1}/_{4}$" red border, u. craft scissors to cut out gift tag. Use p to write message on tag. Glue ivy leave to tag.
8. Place gifts in basket.

HOT REUBEN CASSEROLE

Combining all the ingredients of the popular deli sandwich, our Hot Reuben Casserole is a hearty, satisfying dish that's perfect for greeting new neighbors. Tender corned beef, Thousand Island dressing, and Swiss cheese are layered on a bed of tangy sauerkraut and covered with crispy rye bread crumbs to make this filling entrée. Presented in our quick-and-easy casserole cozy, it's a delicious way to say, "Welcome, friends!"

HOT REUBEN CASSEROLE

    2 cans (10 ounces each) chopped
         sauerkraut, drained
    1 pound thinly sliced corned beef,
         coarsely chopped
  ³/4 cup Thousand Island dressing
    8 ounces thinly sliced Swiss cheese
 5¹/2 cups (about 8 ounces) coarsely
         crumbled rye bread
  ¹/4 cup butter, melted

In a greased 8 x 11¹/2-inch baking dish, layer first 5 ingredients and drizzle with butter. Cover and store in refrigerator. Give with serving instructions.

Yield: about 6 to 8 servings

To serve: Bake uncovered in a preheated 375-degree oven 30 to 40 minutes or until casserole is heated through and bread crumbs are lightly browned.

CASSEROLE COZY

For cozy to hold an 8" x 11¹/2" dish, you will need two 13" x 17¹/4" quilted fabric place mats, thread to match place mats, three ⁷/8" dia. buttons, and three 3¹/2" lengths of ¹/8"w elastic.

1. Position place mats wrong sides together. Leaving 1 short edge open, machine stitch place mats together along inner edge of binding.
2. For closure, evenly space buttons ¹/2" from open edge of top place mat; stitch in place. For each button loop, fold 1 length of elastic in half; sew ends of loop to inside edge of bottom place mat even with button (Fig. 1).

Fig. 1

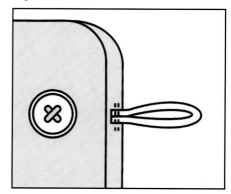

COCK-A-NOODLE SOUP

This basket of goodies will perk up a friend who's feeling a little under the weather. For an old time "cure-all" that's filled with nutritious vegetables, tasty chicken, and egg noodles, we prescribed our Cock-A-Noodle Soup. Then we tucked in crackers, lemon drops, a mug with tea bags, and a packet of tissues to round out the surprise. Left at the door as a get well wish, this offering is sure to lift spirits!

COCK-A-NOODLE SOUP

STOCK

- 1 (3^1/$_2$ to 4-pound) chicken
- 6 sprigs fresh parsley, stems included
- 2 onions, quartered
- 2 celery stalks, leaves included
- 2 bay leaves
- 1 turnip, quartered
- 1 teaspoon salt
- 1 teaspoon black peppercorns, crushed
- ^{1}/$_2$ teaspoon dried thyme

SOUP

- 3 quarts stock
- ^{2}/$_3$ cup finely chopped celery
- ^{1}/$_2$ cup finely chopped carrots
- ^{1}/$_2$ cup finely chopped onion
- 2 teaspoons salt
- ^{1}/$_2$ teaspoon ground black pepper
- 2 cups uncooked thin egg noodles
- 3 to 4 cups shredded cooked chicken

For stock, place chicken in a Dutch oven with 5 quarts water. Add remaining stock ingredients and bring to a boil. Reduce heat to medium and simmer 30 minutes, skimming foam from the top. Partially cover pan; simmer 30 minutes longer or until juices run clear when chicken is pierced with a fork. Remove chicken and set aside to cool. Add 1 quart water to Dutch oven, partially cover, and simmer 1 hour longer. When chicken has cooled, remove skin and shred meat. Cover and refrigerate until ready to use.

Strain stock through a cheesecloth-lined sieve into a large bowl; discard solids. Cover and refrigerate stock at least 8 hours. After refrigerating, skim fat from surface of stock.

For soup, combine 3 quarts stock in large Dutch oven with next 5 ingredients. Bring soup to a boil; cover and reduce heat to low. Cook 30 minutes or until vegetables are tender.

Prepare noodles following package instructions. Add noodles and shredded chicken to soup and simmer 5 minutes.

Yield: about 4 quarts of soup

CHICKEN CORN CHOWDER

This thoughtful gift will bring warmth and comfort to Mommy and her wee one as they arrive home for the first time! Creamy Chicken Corn Chowder is a nutritiously filling meal for the new mother. Wrap a jar of the soup in a receiving blanket and top it off with a cute toy for baby to enjoy, too.

CREAMY CHICKEN CORN CHOWDER

    3 pounds bone-in split chicken
        breasts
    5 cups water
    1 cup chopped onion
    1 cup chopped celery
    2 teaspoons salt
$^1/_2$ teaspoon ground black pepper
    4 cups peeled, diced potatoes
    1 cup thinly sliced carrots
    1 can ($14^3/_4$ ounces) cream-style
        corn
    1 can (11 ounces) whole kernel
        corn, drained
    1 jar (2 ounces) diced pimiento,
        drained
    1 cup half and half

In a large stockpot, combine chicken, water, onion, celery, salt, and pepper. Cook over high heat until mixture boils. Cover and reduce heat to medium low; simmer about 1 hour or until chicken is tender. Remove chicken. Add potatoes and carrots to broth. Bring to a boil over high heat. Cover and reduce heat to medium low. Simmer 10 minutes or until vegetables are tender. While vegetables are cooking, skin and bone chicken; cut into bite-size pieces. Stir chicken, corn, pimiento, and half and half into vegetable mixture. Cook 5 minutes or until heated through. Serve warm. Store in an airtight container in refrigerator.
Yield: about 14 cups chowder

NEW BABY GIFT
You will need a 5" dia. x $10^3/_4$"h jar with lid, receiving blanket, rubber band, $2^1/_2$ yds. of sheer wire-edged ribbon, craft wire, wire cutters, safety pin, and a stuffed toy.
For tag, you will *also* need decorative-edge scissors, card stock, black permanent fine-point marker, and a diaper pin.

1. Place gift in jar. Gather blanket around jar; secure with rubber band. Cut a 28" length from ribbon; knot around rubber band. Notch ribbon ends.
2. Using remaining ribbon, follow *Making a Bow*, page 111, to make a bow with six 8" loops and two 2" streamers. Use wire ends to attach bow around gathers. Pin toy to center of bow.
3. For tag, use craft scissors to cut a $2^1/_4$" square from card stock. Use marker to write message on tag. Use diaper pin to pin tag to blanket.

CRUNCHY CHOCOLATE CANDIES

Only have a few minutes? Great! Because that's all you'll need to stir up a batch of Crunchy Chocolate Candies. This extra-easy two-ingredient confection is made with crispy rice cereal and chocolate-flavored candy coating. Placed in tiny foil cups, the candies make tasteful last-minute gifts for any occasion! To make your offering more special, package the sweets in purchased candy boxes tied with coordinating ribbons.

CRUNCHY CHOCOLATE CANDIES

14 ounces chocolate-flavored candy coating
2¹/₂ cups crispy rice cereal

In a heavy medium saucepan, melt candy coating over low heat. Stir in cereal. Drop by tablespoonfuls into foil candy cups. Place candies in refrigerator to harden. Store in an airtight container in refrigerator.

Yield: about 3¹/₂ dozen candies

BUTTERSCOTCH COFFEE CAKE

Easily created with a package of frozen rolls, this Butterscotch Coffee Cake is a delicious way to extend warm wishes. The sweet cinnamon-spiced topping, enhanced with pecans and butterscotch pudding mix, is sure to please! Take the cake over to a neighbor's house straight from the oven for a treat that's melt-in-your-mouth wonderful.

BUTTERSCOTCH COFFEE CAKE

- 1   cup chopped pecans
- 1   package (25 ounces) frozen white dinner rolls
- $^1/_2$ cup sugar
- 1   package (3.5 ounces) butterscotch pudding and pie filling mix
- 1   tablespoon ground cinnamon
- $^1/_2$ cup butter or margarine, melted

Sprinkle pecans in the bottom of a greased 12-cup fluted tube pan. Place rolls over pecans. In a small bowl, combine sugar, pudding mix, and cinnamon. Sprinkle sugar mixture over rolls. Pour butter over sugar mixture. Cover with plastic wrap and let rise in a warm place (80 to 85 degrees) $5^1/_2$ to $6^1/_2$ hours or until doubled in size. To serve in early morning, coffee cake can rise overnight (about 8 hours).

Preheat oven to 350 degrees. Bake 25 to 30 minutes or until golden brown. Remove from oven and immediately invert onto plate. Serve warm.

Yield: about 16 servings

SNAPPY ANNIVERSARY BASKET

Here's a red-hot gift for a couple whose romance still sizzles years after the honeymoon! Snappy Strawberry-Jalapeño Sauce is wonderfully spicy and sweet —sort of like the deserving couple. For their immediate enjoyment, the sauce is placed in a charming anniversary basket along with crackers and a tangy Cheddar-cream cheese blend.

SNAPPY STRAWBERRY-JALAPEÑO SAUCE

- 2 jars (18 ounces each) strawberry preserves
- 1 jar (12 ounces) pickled jalapeño pepper slices, drained

Pulse process preserves and jalapeño slices in a food processor until peppers are finely chopped. Pour into 4 half-pint jars; cover and store in refrigerator. Give with serving instructions.

Yield: about 4 cups sauce

To serve: In a medium bowl, combine 8 ounces softened cream cheese and 8 ounces finely shredded sharp Cheddar cheese; beat until well blended. Spread into a serving dish. Spoon 1 cup sauce over cheese. Serve with crackers.

ANNIVERSARY BASKET

You will need a basket with handle (we used a 7¹/₂" x 13¹/₂" basket), fabric for basket liner, 1¹/₄"w ribbon, jute twine, and an artificial strawberry stem with blossoms and leaves.

For gift tag, you will *also* need white paper, red paper, blue permanent felt-tip pen, hole punch, and glue.

1. Follow *Making a Basket Liner,* page 110, to make liner; place liner in basket.
2. Follow *Making a Bow,* page 111, to make one bow each from ribbon and twine.

3. Tie a length of twine around strawberry stem; tie ends of twine around center of bows. Tie stem and bows to basket handle.
4. For gift tag, cut a 1¹/₂" x 3¹/₂" piece from white paper. Use pen to write message on paper piece. Glue paper piece to red paper. Leaving a ³/₈" red border, cut out gift tag,
5. Punch hole in corner of tag. Cut a 6" length of twine. Thread twine through hole and tie tag to basket handle.

"TURNOVER" A NEW DAY

Help a hurried friend start the day with a quick, hearty breakfast—deliver a basketful of frozen Sausage Breakfast Turnovers! The savory bites are ready to pop straight from the freezer into the oven. Wrap them in a colorful kitchen towel and deliver with baking instructions.

SAUSAGE BREAKFAST TURNOVERS

1 package (16 ounces) bulk pork sausage

1/3 cup chopped onion

1/3 cup chopped green pepper

3 cans (12 ounces, 10 count each) refrigerated biscuits

1 cup (4 ounces) finely shredded Cheddar cheese

1 egg white, beaten

In a large skillet, cook sausage over medium heat until lightly browned. Add onion and pepper; cook until vegetables are tender. Transfer sausage mixture to a colander to drain; cool.

On a lightly floured surface, use a floured rolling pin to roll each biscuit into a 4-inch circle. In a medium bowl, combine sausage mixture and cheese. Spoon 1 tablespoon sausage mixture on half of each biscuit, leaving edges free. Brush egg white on edges. Fold biscuits in half; press edges with a fork. Prick tops of turnovers with fork. Transfer turnovers to a baking sheet. Place in freezer 1 hour or until firm. Transfer to resealable plastic freezer bag; store in freezer. Give with baking instructions.

Yield: 30 turnovers

To bake: Place frozen turnovers on an ungreased baking sheet. Let stand at room temperature 30 minutes. Bake in a 350-degree oven 13 to 16 minutes or until heated through and golden brown. Serve warm.

RISE AND SHINE BASKET

You will need tracing paper, decorative-edge craft scissors, white and yellow card stock, transfer paper, black permanent fine-point marker, pink and blue highlighters, craft glue, 1/8" dia. hole punch, basket (we used an 8" x 11" oval basket), dish towel, rubber band, 1"w and assorted ribbons to coordinate with towel, and 12" of 1/16"w satin ribbon.

1. Trace sun and cloud patterns, page 112, onto tracing paper; cut out.

Using patterns, cut cloud from white card stock and use decorative-edge craft scissors to cut sun from yellow card stock. Use transfer paper to transfer detail lines to shapes.

2. Use black marker to draw over all transferred lines and to write ". . . have a sunshine day!!" on cloud. Use blue highlighter to draw over lines on cloud and pink highlighter to draw over lines on sun. Glue cloud to sun. Punch hole in tag.

3. Line basket with towel; place gift in basket. Gather towel around gift; secure with rubber band. Tie 1"w ribbon into a bow around gathers to cover rubber band. Use 1/16"w ribbon to tie tag to bow. Knot remaining ribbons around knot of bow.

HAPPY BIRTHDAY COOKIE!

r a delightfully different
thday confection, why not make
giant cookie and deliver it in a
llipop" package! A fun way to
lebrate for young and old alike,
packed with goodies like candy-
ated chocolate baking candies
d crispy rice cereal. To keep the
okie fresh, wrap it with cellophane
d tie off with colorful curling ribbon.

APPY BIRTHDAY COOKIE
OOKIE
- /3 cup butter or margarine,
  softened
- /3 cup granulated sugar
- /3 cup firmly packed brown sugar
- 1 egg
- /4 cup vegetable oil
- 1 teaspoon vanilla extract
- 1 cup plus 3 tablespoons
  all-purpose flour
- /2 teaspoon baking soda
- /4 teaspoon salt
- /3 cup candy-coated chocolate mini
  baking candies, divided
- /3 cup quick-cooking oats
- /3 cup crispy rice cereal

ICING
- $^1/_2$ cup confectioners sugar
- 2 teaspoons cocoa
- 3 to 4 teaspoons milk
- $^1/_2$ teaspoon vanilla extract

Preheat oven to 325 degrees. For
cookie, cream butter and sugars in a
medium bowl until fluffy. Add egg,
oil, and vanilla; beat until smooth. In
a small bowl, combine flour, baking
soda, and salt. Add dry ingredients to
creamed mixture; stir until a soft dough
forms. Stir in $^1/_3$ cup candies, oats,
and cereal. Press dough into a greased
12-inch-diameter pizza pan. Sprinkle
remaining $^1/_3$ cup candies on top of
dough. Bake 23 to 25 minutes or until
top is lightly browned. Transfer pan to
a wire rack to cool completely.

For icing, combine confectioners
sugar, cocoa, milk, and vanilla in a small
bowl; stir until smooth. Transfer cooled
cookie to a 12-inch-diameter cardboard
cake board. Drizzle icing over cookie;
let icing harden. Store in an airtight
container.

Yield: about 12 servings

"HAPPY BIRTHDAY"
LOLLIPOP AND TAG
You will need a hot glue gun, 20" of
$^3/_8$" dia. dowel rod, cellophane, chenille
stem, clear tape, and assorted curling
ribbons.
For gift tag, you will *also* need tracing
paper; card stock; red, green, and black
permanent medium-point markers; and
a hole punch.

1. For lollipop, glue dowel to back of
cake board. Wrap cellophane around
cookie and gather around dowel; secure
with chenille stem. Use tape to secure
sides of cellophane at back of lollipop.
2. Tie several lengths of ribbon into a
bow around gathers; curl ribbon ends.
3. Follow *Making Patterns,* page 110, to
make tag pattern. Use pattern to cut tag
from card stock.
4. Use red marker to draw "stitches"
along edges of tag. Use black marker to
write message on tag and green marker
to draw musical notes on tag.
5. Punch hole in tag; thread one
streamer through hole and knot
to secure.

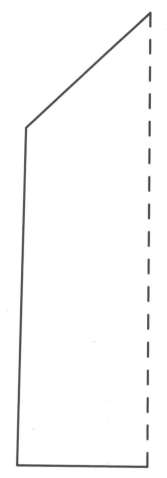

HOLIDAY GIFTS

You'll put a smile on the face of everyone you know with these simple-to-sumptuous holiday presents. The collection of over 20 desserts, snacks, and candies also includes a fruity New Year's beverage and a savory stew for Saint Patrick's Day. Celebrate all through the year by sharing flavorful gifts with friends and family.

RASPBERRY CHAMPAGNE

Welcome the new year in festive style with sparkling Raspberry Champagne Cocktails. To create a ready-made party for two, weave colorful ribbon through a simple wooden crate, then pack it with a bottle of homemade raspberry syrup, a bottle of bubbly, and a pair of champagne glasses. Add a fun gift tag to announce your wishes for a "Happy New Year!"

RASPBERRY CHAMPAGNE COCKTAILS

- 2 cups frozen whole red raspberries
- $^1/_2$ cup sugar
- $^1/_2$ cup Chambord or other raspberry liqueur
- $^1/_3$ cup cognac
- $^1/_2$ teaspoon grated lemon zest
- 1 bottle (750 ml) champagne

In a medium bowl, combine raspberries and sugar. Cover and let stand at room temperature 45 minutes, stirring and mashing mixture occasionally.

In a 1-quart glass container, combine raspberry mixture, liqueur, cognac, and lemon zest; cover and let stand at room temperature 3 days.

Strain mixture; discard seeds and zest. Store raspberry syrup in an airtight container in refrigerator. Give with champagne and serving instructions.

Yield: about $1^1/_2$ cups syrup

To serve: Place $2^1/_2$ tablespoons raspberry syrup in a 6-ounce champagne glass; fill with chilled champagne. Serve immediately.

"HAPPY NEW YEAR!" GIFT TAG

You will need a photocopy of tag design (page 113); lavender paper; pink, green, yellow, and lavender markers; lavender permanent felt-tip pen; decorative-edge craft scissors; and glue.

1. Use markers to color tag design. Use pen to write message on tag. Cut out tag.
2. Glue tag to lavender paper. Leaving $^1/_4$" lavender border, use craft scissors to cut out gift tag.

ALMOND TORTONI

Help a friend start the new year off right! Our Almond Tortoni is an Italian-style frozen dessert created with lightly sweetened whipped cream mixed with almonds and almond liqueur. The luscious confection is garnished with nuts and cherries and presented in a ribbon-tied take-out box. Colorful confetti glued around the edges of the gift tag adds a sparkly touch.

ALMOND TORTONI

2 cups whipping cream
1/4 cup sifted confectioners sugar
1/4 cup amaretto
1/2 cup finely ground almonds, toasted
Toasted sliced almonds and maraschino cherries with stems to garnish

Place a medium bowl and beaters from an electric mixer in freezer until well chilled. In chilled bowl, whip cream until soft peaks form. Gradually add confectioners sugar and amaretto; beat until stiff peaks form. Fold in ground almonds. Spoon mixture into 12 paper-lined muffin cups. Garnish with almond slices and cherries. Freeze until firm; cover. Remove from freezer about 15 minutes before serving.

Yield: 12 servings

Borrowing an old European tradition, Victorian Heart Cookies capture the spirit of the true romantic. The shortbread hearts are cut out in several sizes and feature fancy paper cutouts that are held in place by the pink icing. A heart-shaped box with elegant embellishments is perfect for delivering these little tokens of affection on Valentine's Day.

VICTORIAN HEART COOKIES

COOKIES

  2 cups all-purpose flour
  1 cup pecans
$^1/_8$ teaspoon salt
  1 cup butter or margarine, softened
$^1/_2$ cup firmly packed brown sugar

ICING

  3 cups sifted confectioners sugar
$^1/_4$ cup milk
     Pink paste food coloring
     Paper cutouts to decorate

Process flour, pecans, and salt in a blender or food processor until mixture is a fine powder. In a large bowl, cream butter and sugar until fluffy. Stir dry ingredients into creamed mixture. Cover and chill 1 hour.

Preheat oven to 350 degrees. On a lightly floured surface, use a floured rolling pin to roll out dough to $^1/_8$-inch thickness. Use various sizes of heart-shaped cookie cutters to cut out cookies. Transfer to a greased baking sheet. Bake 12 to 15 minutes or until edges are light brown. Transfer to a wire rack with waxed paper underneath to cool completely.

For icing, stir sugar and milk together in a medium bowl until smooth. Tint icing pink. Ice cookies. Before icing hardens, gently press paper cutouts on tops of cookies. Allow icing to harden. Store in an airtight container. Remove paper cutouts before eating.

Yield: about $3^1/_2$ dozen $2^1/_2$-inch cookies

VALENTINE GIFT BOX

You will need an approx. 8"w heart-shaped box, wrapping paper for side of box, fabric for box lid, $1^1/_2$"w satin ribbon for bow, $^1/_2$"w satin ribbon and decorative trim for side of box lid, silk rose with leaves, desired color spray paint, white paper, spray adhesive, craft glue, and red felt tip pen with fine point.

1. Spray paint inside of box and box lid; allow to dry.

2. To cover side of box, measure around box and add 1"; measure height of box. Cut wrapping paper the determined measurements. Use spray adhesive to apply wrapping paper to side of box.
3. To cut out fabric for lid, use a pencil to draw around lid on wrong side of fabric. Cut out fabric $^1/_2$" outside pencil line. At $^1/_2$" intervals, clip edges of fabric to within $^1/_8$" of pencil line.
4. (*Note*: Use craft glue for remaining steps; allow to dry after each glue step.) To cover lid, center lid on wrong side of fabric. Alternating sides and pulling fabric taut, glue clipped edges of fabric to side of lid.
5. To cover side of lid, measure around lid and add $^1/_2$". Cut $^1/_2$"w ribbon and decorative trim the determined measurement. Glue ribbon to side of lid. Glue decorative trim over ribbon.
6. For bow on lid, wrap $1^1/_2$"w ribbon around lid and tie into a bow at top of lid; trim ends. Glue bow in place. Turn lid over; cut ribbon apart at center on inside of lid. Press ribbon ends flat against inside of lid; glue in place.
7. Tuck rose under ribbon; glue in place.
8. For tag, trace heart pattern onto white paper and cut out. Use pen to write "Happy Valentine's Day" on tag. Glue tag to bow.

RASPBERRY CHOCOLATES

uxurious chocolates are traditional offerings for Valentine's Day, and these Raspberry Chocolates are especially nice. The marbleized candies look (and taste!) like they came from a gourmet shop—but they're easy to make in your kitchen. For an elegant gift, present the chocolates in a doily-lined basket. To coordinate with the candies, marbleize paper to create a pretty valentine.

RASPBERRY CHOCOLATES

6 ounces semisweet baking chocolate, chopped
6 ounces white baking chocolate, chopped
$1/2$ cup raspberry jelly

In separate small saucepans, melt chocolates over low heat, stirring constantly. Pour semisweet chocolate into a warm pie plate. Drizzle white chocolate over semisweet chocolate. Use the end of a wooden spoon to swirl together. Do not over mix. In batches, fill a bonbon mold half full with chocolate mixture. Using a small paintbrush, carefully brush chocolate mixture up sides of mold. Place mold in freezer 2 minutes or until chocolate hardens. Spoon about $1/2$ teaspoon raspberry jelly into each chocolate shell. Spoon a small amount of chocolate mixture over jelly, making sure edges are sealed. Return to freezer 2 minutes or until chocolate hardens. Invert and press on back of mold to release candies. Store in an airtight container in a cool, dry place.

Yield: about $2^1/2$ dozen $1^1/8$-inch bonbons

MARBLEIZED VALENTINES

For each valentine, you will need one 6" x 10" piece of heavy white paper, one 3"w heart-shaped paper doily, and one 13" length each of $1/4$"w and $1/2$"w satin ribbon.

You will also need 1 gallon liquid starch, one 12" x 18" disposable aluminum foil roasting pan, acrylic paints (we used lt pink, dk pink, burgundy, and metallic gold), plain white paper, paper towels, waxed paper, tracing paper, spray adhesive, hot glue gun, and glue sticks.

1. (*Note:* For marbleized paper, follow Steps 1 - 6.) Pour starch into pan to a depth of 1".
2. To apply paint to starch surface, hold bottle of paint near surface and gently squeeze out a small dot of paint (paint will float and begin to spread). Repeat to apply several dots of each color of paint. Remove dots that do not spread with a fingertip or the corner of a paper towel.
3. To form marble design, use a fork or the wooden end of a paintbrush to move paint around on surface of starch, forming desired patterns.
4. Gently place a piece of plain white paper on starch surface (paper will float); immediately pick up paper by 2 corners and lay paper, painted side up, on a layer of paper towels. Using dry paper towels, blot excess starch and paint from paper. Lay paper on waxed paper; allow to dry.
5. After marbleizing each sheet of paper, remove any excess paint from starch in pan by placing a layer of paper towels on starch surface. Lift towels from starch and discard.
6. Use a warm dry iron to press marbleized paper flat.

7. Use heart pattern and follow *Making Patterns*, page 110.
8. For each valentine, match short edges and fold heavy white paper in half. Place pattern on folded paper, matching dotted lines of pattern to fold; draw around pattern. Cutting through both layers, cut out paper along solid lines only.
9. Place pattern on marbleized paper; draw around pattern and cut out. Use spray adhesive to apply marbleized paper heart to front of valentine. Use spray adhesive to apply doily to front of valentine. Tie lengths of ribbon together into a bow; trim ends. Hot glue bow to doily.

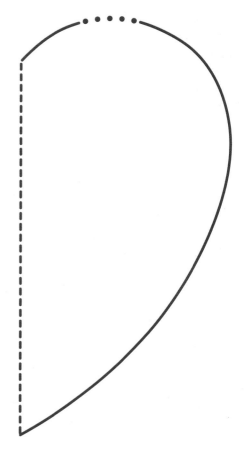

CHOCOLATE-MINT CAKE

This flavorful cake combines rich chocolate with refreshing crème de menthe liqueur. The creamy mint frosting and royal icing shamrocks are tinted green in honor of the day. It's a delicious way to share the luck o' the Irish!

CHOCOLATE-MINT CAKE

Shamrock decorations must be made a day in advance.

ROYAL ICING

- 2 egg whites
- 2/3 cups sifted confectioners sugar
  Green paste food coloring

CAKE

- 1/2 cup butter or margarine, softened
- 4 ounces cream cheese, softened
- 2 cups granulated sugar
- 2 eggs
- 2 teaspoons vanilla extract
- 2 cups all-purpose flour
- 3/4 cup cocoa
- 1/2 teaspoons baking soda
- 1/2 teaspoon salt
- 3/4 cup boiling water
- 1/4 cup crème de menthe

FROSTING

- 1/2 cups sifted confectioners sugar
- 1/4 cups butter or margarine, softened
- 3 tablespoons crème de menthe
- 1 tablespoon vanilla extract
  Green paste food coloring

To make shamrock decorations, trace patterns onto tracing paper, leaving at least 1 inch between patterns. Tape patterns onto a baking sheet. Cover with plastic wrap; secure edges with tape. For royal icing, beat egg whites and sugar in a medium bowl until well blended; tint green. Use a small knife to spread icing inside shamrock patterns. Allow icing to harden at room temperature 24 hours or until completely dry.

For cake, preheat oven to 350 degrees. In a large bowl, cream butter, cream cheese, and sugar until fluffy. Beat in eggs and vanilla. In a medium bowl, sift together flour, cocoa, baking soda, and salt. Add dry ingredients to creamed mixture; beat until smooth. Add water and crème de menthe; beat until smooth. Pour batter into 2 greased and floured 9-inch round cake pans. Bake 25 to 30 minutes or until a toothpick inserted in center of cake comes out clean. Cool in pans 10 minutes. Remove from pans and cool completely on a wire rack.

For frosting, beat sugar, butter, crème de menthe, and vanilla together in a large bowl until smooth. Tint frosting light green. Reserving 1/2 cup of frosting, frost between layers, sides, and top of cake.

To decorate cake, transfer reserved frosting to a pastry bag fitted with a large star tip. Pipe decorative border along top and bottom edges of cake. Invert shamrock decorations onto a flat surface and carefully peel away plastic wrap. Place shamrock decorations right side up on top of cake. Store in an airtight container in refrigerator.

Yield: 10 to 12 servings

served in edible Bread Bowls for a satisfying one-dish meal, hearty Irish Stew is filled with chunks of lamb, potatoes, carrots, and turnips. This traditional fare is the perfect gift for St. Patrick's Day! For an extra bit of Irish charm, deliver your gift in a rustic vine basket decorated with bells of Ireland and other green trimmings.

IRISH STEW

- 1/4 cup vegetable shortening
- 4 pounds boneless lamb, trimmed of fat and cut into 1-inch cubes
- 1 tablespoon salt
- 1 teaspoon ground black pepper
- 1/2 cup all-purpose flour
- 5 cups hot water
- 10 cups peeled and cubed potatoes (about 3 1/2 pounds)
- 2 cups peeled and cubed white turnips (about 13 ounces)
- 2 cups chopped onions (about 2 large onions)
- 2 cups sliced carrots (about 3 medium carrots)
- 4 teaspoons dried parsley
- 2 bay leaves

In a 10-quart stockpot, melt shortening over medium high heat. Sprinkle lamb with salt and pepper. Thoroughly coat lamb with flour. Add lamb to shortening and cook until brown. Add water and bring to a boil. Reduce heat to medium low, cover, and simmer 1 hour. Add remaining ingredients, cover, and simmer 30 minutes or until vegetables are tender. Remove bay leaves. Cover and refrigerate until ready to present. Give

with Bread Bowls (recipe follows) and serving instructions.

Yield: about 8 servings

BREAD BOWLS

- 1 box (16 ounces) hot roll mix
- 1 cup instant mashed potato flakes
- 2 tablespoons dried minced onion
- 1 1/3 cups hot water
- 2 tablespoons butter or margarine, melted
- 1 egg
  Vegetable oil cooking spray

In a large bowl, combine hot roll mix (including yeast), potato flakes, and onion. Add water, butter, and egg. Knead in bowl until a soft dough forms. Turn onto a lightly floured surface and knead about 5 minutes or until dough becomes smooth and elastic. Cover and let rest 5 minutes.

On a large baking sheet, invert six 10-ounce oven-proof custard cups. Heavily spray outside of cups with cooking spray. Divide dough into 6 equal balls. Shape each ball of dough over outside of a custard cup. Spray dough with cooking spray. Cover and let rise in a warm place (80 to 85 degrees) 30 minutes.

Preheat oven to 375 degrees. Bake 20 to 30 minutes or until golden brown. Cool 5 minutes. While still warm, remove bread from cups. Cool completely on a wire rack. Store in an airtight container until ready to present. Give with Irish Stew and serving instructions.

Yield: 6 bread bowls

To serve: Place stew in a large saucepan and cook over medium heat until heated through. If desired, wrap bread in

aluminum foil and reheat. Spoon stew into Bread Bowls. Serve immediately.

ST. PATRICK'S DAY BASKET

You will need a basket; artificial ivy, bells of Ireland, and white hydrangea; green craft ribbon; fabric square to line basket; white paper; green construction paper; spray adhesive; black felt-tip pen with fine point; 1/16"w white satin ribbon; florist wire; hot glue gun; and glue sticks.

1. Arrange ivy around handle and front of basket; hot glue to secure. Arrange bells of Ireland and hydrangea on side of basket; hot glue to secure.
2. Form multi-loop bow from craft ribbon; wrap bow with wire at center to secure. Hot glue bow and streamers to basket. Line basket with fabric square.
3. For tag, trace shamrock pattern onto white paper; cut out. Use spray adhesive to apply tag to green paper; trim green paper 1/8" from tag. Use black pen to write "Happy St. Patrick's Day" on tag. Make a hole in top of tag. Thread 1/16"w ribbon through tag; knot ribbon close to tag. Tie tag to bow.

ORANGE DROP COOKIES

This carrot bag full of yummy Orange Drop Cookies makes a rich reward for the Easter Bunny. The citrusy cookies, shaped like carrot "coins" and brightly iced, are a special treat that anyone would love to find on Easter morning.

ORANGE DROP COOKIES

COOKIES
$^1/_2$ cup butter, softened
$^3/_4$ cup sifted confectioners sugar
  1 egg
  1 teaspoon dried grated orange peel
  1 teaspoon orange extract
$1^3/_4$ cups all-purpose flour

ICING
$2^1/_2$ cups sifted confectioners sugar
  5 tablespoons milk
    Orange paste food coloring

For cookies, cream butter and sugar in a medium bowl until fluffy. Add egg, orange peel, and orange extract; beat until smooth. Gradually add flour; stir until a soft dough forms. Divide dough in half; shape each half into a 12-inch-long roll. Wrap in plastic wrap and refrigerate 1 hour.

Preheat oven to 325 degrees. Cut dough into $^1/_2$-inch-thick slices. Transfer to a greased baking sheet. Bake 12 to 15 minutes or until light brown on bottoms. Transfer to a wire rack with waxed paper underneath to cool completely.

For icing, stir together sugar and milk in a small bowl until smooth. Tint icing orange. Use a fork to dip cookies in icing; return to wire rack. Allow icing to harden. Store in an airtight container.

Yield: about 4 dozen cookies

CARROT BAG
Place two 20" squares of cellophane together and roll into a cone shape; use transparent tape to secure. Fill bag with cookies. Tie top of bag with green curling ribbon; curl ribbon ends. Trim top of bag.

EASTER EGG CAKES

Beautifully decorated with tinted icing, Easter Egg Cakes have a hidden surprise inside—a yummy "yolk" made of sweetened cream cheese! A basketful of the moist cakes will enchant a friend, or you can give the cakes individually for unique little Easter treats.

EASTER EGG CAKES

CAKES
- 1 box (18.25 ounces) white cake mix without pudding mix
- 1/4 cups water
- 1/3 cup vegetable oil
- 3 egg whites (reserve 1 egg yolk for filling)

FILLING
- 4 ounces cream cheese, softened
- 1/4 cup granulated sugar
- 1 egg yolk (reserved from cakes)
  Yellow paste food coloring

ICING
- 1/4 cups plus 2 tablespoons sifted confectioners sugar
- 1/2 cup water
- 2 tablespoons light corn syrup
- 1 teaspoon almond extract
  Pink paste food coloring

ROYAL ICING
- 4 cups sifted confectioners sugar
- 3 egg whites
  Pink, yellow, blue, and green paste food coloring

For cakes, preheat oven to 350 degrees. In a large bowl, combine cake mix, water, oil, and egg whites; beat until moistened using low speed of an electric mixer. Beat at medium speed 2 minutes.

For filling, beat cream cheese, sugar, and egg yolk in a medium bowl until smooth. Tint filling yellow. Spoon about 1 tablespoon cake batter into each tin of a greased and floured miniature egg pan containing six $3^1/_2$-inch-long tins. Spoon about 1 teaspoon filling in center of batter. Continue filling each tin with batter until three-fourths full. Bake 18 to 20 minutes or until cakes pull away from sides of pan and spring back when lightly pressed. Cool in pan 10 minutes. Invert onto a wire rack with waxed paper underneath to cool completely.

For icing, place sugar in a medium saucepan. In a small bowl, combine water and corn syrup. Add corn syrup mixture to sugar and stir until well blended. Attach candy thermometer to pan, making sure thermometer does not touch bottom of pan. Stirring constantly, cook over medium-low heat until icing reaches 100 degrees. Remove from heat; stir in almond extract. Tint icing light pink. Cool icing 5 minutes. Stirring icing occasionally, ice tops of cakes. Allow icing to harden.

For royal icing, beat sugar and egg whites in a medium bowl 7 to 10 minutes or until stiff. Divide icing evenly into 4 bowls. Tint icing pink, yellow, blue, and green. Transfer icing to separate pastry bags and use desired tips to decorate cakes. Allow icing to harden. Store in an airtight container.

Yield: about 2 dozen cakes

s easy to delight a special
omebunny" with this Easter treat!
rst you make the cutout sugar
ookies using refrigerated dough;
en fill fun-to-use squeeze bottles
th pastel icing so your friend can
ecorate the cookies. For delivery,
ck undecorated cookies in our
ever Easter Bunny bag and tuck
in a roomy basket along with the
ottles of icing.

PRINGTIME COOKIES

1   package (20 ounces) refrigerated
      sugar cookie dough
3   cups sifted confectioners sugar
/3 cup milk
/2 teaspoon almond extract
      Yellow, blue, pink, green, and
      purple paste food coloring and
      6 small-tipped squeeze bottles
      to decorate

Preheat oven to 350 degrees. Roll out
ookie dough according to sugar cookie
ckage directions. Use desired cookie
tters (we used bunny, egg, flower, and
by chick cutters) to cut out cookies.
ke 5 to 7 minutes or until edges are
ht brown. Transfer to a wire rack to
ol.

For icing, combine sugar, milk, and
almond extract until smooth. Place
4 tablespoons icing in each of five small
bowls and tint with food coloring.
Pour each color of icing into a separate
squeeze bottle. Pour remaining white
icing into remaining bottle. Store
cookies in an airtight container.
Yield: about 6 dozen cookies

BUNNY BAG

You will need a 6" x 11" pink paper bag,
white poster board, tracing paper, three
8" purple pipe cleaners, 1¹/₂" pink pom-
pom, two ⁷/₈" dia. wiggle eyes, pink
colored pencil, black felt-tip pen with
medium point, drawing compass, hot
glue gun, and glue sticks.

1. Trace teeth and ear patterns onto
tracing paper; cut out. Use patterns to
cut teeth and 2 ears from poster board.
For cheeks, cut two 2³/₄" dia. circles
from poster board.
2. Use pink pencil to color insides of
ears; use pen to outline teeth.
3. For face, overlap cheeks ¹/₂" and
glue together. Glue teeth to back of
cheeks at bottom. Cross centers of pipe
cleaners to form whiskers; glue to center
of cheeks. Glue pom-pom to center of
whiskers for nose. Glue eyes to tops of
cheeks.
4. For flap, fold top of bag 3" to front.
Glue face to flap. Glue bottom of each
ear to back of bag. Fold tip of 1 ear
forward.

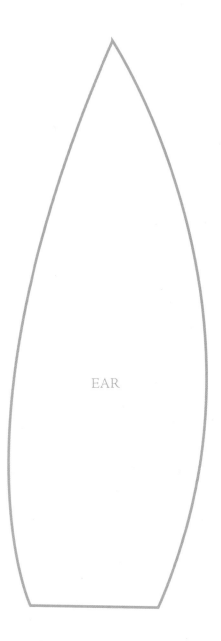

EAR

TEETH

ALMOND COOKIE BARS

his all-American treat makes great gift for the Fourth of ly! Bursting with chocolate chips nd chopped nuts, chewy Almond ookie Bars have a sweet, nutty avor—and they're quick to make the microwave. The "explosive" ontainer is made by covering a canister with patriotic fabric and dding a sparkly "fuse" made from ar-spangled metallic garlands.

ALMOND COOKIE BARS

$3/4$ cup quick-cooking oats
$3/4$ cup firmly packed brown sugar, divided
$1/2$ cup butter or margarine, softened
$1/4$ cup all-purpose flour
1 egg, beaten
1 tablespoon milk
$1/2$ teaspoon almond extract
1 package (6 ounces) semisweet chocolate chips
1 cup finely chopped pecans, divided

In a medium bowl, combine oats, $1/2$ cup brown sugar, butter, flour, egg, milk, and almond extract; stir in chocolate chips and $1/2$ cup pecans. Spread batter evenly in a greased 8-inch square microwave-safe baking dish. For topping, combine remaining $1/4$ cup brown sugar and remaining $1/2$ cup pecans in a small bowl; sprinkle over batter. Lightly press topping into batter. Microwave on high power (100%) 3 minutes; rotate dish. Cook 3 to 5 minutes longer or until sugar topping is melted. Cool completely. Cut into $1^1/2$-inch squares. Store in an airtight container.

Yield: about 2 dozen bars

FIRECRACKER CANISTER

You will need a round tin canister with lid (we used a $4^1/2$" dia. x $6^1/4$"h canister), fabrics to cover canister and lid, polyester bonded batting, $1/4$"w gold trim, satin ribbon same width as side of lid, wired star garland, gold wire garland, fabric marking pencil, hammer, nail, spray adhesive, craft glue, spring-type clothespins, hot glue gun, and glue sticks.

1. To cover canister, leave lid on canister and measure from bottom edge of lid to bottom edge of canister. Measure around side of canister; add $1/2$". Cut a piece of fabric the determined measurements. Remove lid from canister.
2. Apply spray adhesive to wrong side of fabric. With 1 long edge of fabric along bottom edge of canister, smooth fabric onto canister, overlapping short edges.
3. (*Note:* For remaining steps, use craft glue unless otherwise indicated.) With ends of trim at seam, glue gold trim along top and bottom edges of fabric on canister.
4. To cover lid, use fabric marking pencil to draw around lid on wrong side of fabric. Cut out fabric $1/2$" outside pencil line. Clip edge of fabric at $1/2$" intervals to within $1/8$" of line. Use top of lid as a pattern and cut 1 circle from batting; glue batting to lid. Center fabric circle right side up on lid. Alternating sides and pulling fabric taut, glue clipped edges of fabric to side of lid; secure with clothespins until glue is dry. If necessary, trim edges of fabric just above bottom edge of lid. Measure around side of lid; add $1/2$". Cut ribbon the determined measurement. Glue to side of lid.
5. For fuse, use hammer and nail to punch a hole in center of lid. Cut several lengths of each kind of garland. Twist 1 end of garland lengths together; insert twisted ends through hole in center of lid and bend to one side. Hot glue ends to inside of lid to secure.
6. Separate strands of garland. Wrap ends of several garland lengths around a pencil to curl.

PATRIOTIC DESSERT

Give three cheers for the red, white, and blue with this Patriotic Dessert! Perfect for Flag Day (June 14), the delectable treat features fresh strawberries and blueberries layered with a rich mixture of cream cheese and whipped cream. A handsome bowl makes an attractive, reusable gift for your hostess.

PATRIOTIC DESSERT

  2 cups whipping cream
  2 packages (8 ounces each) cream cheese, softened
$^1/_2$ cup granulated sugar
$^1/_2$ teaspoon almond extract
  2 quarts fresh strawberries, halved
  2 quarts fresh blueberries

Place a large bowl and beaters from an electric mixer in freezer until well chilled. In chilled bowl, beat cream until soft peaks form. In another large bowl, beat cream cheese, sugar, and almond extract until fluffy. Gradually add whipped cream to cream cheese mixture; beat until smooth and stiff peaks form.

For garnish, reserve about 20 strawberry halves and $^1/_2$ cup blueberries. In a trifle bowl (we used a 5-inch-high x 8-inch-diameter bowl) or large glass container, layer whipped cream mixture and remaining strawberries and blueberries, ending with whipped cream mixture. Garnish top with strawberry halves and blueberries to resemble a flag. Cover and refrigerate until ready to present.

Yield: about 16 servings

ALL-AMERICAN MUFFINS

This Fourth of July, salute great all-American tastes with our spectacular Red-White-and-Blue Muffins! Maraschino cherries, vanilla baking chips, and fresh blueberries are baked into the moist little cakes for bite after bite of star-spangled flavor. For a dandy delivery, use a flag-inspired painted plate to take the muffins to a get-together.

ED-WHITE-AND-BLUE
UFFINS

 2 cups all-purpose flour
 1 cup quick-cooking oats
/3 cup firmly packed brown sugar
/3 cup granulated sugar
/4 teaspoon baking soda
/4 teaspoon baking powder
/4 teaspoon salt
/4 cup buttermilk
/2 cup butter or margarine, melted
 2 eggs
 1 teaspoon vanilla extract
 1 package (12 ounces) vanilla
     baking chips
 1 cup coarsely chopped maraschino
     cherries
 1 cup fresh blueberries

Preheat oven to 375 degrees. In a
ge bowl, combine flour, oats, sugars,
king soda, baking powder, and salt.
rm a well in center of dry ingredients.
a small bowl, combine buttermilk,
elted butter, eggs, and vanilla. Add
uid to dry ingredients; stir just until
oistened. Stir in vanilla chips, cherries,
d blueberries.

Fill paper-lined muffin cups two-thirds full. Bake 18 to 22 minutes or until lightly browned. Transfer muffins to a wire rack to cool. Store in an airtight container.

Yield: about 2 dozen muffins

FLAG PLATE

Caution: Plate is for decorative use only and is not intended for direct contact with food.
You will need a 10" dia. unfinished wooden plate; white, red, and blue acrylic paint; satin clear acrylic spray sealer; foam brush; paintbrushes; tracing paper; transfer paper; facial tissues; and sandpaper.

Refer to Painting Techniques, page 111, for painting tips.

1. Sand plate, wash with soap and water, and allow to dry.
2. Use foam brush to paint plate white; allow to dry.
3. Trace stars and swirls pattern, page 113, onto tracing paper. Aligning curve of pattern with edge of plate, use transfer paper to transfer background outline (shown in blue) to plate. Use a pencil to draw stripes on plate as desired.
4. Paint background area blue and stripes red. Before paint dries, lightly blot paint with tissues using a clean area of tissue each time.
5. Transfer stars and swirls to blue section of plate. Paint stars and swirls white.
6. Allowing to dry between coats, apply two to three coats of sealer to plate.
7. Wipe plate with a damp cloth after each use.

riends will get a bang out of ese patriotic cookies for the ourth of July. The "firecrackers" e made from purchased wafer ll cookies, and the Stenciled Star ookies have a rich maple flavor. flag-toting basket makes a irited gift container.

FIRECRACKER COOKIES

COOKIES

12 ounces white candy coating
2 dozen purchased wafer roll cookies, such as Pepperidge Farms® Pirouette cookies
24 pieces (2 inches each) red string licorice

ICING

$2^2/3$ cups sifted confectioners sugar
2 egg whites
Red and blue paste food coloring

For cookies, melt candy coating in a small saucepan over low heat, stirring constantly. Remove from heat. Using a fork, dip each cookie into candy coating, coating completely. Transfer to a wire rack with waxed paper underneath. Before candy coating hardens, insert 1 piece of licorice into 1 end of each cookie. Allow candy coating to harden.

For icing, beat sugar and egg whites in a medium bowl 7 to 10 minutes or until stiff. Divide icing into 2 bowls; tint red and blue. Transfer each icing to a separate pastry bag fitted with a very small round tip. Refer to photo and pipe icing on each cookie. Allow icing to harden. Store in an airtight container.

Yield: 2 dozen cookies

STENCILED STAR COOKIES

1 cup butter or margarine, softened
2 cups firmly packed brown sugar
2 eggs
1 teaspoon maple flavoring
$3^1/2$ cups all-purpose flour
1 teaspoon baking soda
$^1/2$ teaspoon salt
1 cup sliced almonds, chopped
Red liquid food coloring

In a large bowl, cream butter and sugar until fluffy. Add eggs and maple flavoring; beat until smooth. In a medium bowl, stir together flour, baking soda, and salt. Add flour mixture to creamed mixture; stir until a soft dough forms. Stir in almonds. Cover and chill 1 hour.

Preheat oven to 375 degrees. On a lightly floured surface, use a floured rolling pin to roll out dough to $1/4$-inch thickness. Use a 3-inch round cookie cutter to cut out cookies. Transfer to a greased baking sheet. Bake 8 to 10 minutes or until edges begin to brown. Transfer to a wire rack to cool completely.

Using star pattern and food coloring, follow *Stenciling*, page 110, to stencil stars on cookies. Store in an airtight container.

Yield: about $3^1/2$ dozen cookies

GOBLIN COOKIES

Packed with flavor, Jumbo Walnut-Chocolate Chunk Cookies are so good it's scary! When you serve these treats at your Halloween bash, your guests will be "goblin" them up. To make our easy edible "ghost," wrap a cookie in tissue paper, then use a felt-tip pen to draw a jack-o'-lantern face. A few ribbon streamers tie it all together.

JUMBO WALNUT-CHOCOLATE CHUNK COOKIES

- 1 cup butter or margarine, melted
- 1 cup granulated sugar
- 1 cup firmly packed brown sugar
- 2 eggs
- 1 teaspoon vanilla-butter-nut flavoring
- 2 cups all-purpose flour
- 1 teaspoon baking powder
- 1 teaspoon baking soda
- $^1/_2$ teaspoon salt
- 2 packages (10 ounces each) semisweet chocolate chunks
- 2 cups coarsely chopped walnuts

Preheat oven to 350 degrees. In a large bowl, beat butter and sugars until creamy. Add eggs and vanilla-butter-nut flavoring; beat until smooth. In a small bowl, combine flour, baking powder, baking soda, and salt. Add dry ingredients to creamed mixture; stir until a soft dough forms. Stir in chocolate chunks and walnuts. Use $^1/_4$ cup of dough for each cookie. Drop cookies 3 inches apart onto a lightly greased baking sheet. Bake 12 to 15 minutes or until edges and tops are lightly browned. Transfer cookies to a wire rack to cool. Wrap cookies individually in plastic wrap.

Yield: about 2$^1/_2$ dozen cookies

ORANGE SLICE FUDGE

Digging up something good to share on Halloween doesn't have to be a "grave" decision—just brew up a batch of microwave Orange Slice Fudge! Studded with pieces of a favorite candy, the creamy chocolates are presented in spray-painted tins that are simple to decorate with fun stickers. For frightfully easy finishes, tie the canisters with ribbon or glue on handmade labels.

ORANGE SLICE FUDGE

$^1/_2$ cup butter or margarine

$^1/_2$ cups sifted confectioners sugar

1 can (5 ounces) evaporated milk

$^1/_3$ cup cocoa

1 package (11$^1/_2$ ounces) milk chocolate chips

1 package (10$^1/_2$ ounces) miniature marshmallows

2 teaspoons vanilla extract

$^1/_4$ teaspoon salt

1 cup chopped orange slice candies

Line a 9 x 13-inch baking pan with aluminum foil; grease foil. Place butter in a large microwave-safe bowl; microwave on high power (100%) 1 minute or until butter melts. Stir in confectioners sugar, evaporated milk, and cocoa. Microwave on high power (100%) 4 minutes or until mixture comes to a boil, stirring every 2 minutes. Continue to microwave 3 minutes longer, stirring every 2 minutes. Add chocolate chips, marshmallows, vanilla, and salt; stir until well blended. Stir in candies. Pour into prepared pan. Refrigerate 4 hours or until firm. Cut into 1-inch squares, cleaning knife frequently. Store in an airtight container in refrigerator.

Yield: about 8 dozen pieces fudge

GOURMET CARAMEL APPLES

This Halloween, treat your grown-up friends to these delectable caramel apples. The traditional fall sweets become gourmet fare when dipped in white or semisweet chocolate and rolled in chopped pecans. The fancy fruit is packaged in sacks decorated to look like grinning jack-o'-lanterns.

GOURMET CARAMEL APPLES

- 12 craft sticks
- 1 dozen medium Red Delicious apples
- 3 bags (14 ounces each) caramels
- 6 tablespoons water
- 28 ounces semisweet *or* white baking chocolate, coarsely chopped
- 5 cups chopped pecans

Insert craft sticks into stem ends of apples. In a medium saucepan, combine caramels and water. Stirring constantly, cook over medium-low heat until smooth. Remove from heat. Holding each apple over saucepan, spoon caramel mixture over apples. Cool completely on greased waxed paper.

Stirring constantly, melt desired chocolate in a small saucepan over low heat. Remove from heat. Holding each caramel-coated apple over saucepan, spoon chocolate over apple. Roll in pecans. Return to waxed paper to cool completely. Store at room temperature in an airtight container.

Yield: 1 dozen caramel apples

JACK-O'-LANTERN SACKS

For each sack, you will need an orange gift sack, graphite transfer paper, black permanent marker, green curling ribbon, green tissue paper, tracing paper, and green construction paper.

1. Trace face and tag patterns, page 116, onto tracing paper. Cut out tag pattern.
2. Use transfer paper to transfer face pattern to sack. Color face with marker.
3. Stuff bottom of sack ¼ full with tissue paper. Place caramel apple wrapped in plastic wrap in sack; trim top of sack 2½" below top of craft stick.
4. Tuck tissue paper in top of sack; gather top of sack around craft stick. Tie curling ribbon around top of sack.
5. For tag, use pattern to cut tag from construction paper. Write name on tag with marker. Make a hole in top of tag and thread tag onto curling ribbon. Curl ribbon ends.

FALL FLAVORS

This fall, share Cranberry Mustard and Spicy Onion Chutney with friends who relish gourmet tastes. An embellished bag makes a nice keepsake.

CRANBERRY MUSTARD

2/3 cup finely chopped onion
2 tablespoons vegetable oil
6 tablespoons firmly packed brown
    sugar
2 teaspoons grated orange zest
2 cans (16 ounces each) whole
    berry cranberry sauce
2/3 cup prepared mustard

In a large skillet over medium heat, sauté onion in oil about 5 minutes or until onion is tender. Add brown sugar and orange zest. Stirring frequently, cook about 1 minute or until sugar dissolves. Add cranberry sauce and mustard; stir until well blended. Remove from heat and cool. Serve at room temperature as a condiment or use as a sauce for grilling. Store in an airtight container in refrigerator.

Yield: about 4 1/2 cups cranberry mustard (4 gifts)

SPICY ONION CHUTNEY

1/3 cup unsalted butter or margarine
1 cup firmly packed brown sugar
6 cups chopped onions (about
    3 pounds onions)
3 cloves garlic, minced
1/2 cup orange juice
1/4 cup apple cider vinegar
2 tablespoons grated orange zest
6 whole cloves

Melt butter in a heavy Dutch oven over medium heat. Add brown sugar; stirring constantly until sugar dissolves. Cook 2 to 3 minutes or until sugar begins to caramelize. Add onions and garlic (sugar may harden a little); stirring constantly, cook about 10 minutes or until onions are tender. Stir in orange juice, vinegar, orange zest, and cloves; cook about 20 minutes or until mixture thickens. Remove from heat. Serve warm as a condiment with meat, breads, or vegetables. Store in an airtight container in refrigerator.

Yield: about 3 cups (3 gifts)

AUTUMN DAYS BAGS

For each bag, you will need a brown gift bag, 2 coordinating fabrics to cover and line bag, paper-backed fusible web, 2/3 yd lengths of assorted ribbons to coordinate with fabrics, and a hot glue gun and glue sticks.

1. Follow manufacturer's instructions to fuse web to wrong side of fabric to cover bag. Cut a piece of fabric slightly smaller than front of bag; remove paper backing. Fuse fabric to bag.
2. Tie ribbon lengths together into a bow; trim ends. Glue bow to bag.
3. Line bag with remaining fabric.

Our Chocolate-Mint Cheesecake makes a divine holiday gift! The easy recipe makes two, so you can share with a friend and still have one on hand for unexpected company. For a clever presentation, a circle of poster board is decorated to resemble a peppermint candy and placed in the clear lid of a disposable pie carrier. A wrapping of cellophane and ribbons completes the look of a giant Christmas candy.

CHOCOLATE-MINT CHEESECAKES

CRUST

2 cups chocolate sandwich cookie crumbs (about 22 cookies)
$^1/_2$ cup butter or margarine, melted
6 tablespoons sugar

FILLING

3 packages (8 ounces each) cream cheese, softened
1 can (14 ounces) sweetened condensed milk
3 eggs
1 tablespoon vanilla extract
$^1/_2$ cup crushed peppermint candies (about 20 round candies)

Preheat oven to 375 degrees. For crust, combine crumbs, butter, and sugar in a medium bowl. Press mixture into bottom and up sides of 2 greased 9-inch aluminum foil pie pans. Bake 6 to 8 minutes. Remove from oven.

Reduce heat to 300 degrees. In a large bowl, beat cream cheese, condensed milk, eggs, and vanilla until well blended. Stir in candies. Pour mixture into crusts. Bake 25 to 30 minutes or until set in center. Cool completely. Store in an airtight container in refrigerator.

Yield: two 9-inch cheesecakes

"PEPPERMINT" CHEESECAKE CARRIERS

For each carrier, you will need a clear plastic lid to fit a 9" dia. aluminum foil pie pan (we purchased our pan and lid from a grocery store bakery), poster board, red paper, tracing paper, clear cellophane, red and white curling ribbon, drawing compass, craft glue, and transparent tape.

1. For peppermint shape, cut a $7^1/_2$" dia. circle from poster board. For stripes, trace stripe pattern onto tracing paper; cut out. Use pattern to cut 5 stripes from red paper. Glue stripes to poster board circle.
2. If necessary, trim peppermint shape to fit inside top of lid. Tape peppermint shape inside top of lid. Place lid on pie pan.
3. Wrap pie pan in cellophane to resemble a peppermint candy; tie lengths of ribbon into bows around ends of cellophane. Curl ribbon ends.

DESSERT SAUCE

Pour our Chocolate-Peanut Butter Sauce over ice cream or cake and watch the desserts disappear! The microwavable sauce can be served warm, so it makes a great addition to winter treats. Pack a jar of the sweet stuff in a snowman gift can for a simple winter offering.

CHOCOLATE-PEANUT BUTTER SAUCE

  1 cup firmly packed brown sugar
  1 cup whipping cream
$^1/_2$ cup crunchy peanut butter
  1 cup milk chocolate chips
  1 teaspoon vanilla extract

Whisk brown sugar and whipping cream in a medium microwave-safe bowl until smooth. Whisk in peanut butter and microwave on high power (100%) 2 minutes. Whisk in chocolate chips and vanilla until smooth. Serve warm or at room temperature over ice cream or cake. Store in an airtight container in refrigerator.

Yield: about $2^3/_4$ cups sauce

SNOWMAN GIFT CAN

You will need a $3^1/_4$" dia. x $3^1/_2$"h can, spray primer, white and blue spray paint, hammer, nail, 14" of 20-gauge white cloth-covered wire, tracing paper, white craft foam, orange and black permanent fine-point markers, $^1/_2$" x 6" torn fabric strip, and a low temperature glue gun.

For jar lid cover, you will also need a $5^1/_2$" square of fabric, pint jar with lid, rubber band, and 16" of $^1/_8$"w ribbon.

Allow primer and paint to dry after each application.

1. Spray can with primer, then blue paint. Lightly spray can with white paint.
2. For handle, use hammer and nail to make a hole on each side of can. Insert wire end into one hole; bend up to secure. Repeat for opposite side.
3. Trace pattern onto tracing paper; cut out. Use pattern to cut snowman from craft foam. Use markers to draw face and buttons on snowman.
4. For scarf, fray short edges of fabric strip. Glue scarf around snowman's neck. Glue snowman to can.
5. For jar lid cover, fray all edges of fabric square. Place fabric over lid; secure with rubber band. Tie ribbon into a bow over rubber band.

NUTTY OLIVE SPREAD

Because everyone's on the go, the holiday season is the perfect time to give quick-to-fix snacks. Nutty Olive Spread served on crackers or toast is a true palate-pleaser. Share jars of this creamy, crunchy creation in hand-painted canvas totes tied with bows, and be sure to include crackers for munching.

NUTTY OLIVE SPREAD

2 packages (3 ounces each) cream cheese, softened
$^1/_2$ cup mayonnaise
1 jar (5$^3/_4$ ounces) stuffed green olives, drained and finely chopped
$^1/_2$ cup finely chopped pecans, toasted
$^1/_8$ teaspoon ground black pepper
Crackers to serve

In a medium bowl, beat cream cheese until fluffy. Beat in mayonnaise. Stir in olives, pecans, and pepper. Cover and chill overnight. Serve with crackers.

Yield: about 2 cups spread

CHRISTMAS MINI TOTES

For each tote, you will need red and green acrylic paint, paintbrushes, small canvas tote, gold paint pen, one 26" length each of 2"w red and red with gold stars sheer ribbon.

1. Use red and green paint to paint desired designs on front of tote. Use paint pen to add details to designs.
2. Tie ribbons into a bow around handles.

TASTY GIFT BASKETS

A basket, brimming with gifts of goodness, is a sight everyone loves to see. Gather a collection of the popular containers and fill them with these snacks, desserts, toppings, and treats for a wide variety of occasions.

RADISH DIP WITH RYE CHIPS

One of the joys of summer is sharing the bounty of your garden. Made with fresh veggies, cool Radish Dip is especially flavorful served with easy-to-make Rye Chips. For an imaginative presentation, line a market basket with a stenciled cloth and tuck in a jar of dip and a bag of chips.

RADISH DIP WITH RYE CHIPS

- 1 container (8 ounces) sour cream
- 1 cup shredded or finely chopped radishes
- $^1/_2$ cup mayonnaise
- $^1/_3$ cup finely chopped celery
- 2 teaspoons dried chives
- 2 teaspoons cream-style horseradish
- $^1/_4$ teaspoon salt
- 1 loaf (16 ounces) sliced cocktail rye bread
- $3^1/_2$ tablespoons olive oil

In a medium bowl, combine sour cream, radishes, mayonnaise, celery, chives, horseradish, and salt. Cover and chill 2 hours to let flavors blend.

Preheat oven to 300 degrees. Brush bread slices with oil. Cut each slice in half diagonally to form 2 triangles. Place bread triangles on a baking sheet. Bake 25 minutes or until bread is crisp, turning pieces after 15 minutes. Cool rye chips on baking sheet. Store in an airtight container.

Yield: about 2 cups dip and about $7^1/_2$ dozen chips

RADISH BASKET

You will need a basket (we used a $5^1/_2$" x $9^1/_2$" basket), torn muslin piece large enough to line and drape over sides of basket, torn fabric piece slightly larger than muslin piece, red and green acrylic paint, stencil plastic, craft knife and cutting mat, stencil brushes, and black permanent felt-tip pen.

1. Use radish pattern, page 114, and follow *Stenciling*, page 110, to stencil re radishes and green leaves at each corne of muslin piece.
2. Use pen to outline and draw detail lines on radishes and leaves, and to dra "stitches" along edges of muslin piece.
3. Center muslin piece on remaining fabric piece and place in basket.

GINGER LIMEADE SPARKLE

When the heat is on, stir up a batch of Ginger Limeade Sparkle and create some summertime relief for two! Fresh ginger lends a sweet, peppery zing to the lime-flavored concoction. Tuck a jug of the refreshment in a basket along with club soda and a pair of stylish glasses for serving.

GINGER LIMEADE SPARKLE

- 3 cups water
- 2 cups sugar
- 1 piece (4 ounces) ginger, peeled and sliced crosswise into 4 pieces
- 2 cans (12 ounces each) frozen limeade concentrate, thawed

In a medium saucepan, combine water, sugar, and ginger. Stirring frequently, bring to a boil over medium-high heat. Reduce heat to medium low and simmer 5 minutes. Remove from heat and let stand 30 minutes.

Strain syrup into a 1-gallon container; discard ginger. Stir in limeade. Cover and store in refrigerator. Give with serving instructions.

Yield: about 7 cups concentrate

To serve: Stir two 1-liter bottles club soda into concentrate. Serve over ice. Garnish with lime zest strips.

Draft our all-star lineup of chili toppings to score taste touchdowns at your game-watching party! The flavorful front line features Cheese Blend, Onion Relish, Mustard Relish, and Creamy Fresh Salsa. Team them up with your favorite chili to tackle even the heartiest of appetites. Jars of the condiments are huddled in a turf-lined basket that's decorated with pictures of the group's favorite team. Matching jar lids, a miniature pennant, and streamers in team colors lend spirit to this "fan-tastic" surprise!

CHEESE BLEND

1 cup (4 ounces) shredded sharp
    Cheddar cheese
1 cup (4 ounces) shredded mild
    Cheddar cheese
1 cup (4 ounces) shredded
    Monterey Jack cheese

Combine cheeses in an airtight
container. Store in refrigerator.
Yield: about 3 cups cheese

ONION RELISH

2 cups chopped onions
1/2 cup apple cider vinegar
1/2 cup sugar
1/2 teaspoon salt
1/4 teaspoon ground black pepper
1/2 teaspoon celery seed
1/2 teaspoon mustard seed
1/4 teaspoon ground turmeric

In a medium bowl, combine onions,
vinegar, sugar, salt, pepper, celery seed,
mustard seed, and turmeric. Cover and
store in refrigerator.
Yield: about 2 cups onion relish

MUSTARD RELISH

1/2 cups prepared mustard
1/2 cup drained hamburger dill
    pickle slices
1/2 cup chopped sweet pickles
1/4 cup drained pickled jalapeño
    pepper slices

Process mustard, pickles, and peppers
in a food processor until mixture is
coarsely chopped. Store in an airtight
container in refrigerator.
Yield: about 2 cups mustard relish

CREAMY FRESH SALSA

1 1/2 cups coarsely chopped and
    drained plum tomatoes (about
    3 tomatoes)
3 tablespoons chopped green
    onions
3 tablespoons chopped green
    pepper
3 tablespoons chopped fresh
    cilantro
1 1/2 tablespoons finely chopped celery
1 clove garlic, minced
1/4 teaspoon salt
1/8 teaspoon ground black pepper
1/3 cup sour cream

In a medium bowl, combine
tomatoes, green onions, green pepper,
cilantro, celery, garlic, salt, and black
pepper. Fold in sour cream. Cover and
store in refrigerator.
Yield: about 2 cups salsa

TOUCHDOWN BASKET

You will need a cardboard box (we used
a 6" x 13" box), football magazines,
corded piping, green artificial turf,
yellow and green (or your team's colors)
curling ribbon, decoupage glue, foam
brush, and glue.
For jar lid and flag, you will *also*
need tracing paper, yellow and green
paper (or your team's colors), black
permanent felt-tip pen, 10"l bamboo
skewer, decorative-edge craft scissors,
and glue.

1. Cut motifs from magazines. Use
foam brush to apply decoupage glue to
wrong side of each motif. Glue motifs
around outside of box, overlapping
motifs as desired; allow to dry.
2. Measure around top edge of box; add
1". Cut a piece of piping the determined
measurement. Gluing raw edge to inside
of box and overlapping ends, glue piping
around top of box.
3. Refer to Fig. 1 and measure length
of inside of box from rim to rim
(shown in red); measure width of box
(shown in blue). Cut one piece of turf
the determined measurements. Glue
to inside of box. Measure length and
height of one long side of box. Cut
two pieces of turf the determined
measurements. Glue each piece to
inside of box.

Fig. 1

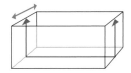

4. Cut several lengths of curling ribbon.
Glue centers of ribbon lengths to top
corners of box; curl ends.
5. For *each* jar lid, remove band from
jar. Trace around inside opening of
band on tracing paper; cut out. Use
pattern to cut circle from turf. Glue
circle to top of jar lid. Draw around
tracing paper circle on yellow (or your
choice) paper. Use craft scissors to cut
out label 1/4" inside drawn line. Use pen
to write recipe name on label. Glue label
to turf circle.
6. For flag, trace pattern, page 114, on
tracing paper; cut out. Draw around
pattern on green (or your choice) paper.
Use craft scissors to cut out flag. Refer
to grey line on pattern to fold tab to
back of flag. Glue one end of skewer
into fold. Use pen to write message
on flag. Cut several lengths of curling
ribbon. Tie ribbons into a bow and glue
bow to top of flag; curl ends.

CHERRY HONEY

Surprise someone with a charming breakfast basket—just "bee-cause!" This sweet thinking-of-you gift features a pot of fruity Cherry Honey, packed with your oven-fresh biscuits. Made of honey and cherry preserves stirred together, the tasty spread provides a great start to a "buzz-y" day!

CHERRY HONEY

1 jar (12 ounces) cherry preserves
$^1/_2$ cup honey

In a small bowl, combine preserves and honey; stir until well blended. Store in an airtight container in refrigerator.

Yield: about $1^1/_2$ cups flavored honey

JUST "BEE-CAUSE!" BASKET AND GIFT TAG

You will need a basket with handle (we used a 9" dia. basket), bee-motif fabric for basket liner, 21" length of 2"w black and white grosgrain ribbon, artificial daisies and cherries, pinking shears, and glue.

For gift tag, you will *also* need a photocopy of tag design (page 115), yellow paper, black permanent felt-tip pen, serrated-edge craft scissors, and an artificial bee.

1. Use fabric and follow *Making a Basket Liner,* page 110, to make basket liner with pinked edges.
2. Glue daisies and cherries to basket handle. Tie ribbon into a bow around handle.

3. For gift tag, use craft scissors to cut out tag. Use pen to write message on tag. Glue tag to yellow paper. Leaving $^1/_8$" yellow border, cut out gift tag. Glu bee to corner of tag.

BANANA SPLIT SAUCE

A perfect topping for ice cream, this delectable Banana Split Sauce is an "a-peeling" way to satisfy a dessert lover! The chocolaty syrup is brimming with dried banana chips, chopped pecans, and cherries. It's easy to mix up, and the recipe yields enough for several gifts. To present, tuck a jar of the sauce and some sundae glasses in a pretty fabric-lined basket. Adorned with a Neapolitan-style bow and a banana tag, it's the sweetest offering you could ever give!

BANANA SPLIT SAUCE

1 jar (18 ounces) cherry preserves
1 container (48 ounces) chocolate-flavored syrup
1 cup coarsely chopped pecans, toasted
1 cup dried banana chips
1 jar (6 ounces) maraschino cherries, drained and coarsely chopped

In a large microwave-safe bowl, microwave preserves on medium-high power (80%) 4 to 5 minutes or until melted. Stir in remaining ingredients. Store in an airtight container in refrigerator. Serve warm or cold with ice cream or cake.

Yield: about 7 cups sauce

BASKET TAG

Trace banana pattern, page 114, onto tracing paper; cut out. Use pattern to cut banana from a piece of heavy yellow paper. Use dark yellow, green, brown, and dark brown colored pencils to color banana. Use brown pencil to write "BANANA SPLIT SAUCE" on tag. Use a ¹/₈" hole to punch a hole at top of tag. Use white satin cord to tie tag to basket handle.

TROPICAL FRUIT SHERBET

A triple fruity frozen fantasy, Tropical Fruit Sherbet offers a fun salute to Air Conditioning Appreciation Day (July 3)! When the dog days of summer arrive, this chilly confection gives you a cool reason to get together with the gang and enjoy the beauty of the great indoors! Add fun to the festivities by presenting the freezer pleaser in a colorful no-sew basket along with whimsical ice cream dishes.

TROPICAL FRUIT SHERBET

1 fresh pineapple, peeled and cored
3 passion fruit
4 kiwi fruit, peeled and sliced
1 envelope unflavored gelatin
$1/4$ cup cold water
1 cup whole milk, divided
$3/4$ cup sugar, divided
1 can ($8^{1}/2$ ounces) cream of coconut
2 tablespoons freshly squeezed lemon juice

Process pineapple in food processor until puréed. Transfer to a medium saucepan. Stirring occasionally, cook over medium heat 8 minutes; remove from heat.

In a small bowl, scrape seeds and yellow pulp from skin of passion fruit; discard skin. Purée passion fruit and kiwi fruit in a food processor; strain to remove seeds. In a heavy large saucepan, sprinkle gelatin over water; soften one minute. Stir in $1/2$ cup milk and $1/4$ cup sugar. Stirring constantly, cook over low heat until gelatin dissolves. Stir in remaining $1/2$ cup milk and remaining $1/2$ cup sugar. Stirring frequently, cook over medium-low heat until sugar dissolves. Remove from heat; stir in fruit, cream of coconut, and lemon juice. Transfer to a metal or plastic bowl. Cover and freeze overnight.

Let mixture stand at room temperature 1 hour. Break into pieces and process in a large food processor until smooth; refreeze in an airtight container. Serve frozen.

Yield: about $7^{1}/2$ cups sherbet

FABRIC-COVERED BASKET

You will need a round basket with handle (we used an 11" dia. basket), fabric to cover basket, two rubber bands, natural excelsior, and glue.
For gift tag, you will *also* need a photocopy of tag design (page 114), green paper, $1/3$ yd of $1/8$"w pink ribbon, purple and green colored pencils, decorative-edge craft scissors, black permanent felt-tip pen, and a hole punch.

1. Center basket on wrong side of fabric.
2. Pulling fabric taut, gather fabric at base of handle on each side of basket; use rubber bands to secure gathers. Tuck ends of fabric and rubber bands between basket and fabric; glue at handle to secure. Turn remaining fabric edges to wrong side with fold even with top of basket; glue to secure.
3. For gift tag, use pencils to color tag design. Cut out tag. Use pen to write message on tag. Glue tag to green paper. Leaving a $3/8$" green border, use craft scissors to cut out gift tag.
4. Use hole punch to punch hole in tag. Loop ribbon through hole and tie ribbon into a bow around basket handle.

ORIENTAL SALAD DRESSING

If you believe that variety is the spice of life, then you'll love sharing our unusual Oriental Salad Dressing with like-minded friends. Simply combine rice vinegar, sesame oil, and Chinese five spice powder with a few pantry staples and, in minutes, you've got it made. Perfect for spicing up a plain salad, the dressing will add Oriental style to any meal. Along with the jar of dressing, include a set of Chinese bowls and some chop sticks for an especially nice gift.

ORIENTAL SALAD DRESSING

- 1 cup vegetable oil
- $^3/_4$ cup rice vinegar
- $^1/_4$ cup plus 2 tablespoons sugar
- $^1/_4$ cup dark sesame oil
- 2 tablespoons dry mustard
- 2 teaspoons salt
- 1 teaspoon Chinese five spice powder

Combine all ingredients in a 1-quart jar with a tight-fitting lid. Shake until well blended. Store in refrigerator. Serve with salad or stir-fried vegetables.

Yield: about 2$^1/_4$ cups dressing

MOCHA CREAMER

Those who enjoy country cow novelties will be charmed by these bags of Mocha Creamer! The mix stirs together quickly, and the bovine-inspired gift bags are simple to make by sponge painting plain white lunch sacks. This fast, friendly present will have everyone in the "moo-o-o-d" for mocha!

MOCHA CREAMER

1 jar (6 ounces) non-dairy powdered creamer
1 cup chocolate mix for milk
$1/2$ teaspoon ground cinnamon

In a medium bowl, combine creamer, chocolate mix, and cinnamon. Store in an airtight container. Give with serving instructions.

Yield: about $2^1/2$ cups creamer (4 gifts)

To serve: Stir 1 tablespoon creamer into ounces of hot coffee.

COW-PRINT BAGS

For each bag, you will need a white lunch bag, white and red paper for tag, 2 yd of $1^3/8$"w wire-edged red and white gingham ribbon, 10" of $1/8$"w black satin ribbon, Miracle Sponges™ (dry compressed sponges; available at craft stores), black acrylic paint, black felt-tip pen with fine point, stapler, 8" hole punch, newspaper, paper towels, tracing paper, craft glue stick, and a hot glue gun and glue sticks.

1. Trace spot patterns onto tracing paper; cut out.
2. Use patterns to cut shapes from dry sponges.
3. Use sponge shapes and follow *Sponge Painting*, page 111, to paint black spots on bag.
4. Place gift in bag.
5. For flap, fold top corners of bag diagonally to center front. Fold point to front. Staple bag closed.

6. Tie wire-edged ribbon into a bow; trim ends. Hot glue bow to bag.
7. For tag, cut a piece of white paper. Use black pen to write the following on tag: IN THE "MOO-O-O-D" FOR MOCHA COFFEE? Use glue stick to glue tag to red paper. Cutting close to tag, cut tag from red paper. Punch a hole in 1 corner of tag. Thread satin ribbon through hole and tie tag to bow on bag; trim ends.

Nutrition-minded friends will appreciate these healthy choices! The salad dressing, orangy fruit dip, herb cheese spread, and baked snack chips in our sampling are low-calorie, low-cholesterol treats. For "high-tech" nutrition with old-fashioned flair, present the entire collection in a country basket with a ruffled gingham liner. Or if you prefer, give one item and include fresh fruit, vegetables, or crackers to enjoy with it.

HERB-YOGURT CHEESE SPREAD

    1 carton (32 ounces) plain low-fat
         yogurt (use yogurt without
         added gelatin)
    3 tablespoons reduced-calorie
         mayonnaise
    1 clove garlic, minced
  1/4 cup minced green onion
    1 tablespoon chopped fresh parsley
    1 teaspoon Worcestershire sauce
  1/4 teaspoon salt
  1/8 teaspoon ground black pepper
  1/8 teaspoon cayenne pepper

To make yogurt cheese, place a colander over a large glass or ceramic bowl. Line colander with 4 layers of cheesecloth; spoon yogurt into colander. Cover with plastic wrap and refrigerate 2 hours to drain. Spoon yogurt cheese into an airtight container; discard cheesecloth and drained liquid. (You should have about 2 cups of cheese.)

To make Herb-Yogurt Cheese Spread, combine 1 cup yogurt cheese with remaining ingredients in a small bowl. Stir well to blend (do not beat or use a food processor). Cover and refrigerate 8 hours or overnight. Serve with crackers or fresh vegetables. Store in airtight container in refrigerator.

Yield: about 1 1/2 cups of spread; 15 calories per tablespoon

Note: Use remaining yogurt cheese as a low-calorie substitute for sour cream. If cooking with yogurt cheese, bring to room temperature before adding to hot mixtures.

SKINNY FRUIT DIP

    1 cup low-fat cottage cheese
    3 tablespoons plain low-fat yogurt
2 1/2 tablespoons low-sugar orange
         marmalade
    1 tablespoon orange juice
    2 teaspoons honey

Place all ingredients in a blender or food processor fitted with a steel blade. Process until smooth and creamy. Serve with fresh fruit. Store in airtight container in refrigerator.

Yield: about 1 1/3 cups of dip; 14 calories per tablespoon

DIET THOUSAND ISLAND DRESSING

    1 cup reduced-calorie mayonnaise
  2/3 cup spicy vegetable juice
    3 tablespoons sweet pickle relish
    1 tablespoon minced onion
    1 tablespoon minced green pepper
  1/4 teaspoon dry mustard
  1/8 teaspoon garlic powder
  1/8 teaspoon ground black pepper

In a medium bowl, use a wire whisk to blend all ingredients. Cover and refrigerate at least 2 hours before serving. Store in airtight container in refrigerator.

Yield: about 2 cups of dressing; 25 calories per tablespoon

GUILT-FREE SNACK CHIPS

    1 package (10 ounces) flour tortillas
  1/4 cup low-calorie Italian salad
         dressing
         Garlic salt or salt-free herb and
         spice blend

Preheat oven to 325 degrees. Cut each tortilla into eighths. Spread on a baking sheet lightly sprayed with cooking spray. Using a pastry brush, brush salad dressing over tops of chips. Sprinkle with garlic salt or herb blend. Bake 10 to 12 minutes or until lightly browned. Cool completely before storing in airtight container.

Yield: about 7 cups of chips; 10 calories per chip

RUFFLED BASKET LINER

You will need two 17" squares of fabric, one 5" x 136" strip of fabric for ruffle (pieced as necessary), and thread to match fabric.

1. For ruffle, press short edges of fabric strip 1/2" to wrong side. With wrong sides together, fold fabric in half lengthwise; press. Baste 3/8" and 1/4" from raw edge. Pull basting threads, drawing up gathers to fit around fabric square.
2. Matching raw edges and overlapping ends of ruffle, baste ruffle to right side of one fabric square.
3. Matching right sides and raw edges, place fabric squares together. Leaving an opening for turning, use a 1/2" seam allowance and sew fabric squares together. Cut corners diagonally and turn right side out; press. Sew final closure by hand.

Yo-Yo Cookies

Celebrate National Yo-Yo Day (June 6) with a friend who's still a child at heart. Our edible toy treats are sure to bring back memories of "walking the dog" with a yo-yo, shooting marbles, and playing ball. The delicious goodies are made from vanilla-flavored cookies sandwiched together with orange cream filling.

Yo-Yo Cookies

COOKIES

- $1/2$ cup butter or margarine, softened
- $1/3$ cup corn syrup
- $1^1/2$ cups granulated sugar
- 1 egg
- 1 teaspoon vanilla extract
  Orange paste food coloring
- $2^3/4$ cups all-purpose flour
- 2 teaspoons baking soda
- $1/4$ teaspoon salt

FILLING

- 3 cups sifted confectioners sugar
- 1 cup butter or margarine, softened
- 1 teaspoon dried grated orange peel
- 1 teaspoon orange extract
  White cotton string to decorate

For cookies, preheat oven to 375 degrees. In a large bowl, cream butter, corn syrup, and sugar until fluffy. Add egg and vanilla; beat until smooth. Tint orange. In a medium bowl, stir together flour, baking soda, and salt. Add dry ingredients to creamed mixture; stir until a soft dough forms. Divide dough in half. On a lightly floured surface, use a floured rolling pin to roll out each half of dough to $1/4$-inch thickness. Use a $1^1/2$-inch round cookie cutter to cut out cookies. Place cookies 1 inch apart on a greased baking sheet. Bake 5 to 7 minutes or until edges are light brown. Transfer to a

wire rack to cool completely.

For filling, beat all ingredients together in a medium bowl until smooth. Spread filling generously on half of cookies; top with remaining

cookies. For each yo-yo string, cut a 20" length of string. Tie one end into a small loop. Wrap remaining end around cookie. Store in an airtight container. Remove string before eating cookie.

Yield: about 3 dozen cookies

TOFFEE COOKIES

On Mother-in-Law Day (the fourth Sunday in October), surprise this special lady with buttery Toffee Cookies. The chewy cookies feature crisp bits of chocolate-covered English toffee. To dress up your gift basket, add a pretty padded lid —she'll enjoy using it long after the cookies are gone.

TOFFEE COOKIES

1 cup butter or margarine, softened
3/4 cup granulated sugar
3/4 cup firmly packed brown sugar
2 eggs
1 tablespoon vanilla extract
1/4 cups all-purpose flour
1 teaspoon baking soda
1 teaspoon salt
2 cups coarsely chopped chocolate-
  covered English toffee bars

Preheat oven to 350 degrees. In a large bowl, cream butter and sugars until fluffy. Add eggs and vanilla; beat until smooth. In a medium bowl, stir together flour, baking soda, and salt. Add dry ingredients to creamed mixture; stir until a soft dough forms. Stir in toffee bars. Drop by heaping teaspoonfuls 2 inches apart onto greased baking sheet. Bake 8 to 10 minutes or until edges are light brown. Transfer to a wire rack to cool completely. Store in an airtight container.

Yield: about 6 1/2 dozen cookies

PADDED BASKET LID

You will need a basket, fabric, pregathered eyelet trim, purchased cording, two 24" lengths of satin ribbon, medium weight cardboard, polyester bonded batting, and craft glue.

1. Measure length and width of basket opening. Cut 2 pieces of cardboard and 2 pieces of batting the determined measurements. Cut 2 pieces of fabric 1" larger on all sides than cardboard.
2. (*Note:* Allow to dry after each glue step.) For lid top, center both pieces of batting, then 1 cardboard piece, on wrong side of 1 fabric piece. At 1/2" intervals, clip edges of fabric piece to 1/8" from edge of cardboard. Pulling fabric taut, glue clipped edges of fabric to wrong side of cardboard.

3. For trim, measure around lid top; add 1". Cut 1 length each of cording and eyelet trim the determined measurement. Glue cording, then eyelet trim, to wrong side of lid top. For ties, fold each ribbon length in half. On wrong side of lid top, glue 1" of 1 folded ribbon end to center of 1 edge of lid top. Repeat to glue remaining folded ribbon end to opposite edge of lid top.
4. For lid bottom, repeat Step 2 (omitting batting) to cover remaining cardboard piece.
5. Matching wrong sides, glue lid top and bottom together. Place lid on basket. Thread ribbon ends through basket. Tie ribbons into bows; trim ends.

PIZZA LOVERS' KIT

Everyone loves fresh homemade pizza, and with these Pepperoni-Veggie Pizza Kits, all the ingredients are included in one handy, taste-tempting gift! You can pack the dough mix, sauce, pepperoni, and mozzarella cheese in a simple basket. Then embellish the carrier with garlic and pepper picks for a presentation that's sure to please at "ciao" time!

PIZZA KITS

The Pizza Kits recipe makes 3 gifts; each gift makes two 12-inch pizzas.

PIZZA DOUGH MIX

11¼ cups all-purpose flour, divided
3 packages dry yeast, divided
3 teaspoons sugar, divided
1½ teaspoons salt, divided

PIZZA SAUCE

3 tablespoons olive oil
1 cup finely chopped onion
5 cloves garlic, minced
1 green pepper, chopped
1 can (29 ounces) tomato sauce
3 large ripe tomatoes, peeled and chopped (about 2 cups)
1 jar (6 ounces) sliced mushrooms, drained
1 can (6 ounces) tomato paste
2 cans (2¼ ounces each) sliced ripe olives, drained
2 tablespoons chopped fresh basil leaves
2 tablespoons chopped fresh oregano leaves
¾ teaspoon salt
½ teaspoon ground black pepper
½ teaspoon sugar
¼ teaspoon crushed red pepper flakes
Three 8-ounce packages shredded mozzarella cheese and three 8.5-ounce packages pepperoni slices to give with gifts

For pizza dough mix, combine the following ingredients in each of 3 resealable plastic bags: 3¾ cups flour, 1 package yeast, 1 teaspoon sugar, and ½ teaspoon salt.

For pizza sauce, heat oil in a large Dutch oven over medium-low heat. Add onion, garlic, and green pepper. Stirring frequently, cook until vegetables are tender. Add tomato sauce, tomatoes, mushrooms, tomato paste, olives, basil, oregano, salt, black pepper, sugar, and red pepper flakes; simmer uncovered 20 minutes or until thickened. Remove from heat and cool. Place 2½ cups sauce in each of 3 containers. Cover and store sauce in refrigerator.

For each gift, give 1 bag Pizza Dough Mix, 1 container (2½ cups) Pizza Sauce, 1 package mozzarella cheese, 1 package pepperoni slices, and recipe for Pepperoni-Veggie Pizza (see Step 2 of Pizza Kit Basket instructions).

PEPPERONI-VEGGIE PIZZA

1 bag Pizza Dough Mix
1½ cups very warm water
2 tablespoons vegetable oil
1 container Pizza Sauce
1 package pepperoni slices
1 package shredded mozzarella cheese

In a large bowl, combine Pizza Dough Mix, very warm water, and oil; stir until a soft dough forms. Turn dough onto a lightly floured surface. Knead about 5 minutes or until dough becomes smooth and elastic, using additional flour as necessary. Cover and allow dough to rest 10 minutes. Divide dough in half and press into 2 lightly greased 12-inch pizza pans. Cover and let rise in a warm place (80 to 85 degrees) 30 minutes.

Preheat oven to 425 degrees. Bake crusts 10 minutes. Spread 1¼ cups Pizza Sauce over each partially baked crust. Place pepperoni slices on each pizza. Sprinkle 1 cup mozzarella cheese over each pizza. Bake 10 to 12 minutes or until crust is lightly browned and cheese is melted.

Yield: two 12-inch pizzas

PIZZA KIT BASKETS

For each basket, you will need a large basket with handle, a red plaid kitchen towel, 2 brown lunch bags, two 9" lengths of 1½"w white and red check grosgrain ribbon, photocopy of recipe (page 115), 2 white 1½" x 2¾" self-adhesive labels, red felt-tip pen with medium point, red paper, artificial garlic and pepper picks, natural raffia, 12" of floral wire, stapler, and a craft glue stick.

1. Place Pizza Dough Mix and Pizza Sauce in bags. Fold top of each bag about 2" to front. Fold 1 length of ribbon over top of each bag; staple ribbon in place. Use red pen to write "Pizza Dough Mix" and "Pizza Sauce" on labels. Adhere labels to bags over ribbons.
2. For recipe card, cut out photocopy of recipe. Use glue stick to glue recipe to red paper. Cutting close to recipe, cut recipe from red paper.
3. Use floral wire to attach garlic and pepper picks to handle of basket. Tie several lengths of raffia into a bow over ends of picks; trim ends.
4. Line basket with towel. Place bags of dough mix and sauce, cheese, pepperoni, and recipe card in basket.

With our spicy Pickled Watermelon Rind, you can preserve some of the fun of a summertime watermelon festival. Perfect for snacks or with meals, the sweet, tangy morsels are real crowd-pleasers—and our recipe makes plenty for sharing. Pack this old-fashioned treat in canning jars topped with pink fabric "fruit" and black button "seeds" to deliver to friends and neighbors. Paper melon slices make cute gift tags.

PICKLED WATERMELON RIND

PICKLED WATERMELON RIND

1 medium watermelon, about 16 pounds
2 tablespoons salt
3 (3 or 4-inch) cinnamon sticks, broken into pieces
1 tablespoon whole allspice
1 tablespoon whole cloves
4 cups vinegar
8 cups granulated sugar
1 lemon, thinly sliced

Remove rind from watermelon. Cut rind into 2-inch squares and remove peel with a paring knife. Place peeled rind in a Dutch oven and cover with water. Add salt and simmer over medium heat until rind is tender, about 25 to 30 minutes; drain. Transfer rind to a large bowl and cover with cold water. Cover bowl and refrigerate at least 4 hours; drain.

Wrap spices in a small square of cheesecloth; tie with kitchen twine. In a Dutch oven, bring vinegar and sugar to a boil. Add rind, spice bag, and lemon. Simmer until rind is transparent, about 35 to 45 minutes. Remove rind with a slotted spoon and pack into hot, sterilized pint jars. Bring syrup to a boil, remove spice bag, and pour hot syrup over rind through a sieve. Seal jars immediately.

Yield: about 5 to 6 pints of rind

WATERMELON TAGS AND JARS

For each tag, use colored pencils to decorate a half circle of paper and write the name with a felt-tip pen. Tie tag to completed jar with ¹/₁₆" wide ribbon.

For each jar, you will need a canning jar and lid with screw ring, one 5" square of pink fabric, one 5" square of craft batting, eight ¹/₄" dia. black buttons, fl. paintbrush, lt green and dk green acryl. paint, matte clear acrylic spray, and cra. glue.

1. Paint side of screw ring dk green and top of screw ring lt green; allow to dry. Spray ring with acrylic spray; allow to dry.
2. Using flat piece of lid as a pattern, c. a circle from fabric and batting. Glue batting to top of flat piece. Glue fabric to batting along fabric edge. Glue lid inside screw ring.
3. Glue buttons to top of lid; allow to dr.

HERB TEA BLEND

The chilly days of January usher in 31 reasons to enjoy our aromatic Herb Tea Blend, a soothing and relaxing beverage. A friend who appreciates the simple pleasure of ~~si~~pping tea will cherish a basket filled with the tea and a pretty cup and saucer. We trimmed our basket with lovely plaid ribbon and a spray of colorful posies.

~~H~~ERB TEA BLEND

~~3~~/4 cup loose tea leaves
~~1~~/4 cup dried sage leaves
  3 tablespoons dried thyme leaves
  1 tablespoon dried lemon peel

Combine tea, sage, thyme, and lemon ~~pe~~el in a resealable plastic bag. Give ~~w~~ith serving instructions.

~~Y~~ield: about 1¼ cups tea blend

~~T~~o serve: Place 2 teaspoons tea blend in ~~a~~ teapot for every 8 ounces hot water ~~desir~~ed. Pour boiling water over tea. Cover ~~an~~d steep 3 to 5 minutes. Strain into tea ~~cu~~ps; serve with lemon slices and honey.

GIFTS BY THE BAGFUL

Bags may be the ultimate gift wrap—they come in lots of sizes and shapes, and are simple to decorate. Embellish a few bags and fill them with these treats, snacks, and mixes for special occasions—or just because!

...ell your sweetie that
...ou care with a batch of
..."Be Mine" Valentine Cookies
...resented in a heartwarming
...ag. The cute cookies, which
...semble conversation heart
...andies, say it all with style
...nd ease! The fanciful gift sack
...fers a window to the heart
...ith its lace and doily trims.

...BE MINE" VALENTINE ...COOKIES

...OOKIES

- $^3/4$ cup butter or margarine, softened
- 1 cup sifted confectioners sugar
- 1 egg
- 1 teaspoon vanilla extract
- 1 teaspoon butter flavoring
- $^1/2$ cups all-purpose flour
- $^1/4$ teaspoon salt
  Red, green, and yellow liquid food coloring

...ING

- 1 cup sifted confectioners sugar
- 1 tablespoon butter or margarine, softened
- $^1/2$ tablespoon vegetable shortening
- 2 teaspoons milk
- $^1/4$ teaspoon vanilla extract
- $^1/4$ teaspoon butter flavoring
- $^1/4$ teaspoons red liquid food coloring

For cookies, cream butter and confectioners sugar in a large bowl until fluffy. Add egg, vanilla, and butter flavoring; beat until smooth. In a medium bowl, combine flour and salt. Add dry ingredients to creamed mixture; stir until well blended. Divide dough into thirds; tint pink, light green, and yellow. Wrap in plastic wrap and chill 1 hour.

Preheat oven to 350 degrees. On a lightly floured surface, use a floured rolling pin to roll out one third of dough to $^1/4$-inch thickness. Use a 3-inch-wide heart-shaped cookie cutter to cut out cookies. Transfer to a greased baking sheet. Bake 8 to 10 minutes or until bottoms are lightly browned. Transfer cookies to a wire rack to cool. Repeat with remaining dough.

For icing, combine confectioners sugar, butter, shortening, milk, vanilla, and butter flavoring in a small bowl; beat until smooth. Stir in food coloring. Spoon icing into a pastry bag fitted with a small round tip. Pipe valentine messages onto cookies. Allow icing to harden. Store in an airtight container.

Yield: about 2 dozen cookies (2 gifts)

SWEETHEART BAGS

For each bag, you will need a medium-size gift bag (about 7"w x 8"h), 6" square of clear cellophane, colored paper for tag, three $1^3/4$"w lace heart appliqués, 20" of $^3/8$"w lace trim, $^3/4$ yd of $2^1/2$"w flat lace, $^3/4$ yd each of five assorted ribbons, candy conversation hearts, tracing paper, craft knife and small cutting mat or folded newspaper, a $^1/8$" hole punch, craft glue, and a hot glue gun and glue sticks.

1. Follow *Making Patterns*, page 110, to make heart pattern. Use a pencil to draw around pattern at center front of bag. Place cutting mat inside front of bag and use craft knife to cut out heart along drawn lines.
2. Center cellophane square over heart opening on inside of bag; use craft glue to glue in place.
3. Beginning at bottom point of heart and mitering lace at center top of heart, hot glue $^3/8$"w lace trim to bag along edges of heart.
4. Hot glue 2 heart appliqués and several candy hearts to bag.
5. Tie $2^1/2$"w lace into a bow; trim ends. Hot glue bow to bag. Tie ribbon lengths together into a bow; trim ends. Hot glue ribbon bow to lace bow.
6. For tag, glue remaining heart appliqué to paper. Cutting close to edges of appliqué, cut appliqué from paper. Hot glue 1 candy heart to center of tag. Punch a hole in top of tag. Thread tag onto 1 ribbon streamer. Knot streamer behind tag.

Nothing tastes better
than fresh homemade bread!
Our Sourdough Baguettes
lend French charm to even
the simplest meal. Present
baked loaves in brown bottle
bags decorated with raffia
and photocopied tags and
labels. You can also include
a batch of the starter and the
recipe so your friends can
enjoy the baguettes anytime!

SOURDOUGH STARTER

  1 package dry yeast
2^1/$_2$ cups warm water, divided
  2 cups all-purpose flour
  3 tablespoons sugar
^{1}/$_2$ teaspoon salt

In a large nonmetal bowl, dissolve
yeast in ^{1}/$_2$ cup warm water. With a
wooden spoon, combine remaining
2 cups warm water, flour, sugar, and
salt. Loosely cover bowl or transfer
starter into a 1^1/$_2$-quart pitcher with lid,
keeping spout open. Place container in
a warm place (80 to 85 degrees) free of
drafts 3 days. Stir mixture several times
each day.

To use starter, remove amount
needed for recipe. To replenish
starter, stir in ^{2}/$_3$ cup warm water and
^{2}/$_3$ cup flour for each ^{2}/$_3$ cup starter
that is removed. Let stand at room
temperature overnight and then store in
refrigerator. Use and replenish starter
every 7 to 10 days.

Yield: about 4 cups starter

SOURDOUGH BAGUETTES

4^1/$_2$ to 5 cups all-purpose flour, divided
  1 cup plus 2 tablespoons warm water
^{2}/$_3$ cup Sourdough Starter, at room
    temperature
^{3}/$_4$ teaspoon salt
   Vegetable cooking spray
  1 tablespoon yellow cornmeal
  1 egg white
  1 tablespoon water

In a large nonmetal bowl, use a
wooden spoon to combine 2^1/$_2$ cups
flour, warm water, and starter. Cover
mixture loosely with plastic wrap and let
rest in a warm place (80 to 85 degrees)
5 hours or until doubled in size.

Stir in 2 cups flour and salt. Turn
dough onto a lightly floured surface.
Knead 5 minutes or until dough
becomes smooth and elastic, adding
additional flour as necessary. Place in a
large bowl sprayed with cooking spray,
turning once to coat top of dough.
Cover loosely with plastic wrap and let
rise in a warm place 12 hours or until
doubled in size.

Turn dough onto a lightly floured
surface and punch down. Knead dough
2 to 3 minutes; divide into thirds.
Shape each piece of dough into a
12-inch-long loaf. Place loaves on
a baking sheet that has been lightly
greased with cooking spray and
sprinkled with cornmeal. Spray loaves
with cooking spray. Loosely cover loaves
with plastic wrap and let rise in a warm
place 4 hours or until doubled in size.

Preheat oven to 400 degrees. Use a
sharp knife to make diagonal cuts across
tops of loaves. In a small bowl, lightly
beat egg white and water; brush on
loaves. Bake about 20 to 25 minutes or
until bread is golden brown and sounds
hollow when tapped.

Serve warm or transfer to a wire rack
to cool completely. Store in an airtight
container.

Yield: 3 loaves bread

"HOMEMADE" BOTTLE BAGS

For each bag, you will need a brown
bottle bag, 1 photocopy each of label
design and tag design (page 116), black
paper, natural raffia, Design Master®
Glossy Wood Tone spray, black felt-tip
pen with fine point, craft glue stick, and
a hot glue gun and glue sticks.

1. Lightly spray photocopies with wood
tone spray. Cut out label and tag.
2. Use glue stick to glue label to center
front of bag.
3. Tie several raffia lengths into a bow;
trim ends. Hot glue bow to bag.
4. For tag, use glue stick to glue tag to
black paper. Cutting close to tag, cut
tag from black paper. Use black pen to
personalize tag. Hot glue tag to bow.

ANGEL CUPCAKES

Flavored with almond and poppy seed, Angel Cupcakes are heaven-sent! They're delightful snacks for anniversaries and a host of other occasions. The glittery gift bag and keepsake clothespin angel are inspirational studies in gift-giving ease!

ANGEL CUPCAKES

- 1 package (16 ounces) angel food cake mix
- 2 tablespoons poppy seed
- $1^1/_2$ teaspoons almond extract, divided
- $^1/_2$ cup chopped sliced almonds
- $1^1/_2$ cups sifted confectioners sugar
- 1 tablespoon plus 2 teaspoons water

Preheat oven to 350 degrees. Line a muffin pan with paper muffin cups. Prepare cake mix according to package directions, adding poppy seed and 1 teaspoon almond extract. Fill muffin cups about two-thirds full. Sprinkle batter with almonds. Bake 14 to 20 minutes or until tops are golden brown. Cool in pan on a wire rack. Transfer cupcakes to a wire rack with waxed paper underneath.

For icing, combine confectioners sugar, water, and remaining $^1/_2$ teaspoon almond extract in a small bowl; stir until smooth. Drizzle icing over cupcakes. Allow icing to harden. Store in an airtight container.

Yield: about $2^1/_2$ dozen cupcakes (5 gifts)

CLOTHESPIN ANGEL BAGS

For each bag, you will need a white lunch bag, a 4"h round wooden clothespin, $2^1/_2$" of $2^1/_2$"w white pregathered tiered lace, 15" of $1^1/_2$"w wired gold ribbon, 7" of wired gold star garland, curly doll hair, gold glitter acrylic paint, iridescent gold dimensional paint, white spray paint, small sponge pieces, newspaper, paper towels, black felt-tip pen with fine point, and a hot glue gun and glue sticks.

1. Use sponge pieces and follow *Sponge Painting,* page 111, to sponge paint front of bag with gold glitter, then iridescent gold paint.

2. For angel, spray paint clothespin white. Use black pen to draw 2 dots for eyes on clothespin.
3. For dress, trim lace so gathered edge measures 1" and finished edge measure $2^1/_2$". Glue gathered edge of dress to clothespin below head.
4. For wings, tie ribbon into a bow; trim ends. Glue bow to back of clothespin.
5. For hair, arrange and glue a small amount of doll hair to head.
6. For halo, coil star garland into an approx. 1" dia. circle; glue to head.
7. Place gift in bag. Fold top of bag about $1^1/_4$" to front; repeat. Clip angel to top of bag.

SPICY VANILLA-PEACH JAM

When your family reunion rolls around, why not award your loved ones a summertime treat—our Spicy Vanilla-Peach Jam. With only six ingredients, this spread is super easy to make. Everyone will think your gifts are just "peachy" when you nestle jars of the jam in stenciled bags!

SPICY VANILLA-PEACH JAM

  5   cups peeled, pitted, and coarsely chopped fresh peaches
$^1/_4$ cup freshly squeezed lemon juice
  9   cups sugar
$^1/_2$ teaspoons ground cinnamon
  2   vanilla beans (3 inches long each)
  1   pouch (3 ounces) liquid fruit pectin

Process peaches in a food processor until finely chopped. In a heavy large stockpot, combine peaches and lemon juice. Stir in sugar and cinnamon until well blended. Split vanilla beans and scrape seeds into peach mixture. Add vanilla beans. Stirring constantly, cook over low heat 4 minutes. Increase heat to high and bring mixture to a rolling boil. Stir in liquid pectin. Stirring constantly, bring to a rolling boil again and boil 1 minute. Remove from heat; skim off foam. Remove vanilla beans. Spoon jam into heat-resistant jars with lids. Store in refrigerator.

Yield: about 10 cups jam (10 gifts)

STENCILED MUSLIN BAGS

For each bag, you will need a 6" x 18" piece of muslin; thread to match muslin; acetate for stencils (available at craft stores); yellow, red, and green acrylic paint; small stencil brushes; craft knife and cutting mat or folded newspaper; black permanent felt-tip pen with fine point; removable tape (optional); paper towels; a $1^3/_4$" square of cream-colored paper and a 2" square of green paper for tag; jute twine; a $^1/_4$" hole punch; and a craft glue stick.

1. Referring to stencil cutting key and color key, page 117, follow *Stenciling,* page 110, to stencil peach at center of muslin about $4^1/_2$" from 1 short edge (top edge of bag).

2. Follow *Making a Sewn Fabric Bag,* page 110, to make bag from stenciled muslin.

3. Fringe top edge of bag about $^1/_2$".

4. For tag, center and glue cream-colored paper to green paper. Use black pen to write the following on tag: Have a "Peachy" Day! Punch a hole in 1 corner of tag.

5. Place gift in bag. Form a multi-loop bow from $1^1/_2$ yds of twine; knot a 12" length of twine around center of bow to secure. Thread 1 end of twine through hole in tag. Knot twine around top of bag.

SASSY BARBECUE SAUCE

The next time you're invited to a cookout, surprise the host with a gift of sassy Bourbon Barbecue Sauce! The fiery blend combines onions, jalapeño peppers, and bourbon in a sweet tomato base. For a gift with sizzle, pack the sauce in a blue jean-inspired bag along with grilling utensils and a handy mitt.

BOURBON BARBECUE SAUCE

$^1/_2$ cup butter or margarine
$1^1/_4$ cups finely chopped onions
1 to 2 fresh jalapeño peppers, seeded and finely chopped
2 cloves garlic, minced
4 cups ketchup
2 tablespoons apple cider vinegar
2 tablespoons Worcestershire sauce
1 cup firmly packed brown sugar
1 teaspoon dry mustard
$^1/_2$ cup bourbon

In a small Dutch oven, melt butter over medium-high heat. Sauté onions, jalapeño peppers, and garlic in butter about 5 minutes or until tender. Reduce heat to medium low. Stir in ketchup, vinegar, and Worcestershire sauce. Add brown sugar and dry mustard; stir until well blended. Stirring frequently, cook 10 minutes. Stir in bourbon; cook about 3 minutes or until mixture is heated through. Store in an airtight container in refrigerator.

Yield: about 6 cups sauce (2 gifts)

BARBECUE GIFT BAGS

For each gift, we filled an empty 24-ounce ketchup bottle with the sauce and decorated the bottle with a label and a corner cut from a bandanna.

For each bag, you will need a large white gift bag (about 10"w x 13"h), 2 back pockets cut from old blue jeans, red bandanna, a 3" x 3$^1/_2$" red paper piece and a 1$^1/_2$" x 2$^3/_4$" self-adhesive label for tag, black felt-tip pen with fine point, and a hot glue gun and glue sticks.

1. With bag flattened, use black pen to draw small circles in each corner on front of bag to resemble rivets on jeans. Draw 2 dashed lines about $^1/_4$" apart between circles along side and bottom edges of bag to resemble stitching.
2. Arrange pockets on bag and glue in place.
3. Tuck bandanna into 1 pocket.
4. For tag, use black pen to write message on label. Adhere label close to 1 long edge of red paper piece. Tuck tag in remaining pocket.

ALPHABET SCRAMBLE MIX

Don't be puzzled about what to give someone who loves crossword puzzles! Our Alphabet Scramble snack mix—as easy as A-B-C to make—combines cereal, dried fruit bits, and honey-roasted almonds. For a presentation that spells fun, a brightly colored gift bag is decorated with a ribbon-tied puzzle book, sharpened pencils, and a thoughtful note.

ALPHABET SCRAMBLE

10 cups sweetened alphabet-shaped cereal

2 packages (6 ounces each) dried fruit bits

2 cans (6 ounces each) honey-roasted whole almonds

Combine cereal, fruit bits, and almonds in a large bowl. Store in an airtight container.

Yield: about 16 cups snack mix (1 gift)

PUZZLE LOVER'S BAG

You will need a large gift bag (about 10"w x 13"h), puzzle book, 1"w grosgrain ribbon, 2 sharpened pencils, 2³/₄" square of white paper for tag, black ball-point pen, tissue paper to line bag, and a craft knife and small cutting mat or folded newspaper.

1. Center puzzle book on front of flattened bag. Use a pencil to draw an approx. 1¹/₄" line at center of top, bottom, and each side of book.

2. Place cutting mat inside front of bag. Use craft knife to cut a slit along each line.

3. To attach book to bag, measure height of puzzle book; multiply by 3. Cut a length of ribbon the determined measurement. From outside of bag, insert ribbon into slit at top of bag and out of slit at bottom of bag. Measure width of puzzle book; multiply by 3. Cut a length of ribbon the determined measurement. Insert ribbon through slits at sides of bag.

4. Center puzzle book on bag between ribbons. Knot ends of 1 ribbon length at center of book. Knot ends of remaining ribbon length at center of book. Trim ribbon ends.

5. Tuck pencils under ribbons.

6. For tag, use black pen to write message on paper piece. Tuck tag into top of puzzle book.

7. Line bag with tissue paper.

GOURMET PRETZELS

Say "I love you" with Gourmet Pretzels that you can make at home! Our treats are doubly delicious because they're double-dipped—first in caramel and nuts, then in chocolate. Deliver them in cellophane bags tied with ribbon and chenille-stem hearts for a sweetheart of a presentation.

GOURMET PRETZELS

- 1 package (14 ounces) caramels
- 3 tablespoons water
- 18 large pretzel sticks (about 6^1/$_2$ inches long)
- 1 cup chopped pecans, toasted and coarsely ground
- 1 package (6 ounces) semisweet chocolate chips
- 6 ounces chocolate candy coating, chopped
- 4 ounces white baking chips
- 4 ounces vanilla candy coating, chopped

Line a baking sheet with waxed paper; grease waxed paper. Combine caramels and water in a heavy medium saucepan over low heat. Stirring frequently, cook about 15 minutes or until mixture is smooth. Holding each pretzel over saucepan, spoon caramel over two-thirds of pretzel. Roll in pecans and place on prepared baking sheet. Chill about 15 minutes or until caramel sets.

Melt chocolate chips and chocolate candy coating in a heavy medium saucepan over low heat. Remove from heat (if chocolate begins to harden, return to heat). Drizzle chocolate mixture over caramel-coated area of

pretzels. Chill about 10 minutes or until chocolate hardens.

Melt baking chips and vanilla candy coating in a heavy small saucepan over low heat. Remove from heat (if mixture begins to harden, return to heat). Drizzle vanilla mixture over chocolate-coated area of pretzels. Chill about 10 minutes or until coating hardens. Store in an airtight container in a cool place.

Yield: 18 pretzels

SWEETHEART GIFT BAGS
For each gift bag, you will need a red chenille stem, white and silver curling ribbon, 16" of ^{5}/$_8$"w white satin ribbon, and a cellophane bag (we used a 4" x 10^1/$_2$" bag).

1. Beginning 3" from one end, shape stem into a heart shape (Fig. 1); twist to secure.
Fig. 1

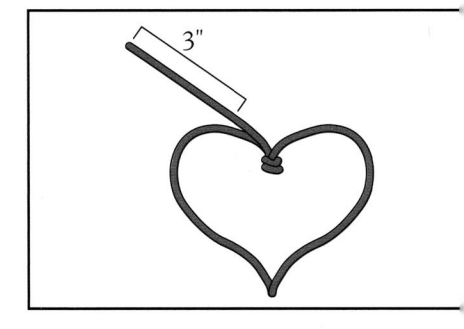

2. Knot three lengths of curling ribbon around stem at top of heart; curl ribbon ends. Tie satin ribbon into a bow around knot; notch ribbon ends.
3. Place gift in bag. Wrap end of stem around top of bag to secure.

VALENTINE'S DAY CARAMELS

Give sweets to the sweet on Valentine's Day with these chewy caramel confections! Made with crisp rice cereal, butterscotch morsels, and candy coating, these treats will become a fast favorite. Our spray-painted doily gift sack features an organdy bow and a handcrafted tag.

BUTTERSCOTCH-CARAMEL CHEWIES

- 1 package (14 ounces) caramels
- 3 tablespoons water
- 1/2 cups coarsely chopped pecans
- 1 cup coarsely crushed crispy rice cereal
- 6 ounces butterscotch chips
- 6 ounces vanilla candy coating
- 2 teaspoons vegetable shortening

Place caramels and water in the top of a double boiler over simmering water. Stir until caramels melt. Remove from heat and stir in pecans and cereal. Drop rounded teaspoons of mixture onto a baking sheet lined with lightly greased waxed paper.

In a heavy medium saucepan, melt butterscotch chips, candy coating, and shortening over low heat. Remove from heat (if butterscotch mixture begins to harden, return to heat). Dip candies in butterscotch mixture; place on waxed paper. Chill until set. Store in an airtight container in a cool place.

Yield: about 5 1/2 dozen candies (5 gifts)

"LACY" PAPER BAGS

For each bag, you will need a white lunch bag, 8" dia. paper doily, pink spray paint, floral-motif sticker for tag, pink felt-tip pen with medium point, 1/2 yd each of 3/4"w white and pink sheer ribbons, 1/4" hole punch, newspaper, and white tissue paper to line bag.

1. Place flattened bag front side up on newspaper.
2. Center doily on bag with doily extending about 1/2" beyond bottom of bag.

3. Lightly spray paint front of bag pink; remove doily.
4. Trim top edge of bag close to edges of stenciled doily.
5. For tag, cut a 1 3/4" x 3 1/4" paper piece with rounded corners from cut-away portion of bag. Adhere sticker to tag. Use pink pen to write "Happy Valentine's Day" on tag. Punch a hole in 1 corner of tag and near top of bag. Thread ribbon lengths through holes and tie into a bow; trim ends.
6. Line bag with tissue paper.

DRESS-UP PARTY POPCORN

Every little girl dreams of being a princess, so on her highness' next birthday, treat her and her guests to a wish come true! Our Peanut Butter Candied Corn will disappear like magic! Present the yummy popcorn in favor bags adorned with fun stickers and shimmering bows. Ponytail holders make pretty dress-up keepsakes.

PEANUT BUTTER CANDIED CORN

    4 quarts popped popcorn
    1 can (12 ounces) lightly salted
       peanuts
    1 cup firmly packed brown sugar
  $^3/_4$ cup dark corn syrup
  $^1/_2$ cup butter or margarine
  $^1/_2$ teaspoon salt
  $^3/_4$ cup smooth peanut butter
    1 teaspoon vanilla extract
  $^1/_2$ teaspoon baking soda

Preheat oven to 250 degrees. Combine popcorn and peanuts in a large roasting pan. In a large saucepan, combine brown sugar, corn syrup, butter, and salt over medium heat. Stirring constantly, bring to a boil; boil 1 minute. Remove from heat. Add peanut butter and vanilla; stir until smooth. Stir in baking soda (mixture will foam). Pour over popcorn mixture; stir until well coated. Bake 1 hour, stirring every 15 minutes. Spread on lightly greased aluminum foil to cool. Store in an airtight container.

Yield: about 20 cups candied corn (10 gifts)

PARTY FAVOR BAGS

For each bag, you will need a white lunch bag, 1 sheet of stickers to fit on front of bag, $^3/_4$ yd of 6"w pink tulle ribbon, a beaded ponytail holder to coordinate with ribbon and stickers, $^1/_4$" hole punch, and transparent tape.

1. Leaving about 4" uncovered at top of bag, tape sticker sheet to front of bag.

2. Place gift in bag.
3. Fold top of bag about 1" to front; repeat.
4. Punch 2 holes about 1" apart at center of folded part of bag.
5. Thread ribbon through holes and tie into a bow over ponytail holder at front of bag; trim ends.

BIRTHDAY PARTY TREATS

The birthday girl and her guests will jump for joy when you present them with fun favor bags filled with toys, candy, and our gooey Birthday Party Treats! The crispy bites are quickly prepared with fruit-flavored cereal and marshmallows. Sure to delight the partygoers, each goody bag is tied with curling ribbon and a jump rope for take-home fun. A hole-punched tag personalizes each gift.

BIRTHDAY PARTY TREATS

3/4 teaspoon *each* of the following coarse decorating sugars: blue, orange, red, violet, green, and yellow
1 package (10¹/₂ ounces) miniature marshmallows
1/4 cup butter or margarine
10 cups round fruit-flavored cereal

Line a 9 x 13-inch baking pan with aluminum foil; grease foil. In a small bowl, combine decorating sugars; set aside. In a large Dutch oven, melt marshmallows and butter over low heat, stirring frequently. Remove from heat. Stir in cereal. Use greased hands to press cereal mixture into prepared pan. Sprinkle with decorating sugar mixture. Let cool. Lift from pan using ends of foil. Cut into 2-inch squares; individually wrap treats. Store in a cool place.

Yield: about 2 dozen treats

TASTY CATFISH SPREAD

ere's an appetizing gift that's sure catch the attention of a fish lover! erved with toast or crackers, Tasty atfish Spread makes a wonderful ack. And there's nothing fishy bout how easy it is to put together e clever bag—just draw the details a paper sack. Next, add a few bbon whiskers and a twisted paper il and fins for "reel" appeal.

TASTY CATFISH SPREAD

      2 pounds catfish fillets
         Salt and ground white pepper
      1 cup sour cream
    1/2 cup mayonnaise
    1/2 cup finely chopped celery
    1/2 cup finely chopped green onions
    1/4 cup finely chopped fresh parsley
      1 jar (2 ounces) diced pimiento,
         drained
      3 tablespoons freshly squeezed
         lemon juice
      1 tablespoon chopped fresh dill
         weed
      1 tablespoon prepared horseradish
    1/2 teaspoon salt
         Toast points or crackers to serve

Preheat oven to 350 degrees. Place fish on a lightly greased $10^1/_2$ x $15^1/_2$-inch jellyroll pan. Lightly sprinkle salt and white pepper over fish. Bake about 20 minutes or until fish flakes easily when tested with a fork. Remove from oven and cool. Transfer fish to an airtight container and chill 1 hour or until thoroughly chilled.

In a medium bowl, combine sour cream, mayonnaise, celery, green onions, parsley, pimiento, lemon juice, dill weed, horseradish, and $1/_2$ teaspoon salt; stir until well blended. Break chilled fish into pieces. Gently fold fish into mayonnaise mixture. Cover and chill 4 hours to let flavors blend. Serve chilled with toast points or crackers.

Yield: about 5 cups spread

CATFISH BAG

You will need a brown paper bottle bag, 10" length of $1/_8$"w black ribbon, black paper twist (untwisted), black permanent felt-tip pen, black colored pencil, 4" length of floral wire, hole punch, and glue.

1. For snout, leaving 1" of center bottom of bag unfolded, fold corners diagonally to back. Glue folds to secure.
2. Use pen to draw eye, gill, mouth, and body details on bag as desired. Shade bag with colored pencil.
3. Punch hole 1" from end of snout. Leaving a 1" tail extending beyond knot, knot ribbon ends together. Thread ends from front to back through hole in bag. Glue ends to back of bag to secure. Cut loop in ribbon.
4. Cut fin and tail shapes from untwisted paper. Glue fins to bag.
5. Place gift in bag.
6. Tightly gather open end of bag; use wire to secure. Glue tail shape to bag, covering wire.

Grandparents' Day (the first Sunday after Labor Day) gives us a wonderful opportunity to celebrate our grandparents and let them know how greatly they've influenced our lives. Packed with a moist, buttery Whipping Cream Pound Cake, our family photos gift bag is sure to prompt memories of special family moments. The unique carrier is covered with photocopies of favorite snapshots and handwritten messages from the children and grandchildren.

WHIPPING CREAM POUND CAKE

- 1 cup butter, softened
- 3 cups sugar
- 6 eggs
- 3 cups plus 3 tablespoons sifted cake flour
- 1 cup whipping cream
- 1 teaspoon vanilla extract

Do not preheat oven. Grease and flour a heavy 10-inch fluted tube pan. In a large bowl, cream butter and sugar until fluffy. Add eggs, 1 at a time, beating thoroughly after each addition. Alternately beat cake flour and whipping cream into creamed mixture until well blended. Stir in vanilla. Pour batter into prepared pan. Place pan in cold oven and set temperature at 300 degrees. Bake 1 hour 15 minutes to 1 hour 40 minutes or until a toothpick inserted in center of cake comes out clean. Cool in pan 10 minutes. Invert cake onto a serving plate; cool completely. Store in an airtight container.

Yield: about 16 servings

FAMILY PHOTOS GIFT BAG

You will need a grocery bag (about 12"w x 15"h), black and white photocopies of family photographs and decorative paper(s), parchment paper, two ⁷/₈ dia. buttons, 20" of brown embroidery floss, Design Master® Glossy Wood Tone spray, stapler, assorted black felt-tip pens, craft glue stick, and a hot glue gun and glue sticks.

1. Place flattened bag front side-up with bottom of bag at top and opening at bottom.
2. Cut out photocopied photographs. Use glue stick to glue photograph cutouts to photocopies of decorative paper(s). Cutting about ³/₄ from edges of photographs, cut out photographs. Lightly spray photocopies with wood tone spray.
3. Cut various sizes of rectangles from parchment paper. Have family members write messages on the paper pieces using black pens.
4. Use glue stick to glue photographs and messages to front of bag to within about 4" from opening edge.
5. Cut away top 4" of each side of bag. Staple a ³/₄" pleat in each side of bag (Fig. 1).

Fig. 1

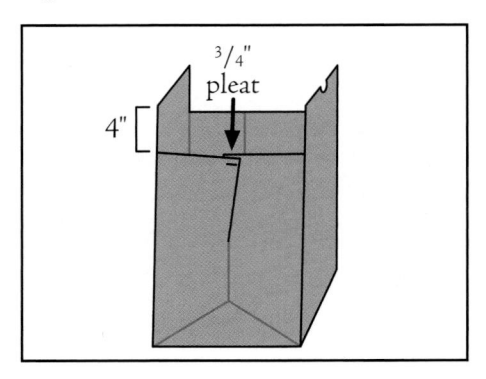

6. Fold corners of bottom flap diagonally toward center; use glue stick to secure (Fig. 2).

Fig. 2

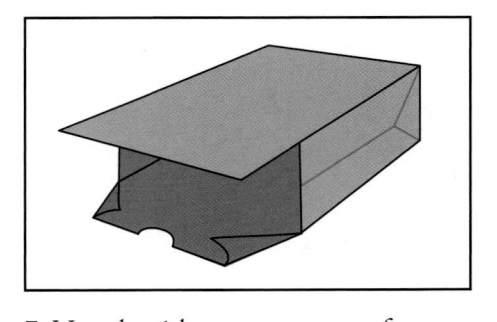

7. Hot glue 1 button to center of top flap at fold line. Hot glue remaining button to center of bottom flap close to edge.
8. Place gift in bag. Close bottom flap over top flap; wrap embroidery floss around buttons to secure.

hildren will love
nding our spunky bunny
ag on Easter morning—
nd the yummy treats hidden
side! The unique bag is
eated in minutes by
ressing up a white lunch
ack with a pom-pom, faux
wels, chenille stems, and
ther basic craft items. The
uttery Easter Egg Cookies
an be painted with swirls,
olka dots, or zigzags using
aste food coloring.

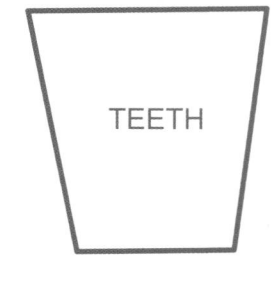

TEETH

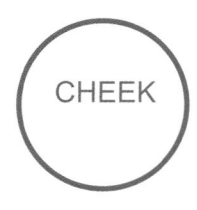

CHEEK

EASTER EGG COOKIES

$1/2$ cup butter or margarine, softened
$1/2$ cup sugar
1 egg
$1/2$ teaspoon vanilla extract
$1/4$ teaspoon lemon extract
$1^2/3$ cups all-purpose flour
$1/2$ teaspoon baking powder
$1/4$ teaspoon salt
Pink, violet, and yellow paste food coloring

Cream butter and sugar in a large bowl until fluffy. Add egg and extracts; beat until smooth. In a small bowl, combine flour, baking powder, and salt. Add dry ingredients to creamed mixture; stir until well blended. Wrap dough in plastic wrap and chill 1 hour.

Preheat oven to 350 degrees. On a lightly floured surface, use a floured rolling pin to roll out dough to $1/8$-inch thickness. Use a $1^1/2$ x $2^1/2$-inch egg-shaped cookie cutter to cut out cookies. Transfer to a lightly greased baking sheet. Bake 7 to 9 minutes or until bottoms are lightly browned. Transfer cookies to a wire rack to cool.

Place 1 teaspoon of water in each of 3 small bowls; tint dark pink, violet, and yellow. Paint desired designs on cookies; allow to dry. Store in an airtight container.

Yield: about $4^1/2$ dozen cookies (3 gifts)

BUNNY BAGS

For each bag, you will need a white lunch bag, white paper for teeth, pink felt for cheeks, $1^1/2$" dia. pink pom-pom for nose, 3 purple chenille stems for whiskers, two 9mm blue acrylic jewels for eyes, $1/2$ yd of $1^1/2$"w wired ribbon, 6" of white twisted paper, black felt-tip pen with medium point, 3" of floral wire, tracing paper, and a hot glue gun and glue sticks.

1. To fringe top of bag, make 2" long cuts about every $1/4$" along top edge of flattened bag.
2. Trace teeth and cheek patterns onto tracing paper; cut out. Use patterns to cut teeth from white paper and 2 cheeks from felt.
3. Use black pen to draw along outer edges of teeth; draw a line at center to separate teeth. Glue teeth to center of bag about 3" from bottom.
4. For whiskers and nose, cut an 8" length from each chenille stem. Glue centers of stems to pom-pom. Glue whiskers and nose to bag. Arrange whiskers as desired.
5. Glue cheeks to bag. For eyes, glue jewels to bag above nose.
6. Place gift in bag. Twist top of bag closed; secure with wire just below fringe. Tie ribbon into a bow around bag, covering wire; trim ends.
7. For ears, untwist twisted paper; cutting with grain of paper, cut paper in half. Twist ends of each paper length. Glue 1 end of 1 paper length to each side of bag at fold.

CARAMELIZED PECANS

Felt flowers blossom on these pretty gift sacks filled with crunchy Caramelized Pecans, sugar-coated nuggets with a rich, delicious taste. To ensure that fond memories of your token will linger long after the snacks are gone, our colorful sack clips double as handy magnets to dress up a message center.

CARAMELIZED PECANS

Recipe does not work well if doubled.

        Vegetable cooking spray
$^3/_4$ cup sugar
    2 tablespoons water
    1 teaspoon vanilla extract
$^1/_4$ teaspoon cream of tartar
    2 cups pecan halves

Spray a sheet of aluminum foil and 2 forks with cooking spray. Combine sugar, water, vanilla, and cream of tartar in a heavy medium skillet over medium-low heat; stirring frequently, cook 10 minutes. Using a pastry brush dipped in hot water, wash down any sugar crystals on sides of pan. Stir in pecans. Increase heat to medium. Stirring occasionally, cook 10 minutes or until sugar begins to caramelize. Stirring constantly, cook 1 to 2 minutes until sugar is caramelized and pecans are golden brown (watch very closely to prevent burning). Spread on aluminum foil. Use forks to separate pecans; allow to cool. Store in an airtight container.

Yield: about $2^1/_2$ cups caramelized pecans (2 gifts)

FELT FLOWER MAGNET BAGS

For each bag, you will need a small sack (about $3^1/_2$"w x 7"h), assorted colors of felt, embroidery floss to coordinate with felt, $^5/_8$" dia. button, spring-type clothespin, 2" of self-adhesive magnetic tape, tracing paper, and a hot glue gun and glue sticks.

1. Trace flower, flower center, and leaf patterns, page 118, onto tracing paper; cut out. Use patterns to cut 1 flower, 1 flower center, and 1 of each leaf from felt.

2. Place leaves on a contrasting color of felt. Use embroidery floss to sew a running stitch along center of each leaf. Cutting close to leaves, cut leaves from felt.

3. Place flower center on flower; stitching through both layers, use embroidery floss to sew button to flower center. Glue leaves to back of flower. Glue flower to clothespin. Adhere magnet to opposite side of clothespin.

4. Place gift in sack.

5. Fold top of sack about 1" to back; repeat. Clip flower to top of sack.

SPECIAL DOG TREATS

Even the pickiest pooch will love home-baked treats made with our special mix! To create a fetching gift for a new pet owner, dress up a brown bag with raffia, a bone-shaped cookie cutter, and puppy cutouts. This package is so "doggone" cute that both owner and canine will howl with delight!

SPECIAL DOG TREAT MIX

- 2 cups whole-wheat flour
- 1 cup all-purpose flour
- 1 cup yellow cornmeal
- 1/2 cup nonfat dry milk powder
- 1/2 teaspoon garlic powder
- 1 package (3 ounces) beef jerky dog treats, finely chopped
- 1/2 cup shredded Cheddar cheese

In a large bowl, combine flours, cornmeal, dry milk, and garlic powder. Stir in beef pieces and cheese. Store in an airtight container in refrigerator. Give with recipe for Special Dog Treats.

Yield: about 5 cups mix (2 gifts)

SPECIAL DOG TREATS

- 2 1/2 cups Special Dog Treat Mix
- 1/3 cup vegetable oil
- 1/4 cup plus 2 tablespoons beef or chicken broth
- 1 egg

Preheat oven to 300 degrees. In a large bowl, combine mix, oil, broth, and egg; stir until well blended. On a lightly floured surface, pat dough to 3/8-inch thickness. Use a 1 7/8 x 3 5/8-inch bone-shaped cookie cutter to cut out treats. Transfer to an ungreased baking sheet. Bake 20 to 22 minutes or until firm and bottoms are lightly browned. Transfer treats to a wire rack to cool. Store in an airtight container in refrigerator.

Yield: about 1 dozen dog treats

DOGGIE TREAT BAGS

For each bag, you will need a medium-size brown gift bag (about 7"w x 8"h), a 1 7/8" x 3 5/8" bone-shaped cookie cutter, black paper, kraft paper, natural raffia, 16" of jute twine, tracing paper, black felt-tip pen with fine point, 1/4" hole punch, craft glue stick, and a hot glue gun and glue sticks.

1. Trace patterns, page 119, onto tracing paper; cut out. Use patterns to cut dogs and small bones from black paper and large bone from kraft paper.
2. Use glue stick to glue begging dog to left side of front of bag; glue square end of remaining dog to inside of bag front at top of bag.
3. Tie several lengths of raffia into a bow; trim ends. Hot glue bow to bag; glue small bones to bow.
4. Place gift in bag. Hot glue top of bag closed.
5. Punch a hole at center top of bag. Tie jute around cookie cutter. Thread 1 end of jute through hole in bag. Knot ends of jute at back of bag.
6. For tag, use black pen to write "Doggie Treats" on large bone. Use glue stick to glue large bone to black paper. Cutting close to bone, cut bone from black paper. Hot glue tag to bag.

FUNNEL CAKE MIX

For a wonderful whiz of a gift, share our four-star Funnel Cake Mix! It's a breeze to prepare fluffy, sugar-dusted treats using the mix, which is delivered in a scarecrow bag. What a clever thought to top the bag with a funnel "hat!"

FUNNEL CAKE MIX

1¹/₄ cups all-purpose flour
  2 tablespoons nonfat dry milk powder
  1 tablespoon sugar
  1 teaspoon baking powder
¹/₈ teaspoon salt

In a medium bowl, combine flour, dry milk, sugar, baking powder, and salt. Store in an airtight container in a cool place. Give with serving instructions.

Yield: about 1¹/₂ cups mix (1 gift)

To serve: Heat about ¹/₂ inch vegetable oil in a large skillet over medium heat. In a medium bowl, combine mix, 1 cup lemon-lime soft drink, and 1 egg; beat until well blended. Cover end of funnel with finger. Hold funnel over skillet and pour about ¹/₄ cup batter into funnel. Remove finger from funnel and, beginning in center of skillet, release batter in a circular motion toward outside of skillet. Using 2 spatulas to turn, fry funnel cake about 1 minute on each side or until golden brown. Drain cake on paper towels. Sprinkle with confectioners sugar. Repeat with remaining batter. Serve warm.

Yield: about 7 funnel cakes

SCARECROW BAG

You will need a brown lunch bag, fabrics for appliqués, paper-backed fusible web, two ⁵/₈" dia. buttons, natural raffia, an approx. 4⁵/₈" dia. metal funnel, 12" of floral wire, black felt-tip pen with fine point, and a hot glue gun and glue sticks.

1. For appliqués, use patterns and follow *Making Appliqués*, page 111, to make 1 nose and 2 cheeks from fabrics; remove paper backing.
2. Fuse nose to center front of flattened bag about 2" from bottom. Fuse cheeks to bag.

3. For mouth, use black pen to draw a curved, dashed line from cheek to cheek.
4. For eyes, glue buttons to bag.
5. Place gift in bag. Twist top of bag closed.
6. Fold several 15" lengths of raffia in half. Place fold of raffia at top of bag; wrap wire around folded raffia and top of bag to secure.
7. For hat, place funnel over top of bag.

ORANGE POPCORN BALLS

There's no trick to scaring up these tasty treats! Individually wrapped and tied with curling ribbon, our marshmallowy Orange Popcorn Balls are quick, yummy bites. The goblin goodies are set out in a spooky fabric-covered bag so that trick-or-treaters can grab their own—if they dare!

ORANGE POPCORN BALLS

- 12 cups popped popcorn
- 6 tablespoons butter or margarine
- 3 cups miniature marshmallows
- 2 teaspoons orange extract
- 1 package (8.2 ounces) candy-coated peanut butter candy pieces

Place popcorn in a large bowl. In a medium microwave-safe bowl, microwave butter on high power (100%) 1 minute or until melted. Add marshmallows. Microwave 1 minute longer; stir until melted. Stir in orange extract. Pour over popcorn, stirring until well coated. Sprinkle candies over coated popcorn; stir just until candies are evenly distributed. Allow popcorn to cool enough to handle. Use lightly greased hands to shape popcorn into 2-inch-diameter balls. Place on waxed paper; cool completely. Individually wrap popcorn balls.

Yield: about 16 popcorn balls

HALLOWEEN TREAT BAG

You will need a large paper grocery bag (about 12"w x 15"h), Halloween-motif fabric, paper-backed fusible web, and four coordinating colors of curling ribbon.

For tag, you will *also* need a photocopy of tag design (page 115), orange paper, purple marker, black permanent felt-tip pen, hole punch, and glue.

1. Draw around front of bag on paper side of web. Fuse web to wrong side of fabric. Cut out along drawn lines. Fuse fabric piece to front of bag.
2. Cut a sawtooth edge around top of bag.
3. Tie several lengths of ribbon into a bow around bag; curl ends.
4. For tag, use marker to color tag design; cut out. Glue tag to orange paper. Leaving a $^1/_8$" orange border, cut out tag. Use pen to write message on tag. Punch hole in one corner of tag. Tie tag to one ribbon end.

AUTUMN POPCORN MIX

Autumn's bounty is richly displayed on these gorgeous bags. Both feature cutout "windows" and colorful ribbons and leaves. Pack the bags with our spiced popcorn mix, which is glazed with brown sugar and molasses. The recipe makes plenty for several gifts.

AUTUMN POPCORN MIX

24 cups popped popcorn
2 cups walnut halves
1 cup butter or margarine
2 cups firmly packed brown sugar
$1/2$ cup molasses
1 teaspoon salt
1 teaspoon vanilla extract
1 teaspoon apple pie spice
$1/2$ teaspoon baking soda
2 packages ($12^1/2$ ounces each) candy corn

Preheat oven to 250 degrees. Combine popcorn and walnuts in a lightly greased large roasting pan. In a heavy large saucepan, melt butter over medium-high heat. Stir in brown sugar, molasses, and salt. Stirring constantly, bring mixture to a boil. Boil 5 minutes without stirring. Remove from heat; stir in vanilla, apple pie spice, and baking soda (mixture will foam). Pour syrup over popcorn mixture; stir until well coated. Bake 1 hour, stirring every 15 minutes. Spread on lightly greased aluminum foil to cool. Sprinkle candy corn over popcorn mixture. Store in an airtight container.

Yield: about 30 cups popcorn mix

LEAF CUTOUT BAG

You will need a brown lunch bag, 2 yds of $5/8$"w wired ribbon, clear cellophane, tissue paper, tracing paper, hole punch, small sharp scissors, and glue.

1. Trace leaf pattern, page 117, onto tracing paper; cut out. Draw around pattern on bag. Use scissors to carefully cut out leaf.
2. Cut a piece of cellophane $1/2$" larger on all sides than pattern. Center cellophane over leaf opening on inside of bag; glue in place.
3. Line bag with tissue paper. Place gift in bag.
4. Fold top of bag $1^3/4$" to back. Punch two holes 2" apart in folded part of bag. Cut one 16" and two 28" lengths of ribbon. Thread short ribbon length through holes in bag and knot at front. Tie long ribbon lengths together into a bow around knot. Arrange bow and streamers on front of bag.

AUTUMN WINDOW BAG

You will need a 4" x $7^1/2$" x 12h" corrugated cardboard gift bag, fabric for border of window, paper-backed fusible web, tracing paper, clear cellophane, poster board, craft knife and piece of cardboard to fit inside bag, yellow and orange curling ribbon, 1 yd of $1/4$"w brown satin ribbon, artificial autumn leaves on stems, and glue.
For gift tag, you will *also* need brown paper, kraft paper, brown permanent felt-tip pen, and a hole punch.

1. For window, trace arch patterns, page 117, separately onto tracing paper; cut out.
2. Center large arch pattern on front of bag and use a pencil to draw around pattern. Place cardboard in bag and use craft knife to cut opening in bag for window.
3. Cut a piece of poster board, web, fabric, and cellophane same width and 1" shorter than front of bag. Fuse fabric to poster board. Draw around small arch pattern at center on wrong side of fabric-covered poster board. Use craft knife to cut opening in poster board. Center cellophane over opening on fabric side of poster board; glue in place. Centering poster board opening in window of bag, glue fabric-covered poster board to inside of bag.
4. Glue one stem of leaves at bottom of window.
5. Cut several lengths of each color curling ribbon. Use curling and satin ribbons to tie a multi-loop bow. Curl streamers of curling ribbon. Glue bow at top of window. Arrange streamers as desired; glue in place. Glue leaves to bow and streamers.
6. For gift tag, tear a $1^3/4$" x $2^1/2$" piece of kraft paper and a $2^1/4$" x 3" piece of brown paper. Center and glue kraft paper piece to brown paper piece. Use pen to write message on tag. Punch hole in tag. Tie tag to end of one streamer.

GINGERBREAD MIX

As the rich aroma of fresh-baked gingerbread fills the air, friends will thank you for the thoughtful gift of Gingerbread Mix. Just write the recipe on a plastic bag, then fill it with the mix and deliver your offering in a gingham sack trimmed with a raffia bow and a cookie cutter. Nothing speaks more of country wholesomeness and simplicity!

GINGERBREAD MIX

7¹/₂ cups all-purpose flour
1¹/₄ cups granulated sugar
 ¹/₂ cup firmly packed brown sugar
  3 tablespoons ground cinnamon
  2 tablespoons baking powder
  2 tablespoons finely chopped
      crystallized ginger
  1 tablespoon ground ginger
  1 tablespoon salt
  2 teaspoons baking soda
  2 teaspoons dried orange peel
  1 teaspoon ground cloves
  2 cups vegetable shortening

In a very large bowl, combine flour, sugars, cinnamon, baking powder, crystallized ginger, ground ginger, salt, baking soda, orange peel, and cloves. Using a pastry blender or 2 knives, cut in shortening until mixture resembles coarse meal. Store in an airtight container in a cool place. To give, follow Step 2 of *Gingerbread Boy Bags* instructions to decorate 4 plastic bags. Place about 3¹/₄ cups mix in each plastic bag.

Yield: about 13 cups gingerbread mix (4 gifts)

Gingerbread Cookie Instructions:
Make Your Own Gingerbread Boys!
1. Pour mix into large bowl.
2. Add ¹/₄ cup molasses, 2 tablespoons brewed coffee, and 1 lightly beaten egg; beat until well blended.
3. Roll out dough ¹/₈-inch thick on a floured surface. Cut out with cookie cutter.
4. Place 1 inch apart on an ungreased baking sheet; bake 6 to 8 minutes at 375°. Makes about 12 cookies.

GINGERBREAD BOY BAGS

For each bag, you will need an 11" x 25" fabric piece for bag, ¹/₂"w paper-backed fusible web tape, an approx. 3¹/₄" x 4³/₄" gingerbread boy cookie cutter, a 1-quart resealable plastic bag, red paper, tracing paper, natural raffia, black permanent felt-tip pens with fine and medium points, and a hot glue gun and glue sticks.

1. Follow *Making a Fused Fabric Bag,* page 110, to make bag from fabric.
2. Place plastic bag over gingerbread boys pattern, page 118, so pattern is centered just below seal of bag. Use medium-point black pen to trace pattern onto bag and copy *Gingerbread Cookie Instructions,* this page, onto bag.
3. Place plastic bag of mix in fabric bag.
4. Tie several lengths of raffia into a bow around top of bag.
5. For tag, trace heart pattern, page 118 onto tracing paper; cut out. Use pattern to cut heart from red paper. Use medium-point black pen to draw along outer edges of heart. Use fine-point black pen to write "oh boy!" on heart. Glue heart to cookie cutter. Glue cooki cutter to bag.

MALTED COCOA MIX

After a winter jaunt outside, what would be more warming than a cup of steaming Malted Cocoa? Surprise a snowbird friend with this chill-busting mix packaged in a jolly snowman bag that's easy and fun to make.

MALTED COCOA MIX

1 package (25.6 ounces) nonfat
   dry milk powder
6 cups miniature marshmallows
1 container (16 ounces) instant
   cocoa mix for milk
1 jar (13 ounces) malted milk
   powder
1 cup sifted confectioners sugar
1 jar (6 ounces) non-dairy
   powdered creamer
$^1/_2$ teaspoon salt

In a very large bowl, combine dry milk, marshmallows, cocoa mix, malted milk powder, confectioners sugar, creamer, and salt; stir until well blended. Store in an airtight container in a cool place. Give with serving instructions.

Yield: about 20 cups mix (10 gifts)

To serve: Pour 6 ounces hot water over $^1/_3$ cup cocoa mix; stir until well blended.

SNOWMAN BAGS

For each bag, you will need a white lunch bag, orange and black craft foam, two $^3/_4$" dia. black buttons, a 2" dia. silk daisy, $4^1/_2$" of $^7/_8$"w plaid ribbon, black felt-tip pen with broad point, tracing paper, and a hot glue gun and glue sticks.

1. Center a saucer upside down at top of flattened bag and draw around edge of saucer closest to opening of bag. Cut bag along drawn line. Fold top of bag about $3^1/_2$" to front.

2. For eyes, glue buttons about 1" apart near fold of bag.
3. Use black pen to draw irregularly shaped dots for mouth.
4. Trace nose and hat patterns, page 118, onto tracing paper; cut out. Use patterns to cut nose from orange and hat from black craft foam.
5. Glue ribbon to hat for hatband; trim ends even with edges of hat. Glue flower to hatband. Glue hat and nose to bag.
6. Place gift in bag. Glue edges of bag closed.

GENERAL INSTRUCTIONS

MAKING PATTERNS

When entire pattern is shown, place tracing paper over pattern and trace pattern; cut out.

When only half of pattern is shown (indicated by dashed line on pattern), fold tracing paper in half and place fold along dashed line of pattern. Trace pattern half; turn folded paper over and draw over traced lines on remaining side of paper. Unfold paper and cut out pattern.

MAKING A SEWN FABRIC BAG

1. With right sides together and matching short edges, fold fabric in half; finger press folded edge (bottom of bag). Using a 1/4" seam allowance, sew sides of bag together.
2. For flat bag bottom, match each side seam to fold line at bottom of bag; sew across each corner 1" from point (Fig. 1).

Fig. 1

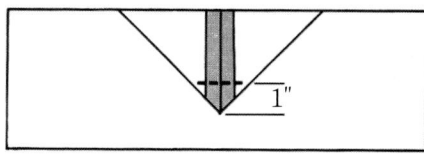

3. Turn bag right side out.

MAKING A FUSED FABRIC BAG

1. (*Note:* We used 1/2" web tape for all fusing steps.) Matching right sides and short edges, press fabric piece in half (fold is bottom of bag). Unfold fabric and follow manufacturer's instructions to fuse web tape along each long edge on right side of fabric piece. Remove paper backing. Refold fabric and fuse edges together.
2. To hem bag, fuse web tape along top edge on wrong side of bag. Press edge to wrong side along inner edge of web tape. Unfold edge and remove paper backing. Refold edge and fuse in place.
3. Turn bag right side out.

JAR LID FINISHING

1. For canning jar lid insert, use flat part of a jar lid (same size as jar lid used in storing food) as a pattern and cut one circle each from cardboard, batting, and fabric. Use craft glue to glue batting circle to cardboard circle. Center fabric circle right side up on batting; glue edges of fabric circle to batting. Allow to dry.
2. Just before presenting gift, remove band from filled jar; place jar lid insert in band and replace band over lid.

MAKING A BASKET LINER

Cut or tear a fabric piece 1/4" larger on all sides than desired finished size of liner. Fringe edges of fabric piece 1/4" or use pinking shears to trim edges.

STENCILING

1. (*Note:* These instructions are written for multicolor stencils. For single-color stencils, make 1 stencil for entire design.) For first stencil, cut a piece of acetate 1" larger than entire pattern. Center acetate over pattern and use pen to trace outlines of all areas of first color in stencil cutting key. For placement guidelines, outline remaining colored areas using dashed lines. Using a new piece of acetate for each additional color in stencil cutting key, repeat for remaining stencils.
2. Place each acetate piece on cutting mat and use craft knife to cut out stencil along solid lines, making sure edges are smooth.
3. Hold or tape stencil in place. Use a clean, dry stencil brush or sponge piece. Dip brush or sponge in paint; remove excess paint on a paper towel. Brush or sponge should be almost dry to produce good results. Beginning at edge of cutout area, apply paint in a stamping motion over stencil. If desired, highlight or shade design by stamping a lighter or darker shade of paint in cutout area. Repeat until all areas of first stencil have been painted. Carefully remove stencil and allow paint to dry.
4. Using stencils in order indicated in color key and matching guidelines on stencils to previously stenciled areas, repeat Step 3 for remaining stencils.

MAKING A BOW

For first streamer, measure desired
length of streamer from 1 end of
ribbon and gather ribbon between
fingers (Fig. 1). For first loop, keep
right side facing out and fold ribbon
over to form desired size loop (Fig. 2).
Repeat to form another loop same size
as first loop (Fig. 3). Repeat to form
desired number of loops. For remaining
streamer, trim ribbon to desired length.

Fig. 1   Fig. 2   Fig. 3

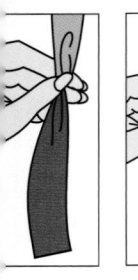  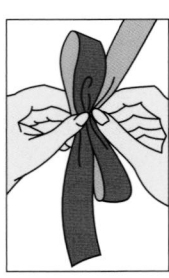

To secure bow, hold gathered loops
tightly. Wrap a length of wire around
center. Hold wire ends behind bow,
gathering loops forward; twist bow to
tighten wire. Arrange loops as desired.
For bow center, wrap a length of
ribbon around center of bow, covering
wire and overlapping ends at back; trim
excess. Hot glue to secure.
Trim ribbon ends as desired.

PAINTING TECHNIQUES

TRANSFERRING A PATTERN

Trace pattern onto tracing paper. Using
removable tape, tape pattern to project.
Place transfer paper coated side down
between project and tracing paper.
Use a stylus or an old ball point pen
that does not write to transfer outlines
of basecoat areas of design to project
(press lightly to avoid smudges and
heavy lines that are difficult to cover).
If necessary, use a soft eraser to remove
any smudges.

PAINTING BASECOATS

*A disposable foam plate makes a good
palette.*
Use a medium round brush for large
areas and a small round brush for small
areas. Do not overload brush. Allowing
to dry between coats, apply several thin
coats of paint to project.

TRANSFERRING DETAILS

To transfer detail lines to design,
replace pattern and transfer paper over
painted basecoats and use stylus to
lightly transfer detail lines onto project.

ADDING DETAILS

Use a permanent marker to draw over
detail lines.

SPATTER PAINTING

*Cover work area with paper and wear
old clothes when spatter painting. Before
painting item, practice painting technique
on scrap paper.*
1. Place item on flat surface.
2. Mix one part paint to one part water.
Dip toothbrush in diluted paint and
pull thumb firmly across bristles to
spatter paint on item. Repeat until
desired effect is achieved. Allow to dry.

SPONGE PAINTING

Use an assembly-line method when
making several sponge-painted projects.
Place flattened bags on a covered work
surface. Practice sponge-painting
technique on scrap paper until desired
look is achieved. Paint all bags with first
color and allow to dry before moving to
next color. Use a clean sponge for each
additional color.

For allover designs, dip a dampened
sponge piece into paint; remove excess
paint on a paper towel. Use a light
stamping motion to paint item; allow
to dry.

For painting with sponge shapes, dip a
dampened sponge shape into paint;
remove excess paint on a paper towel.
Lightly press sponge shape onto project.
Carefully lift sponge. Reapplying paint
as necessary, repeat.

MAKING APPLIQUÉS

1. (*Note:* Follow all steps for each
appliqué. When tracing patterns for
more than 1 appliqué, leave at least
1" between shapes on web. To make
a reverse appliqué, trace pattern onto
tracing paper, turn traced pattern
over, and follow all steps using traced
pattern.) Trace appliqué pattern onto
paper side of web. Cutting about $1/2$"
outside drawn lines, cut out web shape.
2. Follow manufacturer's instructions to
fuse web shape to wrong side of fabric.
Cut out shape along drawn lines.

EVERYDAY PATTERNS

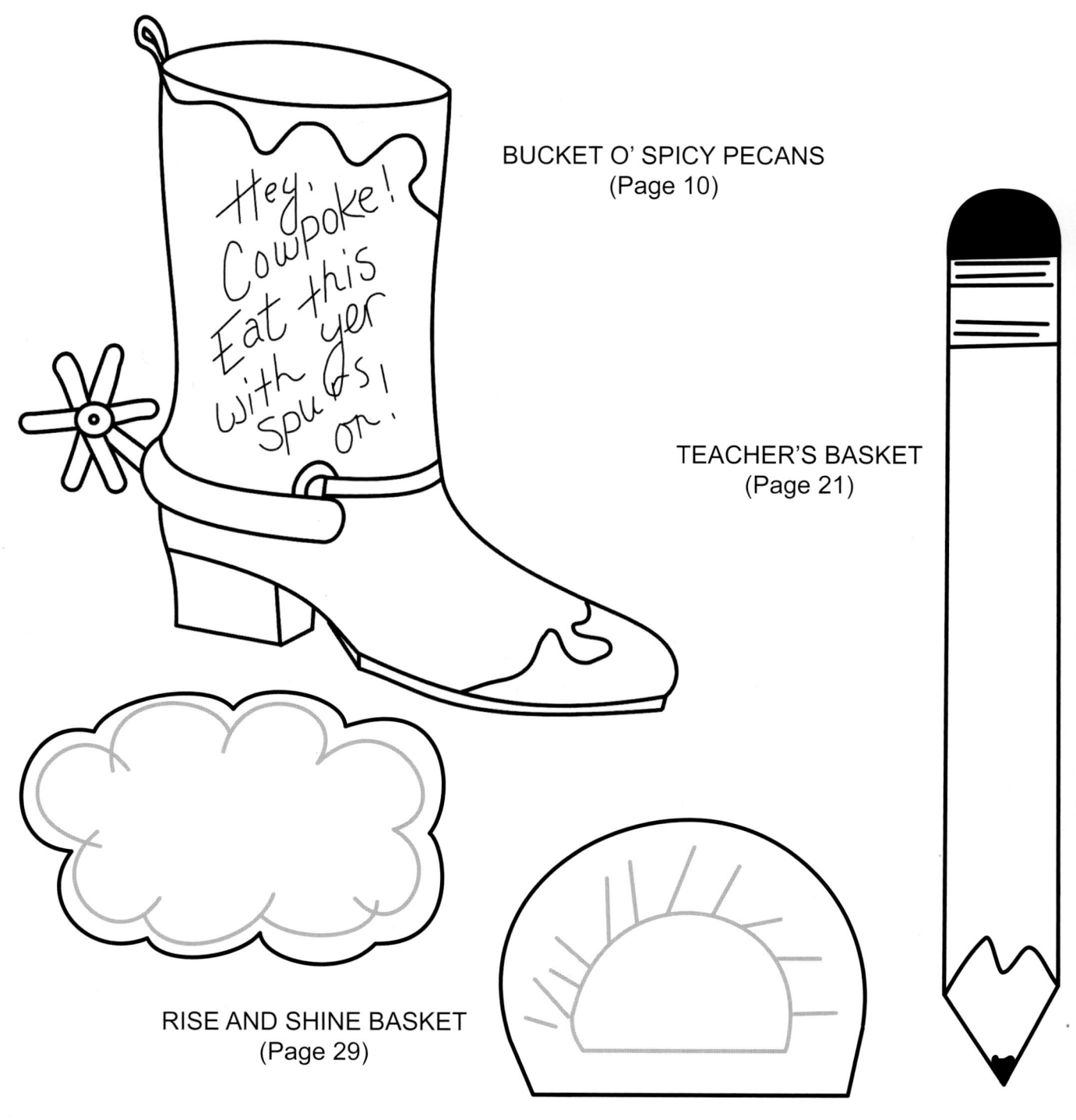

BUCKET O' SPICY PECANS
(Page 10)

Hey, Cowpoke! Eat this with yer spuds on!

TEACHER'S BASKET
(Page 21)

RISE AND SHINE BASKET
(Page 29)

HOT PEPPER SLEEVES
(Page 12)

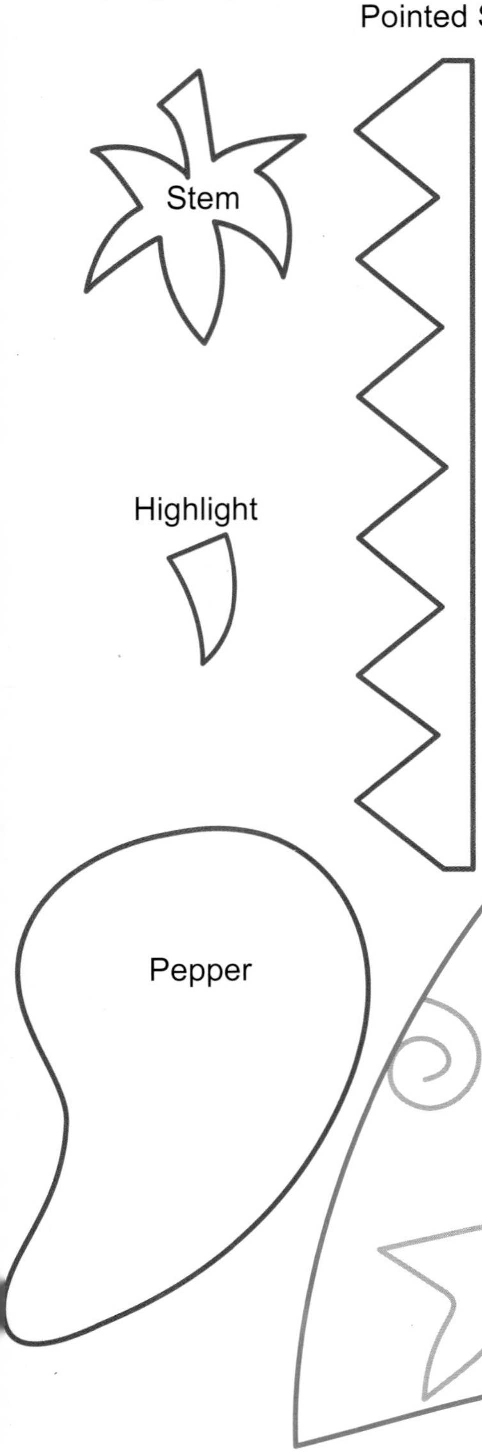

Pointed Strip

Stem

Highlight

Pepper

"HAPPY NEW YEAR!" GIFT TAG
(Page 34)

FLAG PLATE
(Page 51)

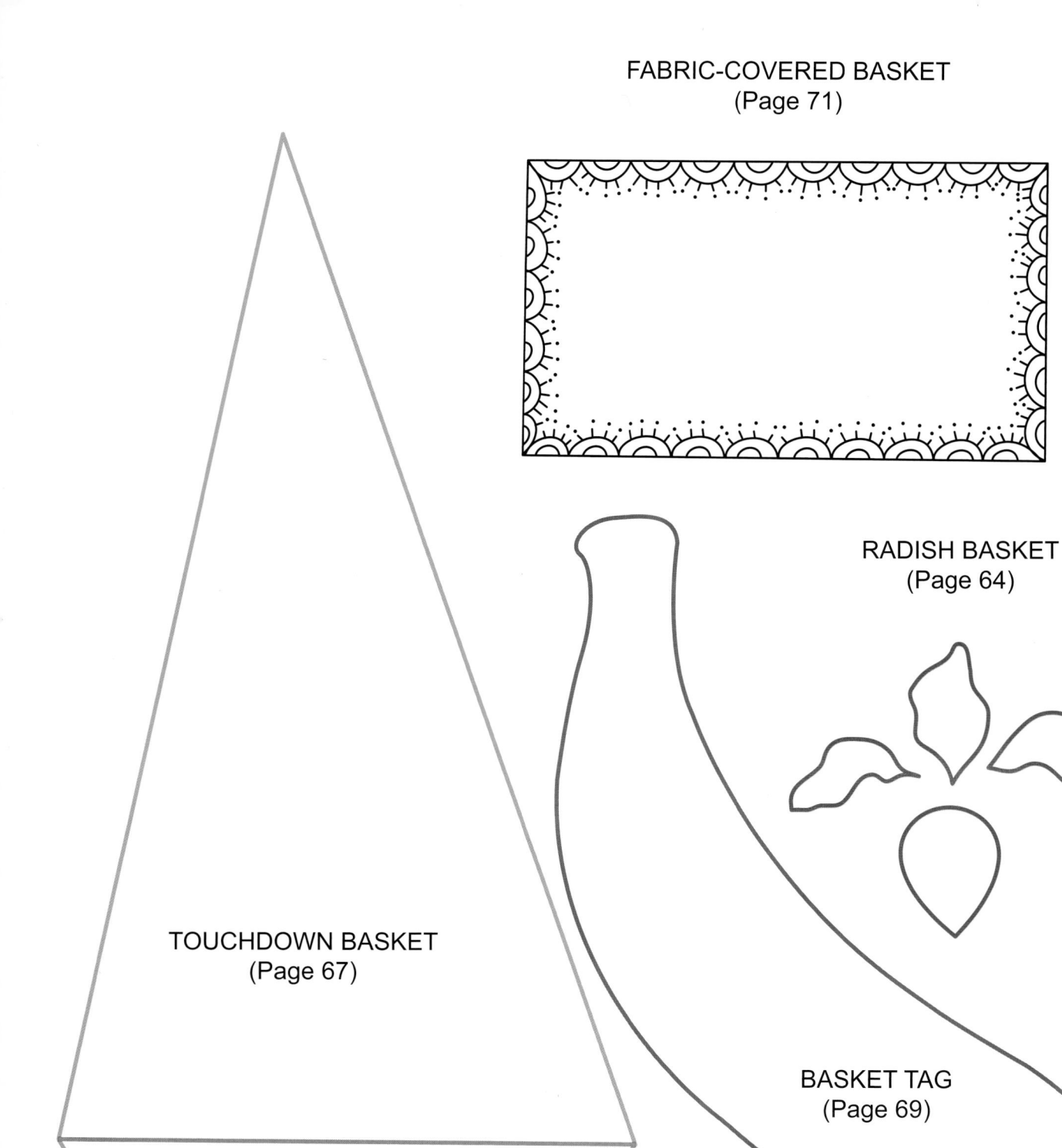

FABRIC-COVERED BASKET
(Page 71)

RADISH BASKET
(Page 64)

TOUCHDOWN BASKET
(Page 67)

BASKET TAG
(Page 69)

Leisure Arts, Inc., grants permission to the owner of this book to photocopy the patterns on this page for personal use on

JUST "BEE-CAUSE!" BASKET AND GIFT TAG
(Page 68)

HALOWEEN TREAT BAG
(Page 105)

PIZZA KIT BASKETS
(Page 79)

PEPPERONI-VEGGIE PIZZA

1 bag Pizza Dough Mix
1¹/₂ cups very warm water
2 tablespoons oil

1 container Pizza Sauce
1 package pepperoni slices
1 package shredded mozzarella cheese

In a large bowl, combine Pizza Dough Mix, very warm water, and oil; stir until a soft dough forms. Turn dough onto a lightly floured surface. Knead about 5 minutes or until dough becomes smooth and elastic, using additional flour as necessary. Cover and allow dough to rest 10 minutes. Divide dough in half and press into 2 lightly greased 12-inch pizza pans. Cover and let rise in a warm place (80 to 85 degrees) 30 minutes.

Preheat oven to 425 degrees. Bake crusts 10 minutes. Spread 1¹/₄ cups Pizza Sauce over each partially baked crust. Place pepperoni slices on each pizza. Sprinkle 1 cup mozzarella cheese over each pizza. Bake 10 to 12 minutes or until crust is lightly browned and cheese is melted.

Yield: two 12-inch pizzas

JACK-O'-LANTERN SACKS
(Page 56)

Tag

Face

"HOMEMADE" BOTTLE BAGS
(Page 87)

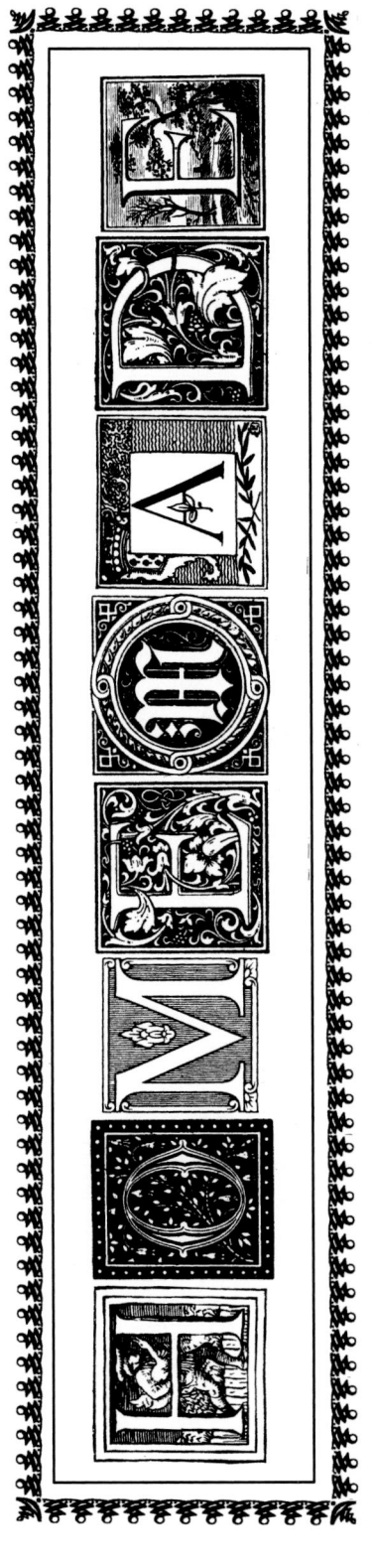

to:
from:

STENCILED MUSLIN BAGS
(Page 89)

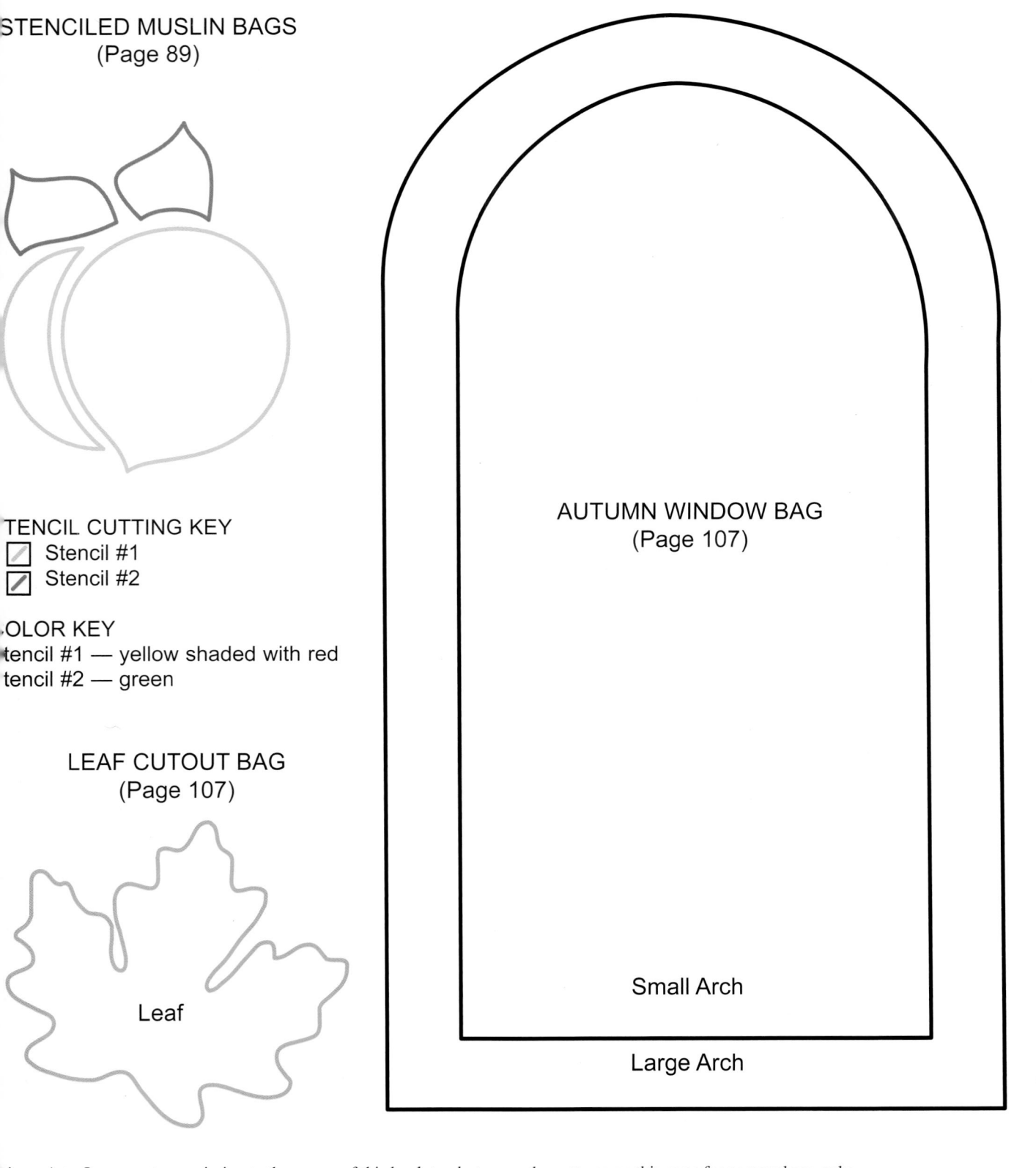

STENCIL CUTTING KEY

☑ Stencil #1
☑ Stencil #2

COLOR KEY

Stencil #1 — yellow shaded with red
Stencil #2 — green

LEAF CUTOUT BAG
(Page 107)

Leaf

AUTUMN WINDOW BAG
(Page 107)

Small Arch

Large Arch

FELT FLOWER
MAGNET BAGS
(Page 102)

Leaves

Flower

Flower
Center

GINGERBREAD BOY BAGS
(Page 108)

Heart

Gingerbread
Boys

SNOWMAN BAGS
(Page 109)

Nose

Hat

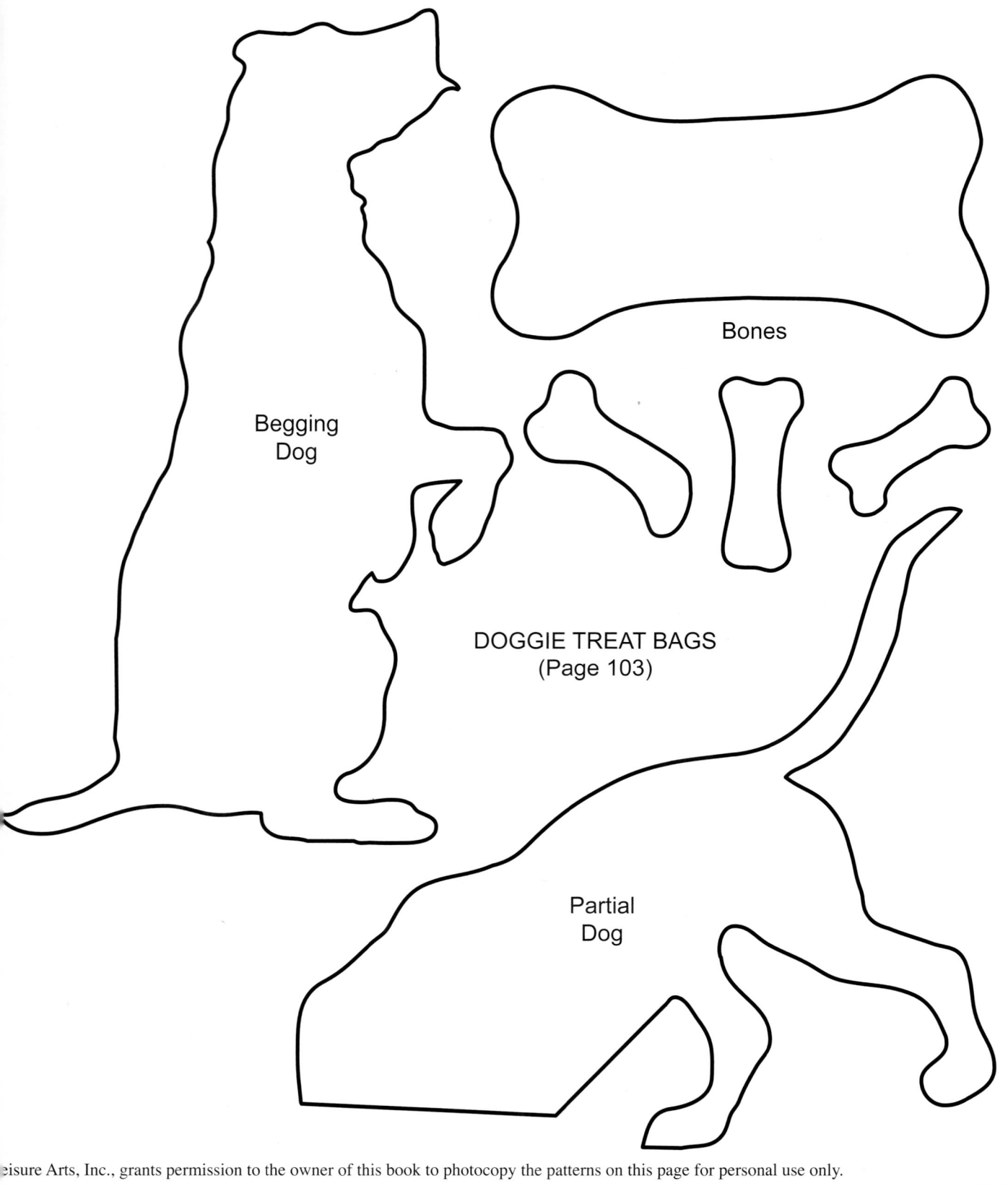

Begging
Dog

Bones

DOGGIE TREAT BAGS
(Page 103)

Partial
Dog

EVERYDAY RECIPE INDEX